CIVIC CENTER

PRAISE FOR
CONFESSIONS OF A WALL STREET INSIDER

"Kimelman is guilty of one thing: writing a helluva book. If you want a front row seat to a Wall Street witch-hunt—read this."

—Turney Duff, bestselling author of *The Buy Side*
and Consultant on the Showtime Original Series *Billions*

"Kimelman delivers a taut page-turner that gives readers an inside seat at the real life Billions that are a daily part of the cutthroat world of proprietary traders. He also exposes a criminal justice system in which prosecutors will do anything to win a case and questions of innocence are far less important than notching a victory. In this disturbing and cautionary tale from the inner sanctums of Wall Street to Federal prison, Kimelman ultimately tells a singular and riveting tale of survival and endurance."

—Gerald Posner, author of *God's Bankers:
A History of Money and Power at the Vatican*

"Kimelman's account as a defendant in the federal criminal justice system provides insights into just how broken and frightening that system has become."

—Walt Pavlo, Jr., *Forbes* columnist and co-author of
Stolen Without a Gun

"If you like wild rides, you'll love *Confessions of a Wall Street Insider*, Michael Kimelman's gripping, well-written memoir of his incredible journey from an associate at the tony law firm Sullivan & Cromwell to the lunacy of day trading, and into the great beyond of Wall Street hedge funds. When he's arrested for insider trading in 2009, the adventure really begins."

—William D. Cohan, best-selling author of *House of Cards: A Tale of Hubris and Wretched Excess on Wall Street*

"When prosecutors place a political agenda and career ambition over truth and justice, people inevitably get trampled. Michael Kimelman is a perfect example of that collateral damage."

—Joe Tacopina, celebrity criminal defense lawyer and owner of the Venezia FC Soccer team

CONFESSIONS

OF A

WALL STREET INSIDER

CONFESSIONS
OF A
WALL STREET INSIDER

A CAUTIONARY TALE OF RATS, FEDS, AND BANKSTERS

MICHAEL KIMELMAN

Skyhorse Publishing

Visit our website at www.skyhorsepublishing.com.

10 9 8 7 6 5 4 3 2 1

Library of Congress Cataloging-in-Publication Data is available on file.

Cover design by Rain Saukas
Cover photo credit: iPhoto

Print ISBN: 978-1-5107-1337-6
Ebook ISBN: 978-1-5107-1338-3

Printed in the United States of America

DEDICATION

For my Mom and Dad, Barbara, and Charles, whose love and courage never wavered. I can't thank you enough or ever repay you for what you gave me. If I am half the parent to my three children that you were to me, I'll know I did all right.

ACKNOWLEDGEMENTS

PETER BOGART WAS MY INVALUABLE PARTNER in editing and structuring this book. His brilliant acumen and generosity helped captain this project to the finish line. Everyone should be lucky enough to have a friend like Pete in their lives.

To Sharon Lord, Allison Oakes, Melissa Kotlen, Eileen Fischer, Claudia Borg, Turney Duff, Walt Pavlo, Ashley Parrish, Meredith Morton, Ilana Kuznick, Dave Fogel, Whitney Korchun, Jason Goldfarb, Jeff Wylde, Darren Lampert, Andrew Herrmann, John Goldman, Kareem Biggs Burke, and others who lent a sharp eye and a kind pen to the manuscript, and whose friendship blessed my life.

To my ride or dies, Stan Horowitz, Randy Oser, Moe Fodeman, Dino Capuano, Phil Berkeley, Pete Izmirly, Brian Hutchison, Chris Johnson, Igor Velikov, Keith Sutton, Mike Borzello, Adam Zutler, Brian Zeft, and anyone else I missed. You know who you are—people whose friendship I measure in decades and would gladly take a bullet for.

To my Lburg crew. I'll take good people in horrible conditions over the opposite every time. Funny how humanity thrives even under the most inhumane circumstances.

To the Skyhorse team, Tony Lyons, Scott Kenemore, Mike Lewis, and Mark Gompertz, who believed in the story and brought it to fruition.

To my brother Andy, who has always been a champion. Big brothers aren't supposed to look up to younger brothers, but I have from day one.

To Lisa, who I have a lot of love for and, with perfect knowledge, would still do it all over again.

And finally, to those who make my heart sing the loudest, my three children, Sylvie, Cameron, and Phineas. When faced with an impossible situation, I tried to make the least worst choice, and to keep my chin up and never forget to smile and be grateful. I hope you can understand one day, and do the same.

CONTENTS

———

PREFACE

—————

WHEN YOU DECIDED TO PICK UP this book, chances are the one thing you knew about me was that I'm a convicted felon.

In America, we're careful to repeat the adage that someone charged with a crime is innocent until proven guilty. But let's be honest. Let's be frank. This is you and me talking here. Most of the time, when someone is indicted and brought to trial for a financial crime, we assume that he (or she, but usually he) is likely to have done something wrong. And if that defendant *is* found guilty by a jury of his peers? Then the assumption becomes an accepted fact. The jury heard all the facts and made an educated pronouncement. The system worked.

Or did it?

It was alleged that on August 8 of 2007, I bought shares of stock in a company called 3Com six weeks before a large takeover deal for that company was announced. It was further alleged that I bought this stock because I had illegal information about the trade. When I was arrested, it was along with several other traders from more than one firm. Some of these men—when convicted—would see prison terms that set new records for sentences given in insider trading cases. These men were charged with making multiple illegal trades and perpetrating a vast conspiracy of illegal insider information.

I was, again, charged with making *one* illegal trade. (And, later on, with "conspiring".) The case against me was so illusory that the government offered me an unprecedented non-cooperation probation/no jail plea deal the day after my indictment, which I later turned down.

It is not my project, here, to convince you of my innocence. What I do hope to convey is *exactly* what it feels like when a routine work decision made years before—which you don't even remember very well—becomes the sole focus of your existence, and the linchpin of your fate and your family's future. What it feels like when the crushing pressure of a federal indictment comes down with all its force on what had been an enduring marriage. What it feels like when you begin to realize that those whom you have trusted are ready to betray you completely.

You probably know that the law prohibits "insider trading." What you may not realize is that there is no clear definition of what "insider trading" actually is. None. Go check. Google away, I'll wait. No statute spells it out. No law book provides a comprehensive accounting of its parameters. (When it came to my case, even the judge got confused.)

In the United States, the law avoids criminalizing conduct that is not clearly defined . . . but securities fraud is an exception. In some quarters, there's a debate over whether it even makes economic sense to criminalize trading on inside information. The market is awash in rumors and insights from all sides, all the time. The line between good information and tainted information is not always clear. The flow of information—of all kinds and qualities—is constant. I was not charged with any pattern of illegal trading. I was charged with a single trade so unremarkable that I could barely remember it.

And it still destroyed my life.

If you are reading this, you are probably curious about what I went through. Well, I went through hell. But what does a man *want* when he is going through hell? When he is in hell, and sees only more hell ahead of him? When there is no foreseeable course except to continue forward through the fire and brimstone?

That one, I can tell you for sure.

He wants to keep on going.

—Michael Kimelman, Fall 2016

CHAPTER ONE

DANGER AT THE DOOR

BEFORE DAWN, NOVEMBER 5, 2009, I was shaken from a deep sleep by a deafening bang with no discernible source. I sat bolt upright in bed, heart in my throat. My first thought was that it must be some sort of mechanical explosion. Maybe that rebellious boiler in our basement had finally had too much. Within seconds, it came again. And then a third time. It became rhythmic.

BANG! . . . BANG, BANG, BANG!!!

I jumped out of bed.

Our front door was being beaten on. Or in. Given the intensity of the blows, it was hard for me to believe the hinges were still holding. I looked over and saw that my wife Lisa was also out of bed, white with fear and cradling our terrified toddler, Phineas. Still in the dazed throes of Ambien and red wine, I half-wondered if this wasn't some sort of bizarre nightmare—the product of stress, drugs, and an overactive subconscious. An hour earlier, I had been floating in a warm nothingness, thanks largely to the sleep meds and several glasses of a mid-priced California Cab.

But now this. Whatever *this* was.

"Oh my God, Michael!" Lisa shouted, instinctively squeezing Phinnie a bit tighter than he was accustomed to. He squirmed uncomfortably. Lisa ran to the window and pulled back the curtain. There, we both saw half a dozen FBI agents in blue and yellow windbreakers fanning out across our front lawn. Each had a holstered firearm. One of them had a K-9 police dog, straining on its leash. I had been attacked by a German shepherd as a kid, and knew precisely what they were capable of.

An avid viewer of shows like *Law & Order* and *CSI: NY,* Lisa initially figured that the Feds were there to hunt down a violent criminal that might be fleeing through our neighborhood. That the FBI agents were there to somehow "help us." But this wasn't TV Land; it was Larchmont Village, New York, as quaint and safe a spot you can find within twenty minutes of the Big Apple. Escaped convicts didn't haunt these mansions and manicured lawns. Lawyers and bankers did.

I was no expert, but it looked like the FBI agents were watching for movement in the windows and doors to our home. After a moment, an agent saw Lisa peeking out from behind the curtain and pointed at her face. Scared and confused, Lisa dropped the curtain and turned back to me.

"Go check on the kids!" she yelled, gripped by a shrill, pure panic.

I sprinted down the hallway and opened Cam's door. Our three-year-old had just moved into his own bed. He was still scared of thunder, and my heart sank as I wondered how he would handle this sledgehammer-like crashing on the front of his home. He was wide awake and crying by the time I burst in.

"It's okay, sweetie. Mommy will be here in second. You are safe."

I quickly kissed him on his forehead. Five-year-old Sylvie was in the room adjacent. I checked on her next. She was starting to stir, but not yet upset. Only curious.

"It's okay, Syl. Don't worry about the noise. Try to go back to sleep."

Lisa arrived in Sylvie's room.

"They're fine, honey," I said.

Then an absurdity. I thought to myself: Someone is knocking on my door. What do you do when someone knocks on your door? You go answer it.

"I'm going to answer the door," I said to my wife, as calmly as if I anticipated a delivery from Amazon or neighborhood kids selling Girl Scout cookies.

I began to walk downstairs. Through the windows of the house, I noticed several more FBI agents moving furtively across our backyard. The trees had lost enough foliage to leave the agents mostly exposed, but they were still trying their best to conceal themselves.

I reached the door and called out, "Okay, I'm opening it."

I swallowed hard and prepared myself for an overzealous agent ramming the door into my face and shattering my nose, or maybe anxiously discharging a chambered round into my chest.

It wasn't until my hands were fiddling with the brass deadbolt that I remembered I was standing in only my Hanes boxer briefs and a dingy V-neck undershirt. I had a quick flashback to the TV lounge in college, watching *COPS* with my buddies and asking, *"Why do these white trash criminals always get arrested in their undershirts and slippers?"*

Now, perhaps, it was no longer such a mystery.

Heart racing, ears ringing, I undid the last latch, twisted the handle and opened the door.

"Mr. Kimelman? Mr. *Michael* Kimelman?"

The agents were right out of Central Casting. Tall. Bulletproof vests. No-bullshit expressions. One was a middle-aged white guy, wearing the traditional navy blue windbreaker with yellow FBI lettering. He was in good shape, and kept his hair meticulously short.

His young black partner was handsome and likewise athletic, and appeared to relish sternly shining his magnum flashlight directly into my eyes.

Squinting, trying reflexively to block the blinding beam with my hand, I said that that was indeed my name.

"I have a warrant here for your arrest," one of them said.

I just stood there, blinking and squinting. In the movies, this is when the accused angrily demands to see the warrant, and then snatches it from the agent's hands when it's produced. But that's the movies. In real life, your brain is like a car that won't start. No matter how hard you pump the accelerator and twist the key in the ignition, there's nothing. Three years of law school and several more at a fabled law firm, and all I could think of to say was: "Uh, for what?"

"Securities fraud. This warrant gives us permission to search your house. Please step aside, sir."

My legs nearly buckled. So this was it. This was how it happened. This was what it looked like, what it sounded like, what it smelled like.

This was how you became one of those guys. A bankster. The people that good folks in the Midwest somewhere—who didn't know a thing about banking beyond their checking accounts—knew they should hate. This was how you became a bad guy, I thought.

It was too much to begin thinking about what decisions, or what people, had brought me here. But something in me knew. One word resounded in my brain. One word. Zvi. (It rhymed with "me" or "flea.") One word over and over again.

Zvi. Zvi. Zvi.

So this was how you became one of the bad guys.

Zvi.

After regaining a semblance of composure, my first thought was that this was an incredible and outrageous invasion of my space. What about securities fraud could possibly give the FBI agents and a police attack dog the need to search my house full of children in the middle of the night? What the hell were they searching for, the *fraudulent securities*?

It made no sense, and I said something to that effect.

"The search is just standard procedure," the white agent said. "We need to make sure there is no imminent danger."

The two agents brushed past me and entered my home.

The white one looked a little like a teacher I'd had in grade school, and the black one reminded me of a certain leading man from the movies. I silently dubbed them Teacher and Hollywood. They never gave me their names.

Teacher sidled up to me as Hollywood began to explore my house and turn on lights.

"So, I really hope you'll agree to talk to us," Teacher said, as he entered and began to look around. "This'll be a hell of a lot easier on you, Mike, if you cooperate."

Mike? Did he really just call me Mike? Hey, can I brew some coffee for you guys? Maybe you want a Danish or donut with that, since apparently you're my new pals?

Before I could respond, several other agents *and the dog* were inside the house. I was actually relieved to get them off our lawn. Our four-bedroom home sat on a quarter of an acre at the top center of a "T" type block with very little privacy where one quiet street intersects another. The kind of place where, in a nation of pedophiles and serial killers, kids can still ride bicycles without fear and walk to each other's houses or to the park alone. The parcels are modest and close together. A friend from Connecticut once told me that he could rake my lawn with a dinner fork. This close proximity meant that there were at least six homes with a direct line of sight of the heavily armed SWAT team that had now occupied my house. I didn't know what the neighbors would think, but I knew it wouldn't be good.

Teacher's voice came again, still palsy-walsy.

"Mike, I've got some really simple questions. If we could slip into the other room and sit down to chat, I'm sure we could clear this up."

I was shaken, but beginning to think on my feet.

Do some people actually fall for this stuff?

"I'm represented by counsel," I blurted out. "If you want to talk, you can speak to him."

Teacher gave it one last shot.

"Listen *very* closely to me. You can help yourself right now. You're not going to get another chance like this. If I have to bring you in and put you through booking, then it's out of my hands. You can cooperate now, with me, or you can see your kids in ten years."

Fucking Zvi! I screamed silently inside my head. *What the fuck did you do?*

Yet my reply betrayed none of my inner emotion. I was calm. Cold. Detached. I sounded like a lawyer. Which, of course, was exactly what I had been trained to be.

"Unless you tell me what's going on, I'm afraid I can have nothing to say to you. Can you tell me anything? Is this because of the Raj thing?"

Ahh, the Raj thing.

By now, November 2009, everyone on the Street, anyone with even a remote interest in investment and finance, was talking about the arrest of Raj Rajaratnam.

Raj was a heavyset, self-made Sri Lankan billionaire, head of a hedge fund called the Galleon Group. (Don't let my use of his first name imply that we were tight. Everybody called him Raj.) Raj was morbidly obese, and had a penchant for all the fabled Wall Street excesses. When the news had first broken of his arrest, I assumed they'd probably gotten him for some sort of sex or drug crime. I'd seen nothing firsthand, but stories of Raj's lifestyle were many and legendary. And who knew how many of them were true?

Then it had come out that Raj's perp walk was not for a sex crime, but for insider trading. And the United States Attorney in charge of the case, Preet Bharara, had used the occasion to do quite a bit of grandstanding around the fact that more arrests would be forthcoming. Lots of people on Wall Street were nervous. My own father had heard what was being bandied about, and had asked me if I was concerned. I'd told him that I was—but not about getting arrested. My concern was for the survival of my firm, Incremental. This was because one of our smooth-talking leaders was a gent named Zvi Goffer. Zvi had once worked directly for Raj at Galleon. Because of this connection, some folks had started referring to us as "Baby Galleon"—which had worked phenomenally in our favor . . . until Raj's arrest.

But that, I told my dad, was where any similarity between myself and Raj ended.

Raj was a billionaire who flew private on Gulfstream Fives and lived in a vast spread on the Upper East Side, with a stately weekend retreat in Greenwich, Connecticut to boot.

Me? I was doing okay, but I still flew my family coach on JetBlue when we went to visit the in-laws in Florida. My tastes did not run to the exotic or illegal. I was not in the same weight class as Raj, in any sense of the term. Hell, I wasn't in the same universe.

The idea that I might be connected to someone like Raj Rajaratnam in the eyes of the law was a sobering, terrifying thought. How had this happened?

But, of course, some part of me already had a sneaking suspicion.

Fucking Zvi!

"I can tell you that it's a securities fraud case," came the reply to my question about Raj. It was Agent Hollywood, who had finished his walkabout and now joined Teacher back at the door to my home. Meanwhile, Lisa had tiptoed down the stairs, wearing a bathrobe now and holding Phinnie on her shoulder. The poor little kid was all snot and tears, terrified by the stern, armed strangers who were tracking dirt onto our carpet and kicking errant toys out of their way.

"Why are you in my house?" Lisa asked, voice trembling.

"Ma'am, your husband is being arrested for securities fraud," said Teacher.

Remarkably, this was all it took: Lisa was speechless, but satisfied. I could also tell that she was suddenly furious, and not just with the agents. She did not have to speak further for me to sense her growing anger.

"Mr. Kimelman, please follow me up the stairs. I need to secure the rest of the house."

Secure the house? Were he and his team here to help us "lock it down"? By now, Phinnie was squirming and screaming inconsolably. All of this at such an ungodly hour was too much to bear. Not to mention the big German shepherd prowling the house, ears pointed, looking ready to attack. Waves of fear and nausea began to build inside me as my adrenaline spike abated. I tried dialing my attorney's number while marching from room to room, but my hands shook, my fingers felt numb, and I had trouble finding him in my contacts. Lisa followed us upstairs to check on Cam and Sylvie.

I can't recall if Agent Hollywood beat me to Cam's room, but he asked me to open the door. Teacher, looking angry, was right behind, along with a third agent, an ex-Marine type, complete with a jarhead haircut and bulging biceps barely contained within his FBI windbreaker.

I hurried over to Cam, stroked his frightened bloodless face, and told him he was okay, that Mommy was coming to get him. On to Syl's room, where she was sitting up in her bed, the covers pulled up to her neck. Hollywood flashed her with the blinding beam of light, and she looked at us with a terrified smile. Syl was accustomed to some craziness in our house: the chickens getting loose from their coop out back, a symphony of smoke alarms going off from the kitchen because Mommy the caterer almost burned the house down. You know, stuff like that. But waking up at 5:00 a.m. to uniformed men with Magnum flashlights, guns, and a huge attack dog roaming around was flat-out terrifying. Yet Sylvie was remarkably composed, all things considered.

"What's going on, Daddy?" she asked, almost matter-of-factly.

"Sweetie, these are just people inspecting the house. They are . . . friends of Daddy's. It's okay."

Did she buy that? I'll never know, but it was all I could come up with.

Lisa was standing right behind me and herded our terrified brood into our bedroom, all at once, and put them all in our bed. Now Lisa turned to me, fighting back her own tears—and asked me the same question as our five-year-old daughter, her voice much less steady than Sylvie's.

"What's going on Mike?"

"Sir, do you have any firearms in the house?" Teacher politely interrupted, which meant I didn't have to answer Lisa right away—and at that moment, I really didn't have an answer anyway. The instant I began to speak to Hollywood, however, Teacher was in my face, demanding a response.

"We asked you a question, sir. Do you have any firearms in the house?"

And the damn ruse worked, catching me off balance. Teacher's right hand rested nervously on his holstered Glock 22. I looked around at the other agents, and they each had their right hands on their firearms. I was suddenly, acutely aware of the large artery pulsing in the left side of my neck. What the hell was going on here? I thought. I've done nothing wrong . . . so why am I sweating so profusely? Why is the artery in my neck about to explode?

"Uh." I hesitated.

I had a legally licensed shotgun in my bedroom closet, hidden from the kids and protected inside a gun case. This was my constitutional right . . . right? Too many questions raced through my mind: Did I really need to tell them? What difference does it make whether I have a shotgun? Will they confiscate it? Is this a Second Amendment violation? A Fourth Amendment violation? Are they trying to trick me into picking up the gun so they could shoot me down on the spot? Surely they wouldn't just execute me right here . . . would they?

I recalled an A&E *True Story*, the one where FBI snipers killed Randy Weaver and then shot his wife Vicki in the head as she held their ten-month-old daughter while standing at their front door. But that was Ruby Ridge, Idaho, where Uncle Sam's federal authority was not always accepted. Surely the rules of engagement were different here, in leafy Larchmont, New York. Weren't they? We paid our hefty taxes in full, gave generously to the local police and fire department.

With some difficulty, I cleared my throat. "Uh, yeah. I do. Upstairs, in the bedroom closet, on the very top, above my dresser. The gun's locked in its case, with a trigger lock as well. It's not loaded."

"Sir, please show me exactly where you keep the shotgun."

We entered my bedroom and I opened the closet. Agent Hollywood got a step stool and asked me to take the shotgun down and to give him all the necessary keys. One set was hidden in my sock drawer, the other inside the pages of an old Criminal Law textbook. The irony of that one almost made me smile. Agent Hollywood snatched the keys from me, removed my shotgun from its black plastic case, examined it closely, and then locked it back in its case. Still in a state of shock, I didn't even notice that he had returned the weapon to the closet. More than a year would pass before I discovered that I still had my Remington.

Then Teacher said: "You need to get dressed. We have to take you downtown."

I risked a glimpse of myself in the mirror. I was disheveled and my face was pasty and pale with fear. I asked if I could take a shower.

"No," said Teacher. "We don't have time. I suggest you put on something comfortable. It's going to be a long day. I'd throw on like a T-shirt, sweatpants, and slippers, or maybe sneakers with no shoelaces."

No shoelaces. That one hit hard. This was happening. This was real.

Ignoring the agent's advice, I grabbed one of my three suits that still fit me, since I rarely wore one anymore. (Believe it or not, the dress code for the trading/hedge fund world is much more Casual Friday than the white-shoe law firms and investment banks.) When he was selling it to me, my friend Ken Giddon of Rothman's had told me that this off-the-rack suit, a solid dark gray would be perfect for weddings, bar mitzvahs, and funerals. He'd never said anything about criminal arraignments.

Hollywood looked at me and said: "Sir, you are going to be very uncomfortable. Trust me. You don't want to wear a suit."

All of sudden something snapped inside me. Something sharp. Just like that, I was extremely pissed off.

"*Trust* you?" I boomed. "You want me to put on jeans and a hoodie, or maybe a track suit? Will there be press there? Is this something the public can see? Will I be in front of a judge? You don't want me to be comfortable—you want me to be embarrassed! Let's stop pretending like you're looking out for me. I'm wearing a damn suit."

Agent Hollywood said nothing, and merely averted his eyes.

"It's your call," Teacher said. "But you can't wear a belt or a tie."

"Right, because I might hang myself in the holding cell," I all but shouted. "And no shoelaces, right? Can I please shave?"

"No, you may not."

I angrily threw on my gray suit, white button-down shirt with the dry-cleaning creases, and black Ecco shoes. (The entire outfit was worth less than one of Raj's Prada loafers.) While I was dressing, I used the moment to dial my attorney, Michael Sommer. It bounced to voicemail.

Jesus. At least someone's still sleeping.

As the agents looked on, I left a message.

"Hey Michael, you're not going to believe this, but the FBI is at my house, arresting me. Please call me or my wife Lisa as soon as you get this."

In the master bedroom, I kissed the kids goodbye. They were huddled together in our bed, Lisa was trying to comfort Phinnie with a bottle, and the ever-inquisitive Syl was determined to know what was happening.

"God, Michael, what's going to happen?" Lisa said.

I told her to call Sommer at his office, and if he didn't call her back by nine to call Moe, my old college roommate who was now Assistant US Attorney for the Eastern District of New York. I told her that Moe would know what to do.

I was trying my best to sound confident, to let her know that someone out there would have answers. I certainly didn't. I walked downstairs, pushing past the gate at the top of the stairs, meant to keep our kids from tumbling down, and the display of cheerful watercolors painted by my recently deceased mother-in-law. There were still four, maybe five FBI agents in the house. I didn't know if the others had left, or were still searching other places in my home, looking for those fraudulent securities.

Teacher said: "Mr. Kimelman, we're going to handcuff you and place you in a car. You'll be taken downtown to be booked."

"Is that really necessary?" I asked. "I'm willing to go wherever you want."

"It is necessary. You're under arrest. And the longer we take here, the more likely you'll be spending the night in lockup."

I nodded. The panic had drifted away, and I felt nothing but hollow, horrifying dread.

Some part of my psyche was still holding out hope that this was not really real, that it was some sort of mistake.

But when I saw Teacher take the metal handcuffs out of his jacket pocket, any last remnants of hope faded away, fast. He turned me around and snapped the cuffs on my wrists. He was firm, but not overly rough—I'll give him that. But the grinding click of the cuffs was the purest articulation of fear and despair I've ever heard—and I knew it was the sound of my life being taken from me.

We walked outside. At least a dozen of my neighbors were out on their porches. I took a long, slow look from house to house. Jesus, it was all of them. The Magazinos, the Holtbys, the British ex-pats, the empty nesters and biking fanatics, the stereotypical overwhelmed couple with the newborn—all of them were looking at me. I forced my shoulders upright and kept my chin up, refusing to display the body language of a guilty man. At least three FBI cars were blocking the street, a predictable mix of navy blue and maroon Crown Vics. One of the agents had the police dog on a leash, but it was furiously barking at Moose, the next-door neighbor's chocolate lab. Mr. Magazino, my elderly neighbor directly across the street, was in his driveway holding his morning newspaper. He was just about the nicest human being in the world. He had watched my children grow, and always had a friendly smile and a kind word.

"Mike" he yelled, slowly ambling toward the street. "You okay? You need anything?"

Before I could answer, Teacher put his hand on his holster and shouted, "Sir, go back inside! This doesn't concern you!"

But clearly it did *concern* Mr. Magazino; that's why he was asking.

"You guys need anything, you just let me know," he said, and pointed at Lisa, now standing in the doorway holding Phinnie.

Another agent pulled the K-9's leash, the dog now squarely in between Mr. Magazino and me. They were acting like this sweet old man was actually a real threat. The new agent's voice was even louder than Agent Teacher's: "Sir, I'm going to tell you one last time. Go back inside your house right now."

It was so utterly ridiculous and unnecessary.

"Thank you, Mr. Magazino," I called, hoping to diffuse the situation. "I'm okay."

Teacher and Hollywood led me to the FBI cruiser, opened the back door, and told me to watch my head. Teacher nudged me into the backseat, and Hollywood fastened my seatbelt.

I leaned forward and stared out the window, totally numb. Silhouettes of more neighbors were framed in their windows, and I caught a glimpse of my son Cam, gingerly looking out from behind the second floor window's curtains with a blank face. As we pulled out of my driveway, Teacher pulled out a walkie-talkie and reported the exact time—5:55 am—and precise mileage on the car to some back office person at FBI headquarters. I had been arrested by a vast federal bureaucracy, where employees needed to check in with their whereabouts and were responsible for each and every mile on their government-issued cars. Knowing I'd been taken by the tendril of the immense, faceless machine like that was additionally unsettling.

Lisa stood at the front door—still holding Phinnie, still fighting back tears—as the vehicle pulled away. I have no idea how long it took us to drive downtown. My mind was a blur from that point. All I remember for certain about the trip is that I didn't sleep. I had no idea what to expect when we "got downtown." The only thing I knew for sure was that my beautiful life had just ended.

If I said a word, it was probably "Fuck."

But if I said two words, they were probably: "Fucking Zvi."

CHAPTER TWO

THE HUMAN SHREDDER

WHEN I MARCHED INTO THE HOLDING cell later that morning, he was already there waiting for me.

Zvi sat there, handcuffed to a bench. Instead of a suit, I saw that he'd taken the advice of the FBI men and gone with a track suit. Zvi was in his early thirties and very handsome, albeit in an Eastern European street thug sort of way.

He seemed surprised to see me.

"What? Kimelman? What's *he* doing here? You've got to be kidding!"

Zvi spoke as though he had an audience. Who he thought he was addressing was never clear to me. Zvi's brother Nu, who worked with us, was also present. He stuck by Zvi and did not say much.

A few other tough-looking characters shared our holding cell. Before I could say anything, one of them sat down next to Zvi and me and eyed my gray Rothman's suit.

"You Wall Street, ain't cha? All a yous. That's right. You Wall Street."

He had a mouthful of stained gold teeth.

Jesus, I thought, another person in this horrible ordeal who is straight out of Central Casting.

I put my head down and said nothing. Eventually, he got up and left me alone.

In the corner of the holding cell was a surveillance camera, a single bright red light telling us that we were being recorded and listened to at all times. Zvi spoke as though he were oblivious to this. Or maybe he was just reckless. Another sign that I had trusted the wrong man.

For my part, I was quiet and measured. I had a thousand things I wanted to say to Zvi.

What do you say to the man who has likely betrayed you, but also, you don't totally know what is going on? How do you let him understand the anger and frustration you are feeling? Is it even the time or place for that? Moreover, how do you do any of this when anything you can say can and will be used against you in a court of law?

Zvi, for his part, appeared to have no such qualms.

As we sat there, Zvi—aloud—began trying to determine who was the rat, or rats. He was convinced that they must exist in our organization. He began to mention the names of our friends and business partners. It did not seem sincere. As he spoke, Zvi would wink and smile my way. I returned neither gesture. It was all I could do to repress the urge to gouge out his eyes.

Later that morning, a group of guards came and opened the cell. Still handcuffed, we were marched down the hall to a room where we were photographed and ID'd. At one point, Zvi looked at me and raised his shackled fist in solidarity and smiled, nodding as if he was Tommie Smith on the '68 podium. I did not respond.

They kept us together as we were processed. When the agents were filling out our paperwork, I heard them ask Zvi his highest level of education. He locked eyes with me and grinned: "High school."

High school?

That was a surprise. Zvi had always boasted about graduating *summa cum laude* from SUNY Binghamton. I had never doubted this claim, or thought to investigate it. (Who, after all, would make that up?) Zvi had once even produced what had appeared to be an acceptance letter for Harvard's dual JD/ MBA program.

Again, I had that sinking feeling. The wormhole went deeper. Nothing was as it seemed.

Next we were taken to a dingy arraignment cell. We were extracted one by one and brought before a pretrial services employee who read us the charges against us. As I listened to mine, I understood that they involved criminal stock trading—at least in part—but mostly they seemed like nebulous, official-sounding nonsense. And they included a dollar figure that just didn't sound like it could be correct. At the end of it, they asked me if I could post bond. (While all this was happening, Lisa was scrambling frantically to contact Sommer, my lawyer, who it turned out was in the Bahamas. I didn't yet know this.) I said I thought I could.

Some hours passed. Later in the day, I was brought before a magistrate— marched into a packed courtroom where, much to my relief, I saw Lisa and some other people I knew, including a lawyer named Mitch Epner who had been sent to fill in for Sommer.

When it came to arranging my release, I would later learn my brother-in-law had put up his house as collateral. My bail was $250,000.

After the bail was decided, my handcuffs were removed. A marshal pointed to Epner and said: "He knows where you go."

He did. We went to another room side and filled out paperwork. Then I was finally free to go. By the time I remembered to look around for Zvi and Nu, they were gone.

We exited through a back door of the facility, but there was still a mob of reporters. We hurried into a black rented towncar that drove us back to Larchmont. Epner told me not to talk about my case in front of the driver, but I did anyway.

Epner had seen the charges. I had to ask him: What was up with that typo? He must know the one I meant. The one that said I had done something to illegally make $16,000. Surely they had meant to write $160,000, I said. Or perhaps even $1.6 million.

No, Epner assured me.

My life had just been upended over $16K.

My arrest was the confirmation that the story was not going to have a happy ending. That was the worst part. For so, so long I had been able to tell myself that it would. For the past year I had been weathering a storm professionally. A horrible, epic storm. But it was to the point that I was telling myself that maybe we *had* weathered it. It was that point where you look around and think, damn, maybe we really are going to make it. That maybe everything really is going to be okay.

The firm I had founded, Incremental Capital LLC, had artfully dodged Trading Armageddon, as the general economic and financial decline of 2008 had set in. We maintained our profitability at a time when Bear Stearns, Lehman Brothers, Merrill Lynch, AIG, and a host of other big banks and publicly traded financial institutions were imploding on a terrifyingly regular basis. Many were the not-so-innocent victims of a reckless credit bubble which had popped, as financial bubbles of every kind over the last few hundred years have tended to do. At that time, every trading day was a short-seller's wet dream; an oozing bloody mess. Yet we couldn't look away, watching the destruction of capital on a scale never seen before in American history—billions of dollars of market value disappearing to Money Heaven on a nearly hourly basis—you felt, if nothing else, like at least you were witnessing something historic.

The market action was exacting a massive psychological toll on almost everyone in the business. For some, it engendered borderline hysteria. Looking out office windows at the concrete far below, it was easy for a lot of us to commiserate with those boys who had leapt from their ledges on Black Tuesday, October 29, 1929. The most hardened, experienced traders still felt sick to their stomachs most days, and even those managing to make some money trading on the short side watched, hopelessly, as their 401(k)s and children's college funds got decimated. Wherever you looked, odds were good that friends and family members were losing their jobs and homes. Up and down Wall Street, firms and traders were looking to simply survive, not thrive. We were all just trying to hold on until tomorrow.

My firm, however, was an exception.

Incremental had weathered the storm well. We'd been smart or lucky enough to increase our risk and press our short exposure some eight months before the market bottomed at the devilish 666 level in the S&P 500 index. Yet despite our impressive performance, the Royal Bank of Canada (RBC), our capital partner, panicked when the global financial markets went haywire. Word came down from their Toronto headquarters to wind down the US proprietary trading business. In retrospect, we should not have been surprised by this. Canadian banks were generally more conservative than their American counterparts when it came to managing balance sheet risk. When it came to underwriting mortgages, they'd even had the foresight to ask their citizens to pass a credit check and submit proof of income.

Even so, they had decided to get out of the business, lick their wounds, and retreat. In so doing, RBC also chose to renege on a deal which had required them to absorb all of Incremental's losses in exchange for a share of profits and commissions. It had seemed a too-good-to-be-true deal when we'd struck it. Still, it felt like a betrayal when RBC pulled out, and it took about nine months to find a suitable capital partner to replace them. We eventually did so by raising capital from several sources, including a billionaire real estate investor's family. The wealthy investor's son, Adam Gittlin, an accomplished businessman in his own right, also agreed to be our new COO.

As an augment to this recapitalization, I lined up significant equity commitments from several well-known hedge fund moguls, all-star heavy-hitters such as Todd Deutsch and Gary Rosenbach, along with a handful of other prominent investors, including the granddaddy of them all, Steve Cohen's SAC Capital. By the fall of 2009, we were employing about fifty traders, many of whom were so-called "fallen angels," experienced and highly talented individuals recently fired from Goldman Sachs or the late Lehman Brothers, or from top-tier hedge funds like Galleon and SAC—all of them casualties of the financial meltdown.

These traders were comfortable taking substantial risk, and with suitable leverage, the firm's daily exposure to the market ran in excess of $200 million. The stress of raising money while also navigating the most treacherous and discouraging trading markets since the Great Depression had begun taking a toll on my marriage and on me personally. I was drinking far too much, and hiding my feelings and frustrations from my wife more than usual. But now, in the fall of 2009, things were looking up. At last! Our firm would once again sink or swim solely on its performance. I was pleased with the business, but then again I was a trader at heart, and knew, deep down, that the Trading Gods often have their own agenda.

I arrived home after 10 p.m. and shut myself away from everyone in Lisa's office. I paced and moped. I fought off waves of nausea. Around midnight, I got up the courage to go online and see if it was in the news.

It was, in the Department of Justice and SEC public press releases.

Manhattan U.S. Attorney Charges 14 Defendants with More Than $20 Million in Insider Trading

Charged Defendants Include Hedge Fund Managers, Trading Firm Executives, Lawyers, and Corporate Insiders; Five Already Have Pleaded Guilty To Insider Trading Charges

PREET BHARARA, the United States Attorney for the Southern District of New York, and JOSEPH DEMAREST, JR., the Assistant Director-in-Charge of the New York Office of the Federal Bureau of Investigation ("FBI"), today announced charges against 14 additional Wall Street professionals and attorneys arising out of their ongoing investigation of insider trading at hedge funds and stock trading firms. The charged defendants include hedge fund managers and trading firm executives, lawyers, and corporate insiders. Five of the charged defendants previously pleaded guilty to insider trading charges in Manhattan federal court. The defendants collectively are charged with allegedly participating in insider trading schemes that generated more than $20 million in illegal profits.

1. ZVI GOFFER, who formerly worked at The Schottenfeld Group LLC ("Schottenfeld"), a broker dealer in New York, New York, and currently operates a trading firm called Incremental Capital ("Incremental"), in New York, New York;

2. ARTHUR CUTILLO, an attorney at the law firm of Ropes & Gray LLP in New York, New York;

3. JASON JENKINS, an attorney in New York, New York;

4. CRAIG DRIMAL, who worked in the offices of the Galleon Group ("Galleon"), in New York, New York, but is not employed by Galleon;

5. EMANUEL GOFFER, who formerly worked at Spectrum Trading LLC, a trading firm in New York, New York, and currently is associated with Incremental in New York, New York;

6. MICHAEL KIMELMAN, currently associated with Incremental in New York, New York;

7. DAVID PLATE, formerly employed by Schottenfeld, and currently associated with Incremental in New York, New York; and

8. ALI HARIRI, a Vice President of Atheros Communications, Inc. ("Atheros") in California.

A ninth charged defendant, DEEP SHAH, who was formerly employed by Moody's Investors Service, Inc. ("Moody's"), in New York, New York, remains at large.

ZVI GOFFER, JASON JENKINS, EMANUEL GOFFER, and DAVID PLATE were arrested at their homes in New York, New York. ARTHUR CUTILLO was arrested at his home in Ridgewood, New Jersey. CRAIG DRIMAL was arrested at his home in Weston, Connecticut. MICHAEL KIMELMAN was arrested at his home in Larchmont, New York. ALI HARIRI was arrested in San Francisco, California. All of the defendants except HARIRI are expected to be presented in Manhattan federal court later today; HARIRI is expected to appear in San Francisco federal court later today.

Of the names of those arrested, the only two whom I knew at all, really, were Zvi and Nu Goffer.

Knew. Was that even the right word? Did I even actually know them at all? Who, really, were they? Until that day, I had never thought to seriously question anything about them. Now, it seemed, I was asking questions about them that would be too little, too late.

These others . . . I'd met Plate a couple of times, tops; Drimal just once; Jenkins and Cutillo, never.

Next, I had a look at what the Securities and Exchange Commission had to say:

SEC Charges Wall Street Lawyers and Traders in $20 Million Insider Trading Scheme

Washington, D.C., Nov. 5, 2009—The Securities and Exchange Commission today charged a pair of lawyers for tipping inside information in exchange for kickbacks as well as six Wall Street traders and a proprietary trading firm involved in a $20 million insider trading scheme.

The SEC alleges that Arthur J. Cutillo, an attorney in the New York office of international law firm Ropes & Gray LLP, had access

to confidential information about at least four major proposed corporate transactions in which his firm's clients participated. Through his
friend and fellow attorney Jason Jenkins, Cutillo tipped this inside
information to Zvi Goffer, a proprietary trader at New York-based
firm Schottenfeld Group. Goffer promptly tipped four traders at three
different broker-dealer firms and another professional trader Craig
Drimal, who each then traded either for their own account or their
firm's proprietary accounts.

Goffer was known as "the Octopussy" within the insider trading
ring due to his reputation for having his arms in so many sources of
inside information. Cutillo, Jenkins, and Goffer at times used disposable cell phones in an attempt to conceal the scheme. For example, prior to the announcement of one acquisition, Goffer gave one of
his tippees a disposable cell phone that had two programmed phone
numbers labeled "you" and "me." After the announcement, Goffer
destroyed the disposable cell phone by removing the SIM card, biting
it, and breaking the phone in half, throwing away half of the phone
and instructing his tippee to dispose of the other half.

The charges contained in the Complaints are merely accusations,
and the defendants are presumed innocent unless and until proven
guilty.

This read from start to finish as though it was established fact. The word
"alleged" was buried in the second paragraph, and that all-important phrase
"presumed innocent" saved for the very end.

Despite the circumstances, I had to smile at their portrayal of Zvi. When
you read about a guy labeled "Octopussy" who's biting cell phones in half . . .
well, you remind yourself that at least you're not that guy.

I clicked around some more and found New York magazine had also
published a piece about us. It was titled "White Collar Crime, Without the
Collar." While the writer did qualify the fact that none of those rounded up
had been proven guilty of a crime, she cited Zvi and Nu, "the Brothers Goffer",
as guilty of crimes against fashion for having shown up for the arraignment in
track suits.

Here, too, I had to laugh, even though my world had crumbled.

So, so much of this was so very absurd.

Octopussy? Really? I had known the guy for several years, and worked with him every day for the last year. I had *never* heard that name used. It didn't even make any sense. I mean, Octopussy was a female arms dealer in a Roger Moore James Bond movie released before Zvi was even born.

And biting the cell phone in half? Who the hell *could* even bite a cell phone in half? With the exception of the character Jaws from *Moonraker* (to stay with the Bond theme), and the guy dragging the train with his teeth in the *Guinness Book of World Records*, and maybe, just maybe, my high school buddy Big Zut, who would rip the caps off non-twist beer bottles with his teeth, I couldn't imagine anyone tearing into a Motorola and spitting out a Qualcomm chip like a watermelon seed.

Then, suddenly, a very specific memory went shivering up my spine. A few months back, on Incremental's trading desk, I'd been walking over to Zvi when I saw Nu pass him a yellow Post-it. When I reached Zvi's seat, I saw him crumple the note and pop it in his mouth, like a Tic-Tac. He was still chewing on it. Zvi sat at the end of the trading desk, within his mini cubicle. (It wasn't even remotely private, but on the phone with RBC, investors, or recruits, it gave him modicum of shelter from prying eyes and ears. He chewed a few more seconds and swallowed.) I looked at him point blank.

"Did you just eat a Post-it?"

He looked at me with his trademark glare, smirked, and then went back to typing up charts without answering.

"Why would you eat a Post-it?" I pressed.

Zvi raised an eyebrow, rocked back in his swivel chair, and smiled.

"Because I don't have a shredder at my desk?" he reasoned.

And I have to admit, it somehow made sense at the time.

"The Human Shredder," I said with a laugh.

Zvi didn't laugh quite as hard, instead offering a softer version of one of his famous glares. By then, I knew all of this was part of his grand shtick, boasting about how he had Raj and other billionaires on autodial, and had access to the best intel around. I only wish I'd known more, and earlier, about what and who I was dealing with. I always thought of myself as a good judge of character, with a solid built-in bullshit detector—but I was never more wrong than when it came to Zvi. And the details, not to mention the consequences, of my misjudgment and his deceit were only just beginning to hit me where it hurt.

When I could no longer bear to look at the Internet, I took drugs and drank Ketel One and fell asleep.

I awoke in the vise grip of an Ambien-Klonopin hangover. My daughter Sylvie was asleep next to me, snoring gently, mouth wide open. She'd crawled into our bed at some point during the night. The Klonopin was typically able to construct a pontoon system that suppressed my waves of agony and anxiety, but it couldn't mute the incalculable uncertainty, the terrifying prospect, of what my life had now become.

I propped myself up and stared at Sylvie's sweet elfin face, a tangled mess of freckles and wheat-brown hair, all meshed into benign perfection. If I went to prison, would she even know me? How could I possibly explain to her what happened yesterday? How can I explain it when I don't totally understand it myself? I'd never wanted to get out of bed less. Walking to the bathroom and turning on the shower seemed an insurmountable task.

The door popped open and my three-year-old son, Cam, all wild curly red hair, bounded into the room, shouted "Daddy!" and leapt into my arms.

Being a parent is tough, the toughest job most of us will ever have. Every halfway decent parent knows this. The pendulum between good times and bad doesn't always swing symmetrically. Unfettered sleep is a distant memory from a younger, less complicated life. Your freedom becomes subjugated to the whims of someone else's existence. But there are those moments you wouldn't trade for anything: a child jumping into your bed, or seeing you at the school pickup line and breaking into a run while yelling your name—these are among the finest experiences life has to offer. They wash away the tough times in an instant—but, unfortunately, they also don't last very long. At five years old, Sylvie was already too cool for emotional displays, and would offer only a placid smile when I would pick her up from school or camp.

But all of this—everything—had changed. It felt irrevocable, precisely because it was. Yet even then, on that first horrible morning after my arrest, when the entire world felt like the darkest depths of Mordor, a palpable, tangible joy had survived. I knew I had to be strong, now and for what followed. I had to be strong for *them*.

With Cam in my arms, I put a finger to my lips, to let him know to be quiet. He looked around and saw the two girls starting to stir. Phin was still asleep.

"The whole family is here," he whispered with a smile, as if we were the only two people sharing this secret.

"Shower?" I whispered back.

"Yes!" he yelled, thrilled at the prospect of a rare early morning, pre-breakfast shower. Bathing was usually a nighttime activity in our household, but a nice warm shower with Dad wasn't a half-bad way to start the day.

This isn't real, said a voice inside my head. *None of it.*

I blocked it out and followed my son to the bathroom.

CHAPTER THREE

SUNDAY WITH MOE

ONE THING YOU LEARN AS A potential felon is that there are many more people than you'd ever expect who have been though a tribulation similar to yours. As it turned out, I could swing a bat and hit a dozen people who were felons or had a family member who served time, something I had no idea about until my case broke. During those first forty-eight hours, numerous friends called me with stories about their dads, their brothers-in-law, their friends, or friends of friends. A few were dark tales, but most offered glimpses of redemption and second chances. Some were as simple as "I never told you this, but my father went to prison for a few years when I was growing up." Some were more in depth and complex. Friends I had known for twenty years unexpectedly opened up their painful, hidden pasts to me. My friend, let's call her Kelly, whom I hadn't spoken to in close to fifteen years, called to tell me about her father and a business gone bad. "Remember when I had to 'rush home' right after graduation? It wasn't because my mom was sick. My father had just lost at trial and was going to prison. We didn't know what to expect or how our family would survive."

My college friend Randy Oser had one of the darker tales. His father had gotten into trouble and tried to navigate the system with an incompetent lawyer. In doing so, he became a pawn in a much bigger case. When he refused to cooperate, they crushed him and added charge after charge. His original sentence had been less than three years. The government brought new charges while he was locked away and broke, unable to defend himself. He didn't walk out of prison for another twelve years, a shell of his former self.

Perhaps because of his story, Randy was one of the fiercest proponents of my making a deal, any deal. He said he had seen a legion of dirty tricks, of empty promises, incompetent lawyers, and corrupt judges and prosecutors. His father's story would've come as no shock to any citizen of the former Soviet Union. But for it to happen *here*, to an American, to someone raised on the goodness and fairness of our system, to a man who still choked-up at the Star Spangled Banner . . . that was a terrifying, eye-popping slap in the face.

The biggest shoulder to lean on came, initially, from another college roommate and great friend, Moe Fodeman. Since our halcyon days at Lafayette College in Pennsylvania, our lives had been inextricably linked. He had always been a selfless friend. He asked for nothing and offered everything he could.

The day after my arrest Moe called and performed a kind of psychological CPR, talking me down from my emotional cliff. I was facing the full wrath and resources of the Feds, and Moe was, technically, one of their lieutenants. An accomplished and respected Assistant US Attorney (AUSA) for the Eastern District of New York, Moe had the experience, the map, and the contacts to know exactly what I was facing. He made up some excuse about being in my area on the Sunday after my Thursday arrest, but I knew he had rearranged his day just to drive up from the city to Westchester to hold my trembling hand.

Since Moe was bringing his son, Lucas, I recruited Cam for our outing. We would have lunch at Molly Spillane's, a new bar on Mamaroneck Avenue. It was better known for Yankee games on the tube and prowling cougars in tube tops than as a place one might dispense sage legal advice. And I was acutely aware that that advice might not be purely legal. Moe was risking a lot by even being with me. Had a newspaper reported or one of his FBI buddies noticed us together, it would have damaged his career. At the very minimum, he would have been reprimanded for trying to help me.

"You shouldn't be here," I said as he greeted me with a much-needed bear hug.

"What are you talking about?" he said with a grin. "I'm not allowed to get lunch with one of my oldest friends?"

"You're a superstar, Moe. You've got a job that you've worked your whole life towards. First federal death penalty in 100 years. Joint Terrorism Task Force. Organized Crime unit. You're a future US Attorney or senator. You shouldn't even be taking my phone calls."

"Listen. This is still America. I'm not currying favor or using my influence to mitigate your case. This is just two friends hanging out."

"Yeah, and I'm sure Charlie Manson and Vince Bugliosi shared a Cobb salad at the Brown Derby post-arrest."

"It's good to see the threat of federal prison hasn't made you lose your sense of humor," Moe said with a smile.

His words brought me back to a reality that I still couldn't fully fathom.

"I'm looking at fifteen years—my kids won't even know who I am when I get out," I said, *sotto voce*, on the verge of tears, first making sure that Cam and Lucas were preoccupied tearing open Splenda packages.

"You're not getting fifteen years," Moe said in a tone that dismissed my concerns.

"I know I'm not. I'll put on a 'David Duke for President' T-shirt and walk around the South Bronx before I'd go away to prison for fifteen years."

I was serious, too. At night, my closed eyelids bombarded me with fearful, deranged fantasies of suicide. But kids need a father, even if the relationship is thirty minutes a month on the phone with a bitter old felon. In my heart, I knew a father was irreplaceable, whatever the circumstances. I knew that my family would be better broke, in a grim one-bedroom apartment by the train tracks in New Rochelle, surviving together on food stamps, than any alternative that took me out of the picture permanently.

"Stop it, Mike," Moe said, sounding far too chipper, casually tipping back his second Diet Coke. "Remember, I don't put *murderers* in jail for fifteen years. You're not looking at anything remotely close to that."

"You read the complaint," I countered. "Twenty years per count on the substantive insider trading charge and five years for conspiracy. That's twenty-five years if it all goes bad."

"That's not how it works," Moe said, waving my concerns away. "Those are statutory *maximums*. That's not what you're facing. In a white collar case, it typically goes by the amount of money a victim loses. With insider trading, there are no victims. So they flip that and it's the 'money you made.' They may have additional charges or bring in other items . . . but Mike! . . . the complaint says you made $16K."

Moe paused as if his own words had puzzled him.

"Honestly, I've never even seen a complaint in a Federal case for a number like that, Mike. You belong on the *People's Court*, not up in Leavenworth. I don't even think five years is realistic, and that's based on a worst-case scenario.

I think you'll have to do about seventy-two hours in Brooklyn MDC or three months of home confinement. Although if I were you, I might opt for prison over being locked at home with Lisa for the next three months."

He made me smile with that one. Both of our wives were equally capable of moments of incredible, unconditional love, but also of terrifying wrath. Moe might not know exactly what I was facing at home, but he probably had a damn good idea.

For the first time in the last seventy-two hours, it felt like the boot heel had been lifted ever so slightly from my throat; Moe, God bless him, was the first one to give me any clue about how the process actually worked. All at once, it dawned on me that the FBI's threat about me not seeing my children for a very long time was not going to be measured in decades.

"In fact, five years is a long time in most circumstances," Moe continued, biting into a cheeseburger. "There are plenty of rapists and gang members that do less than a nickel."

He took another bite of cheeseburger.

"Talk to Michael on Monday," he said, referring to Sommer, my lawyer I'd not yet met with. "He'll be able to really drill down with you on specifics. At a high level, your options will come down to this: Plead 'not guilty' and go to trial, plead 'guilty' and offer to cooperate, or plead 'guilty' and *not* cooperate. You need to think hard about cooperation and if you can provide something the FBI wants. It will mean no jail time, probably. Do you have something you can trade? Don't answer that, but think about it for your meeting."

"Like what, generally? What do I trade?"

"Something on a person. Something on Zvi or one of the other codefendants. Something that makes the case easier for the prosecutors to prove."

I paused for a second to think.

"I don't have anything," I said. "And even if I did, something feels disgusting about a guy stepping down on others to save his own ass. I don't think I did anything wrong and I'm not about to start making shit up."

"I don't want to know details," Moe said. "Remember, I'm your friend. Not your lawyer. If I get subpoenaed and they put me on the stand, I can be forced to repeat anything you've told me. Same goes for everyone else you speak to, with the exception of your wife, who has spousal privilege, or your lawyer. So don't talk to *anyone* else about this case. Not even casually, not even in very general terms. Not your parents. Not your friends. And definitely not any of your codefendants. At this point you need to assume that every phone call, every conversation is being recorded."

"Actually, I think I can also talk with a priest or a shrink," I said, adding the other two privileged conversants.

"See, that $75,000 for law school wasn't a total waste," Moe said with a wry smile. "I'm not here to tell you what to do, Mike. I'm here to be a friend and let you know you'll find a way through this. I've seen guys in your situation dozens of times. Stay positive. Know it will end one day. And know you're a good person. You've been a great friend, and you're an incredible father. Although we both could probably use some improvement on the husband front."

We both laughed.

"Remember," Moe said, "you didn't hurt anyone. You violated a regulatory statute. The complaint I read seems paper thin. That doesn't mean you don't go to jail, but it will be at a level you can recover from."

You better believe I lapped up this "good news" that my predicament would end one day and I probably wouldn't get gang raped like it was oxygen. For the last two nights, only heavy doses of sleeping pills had allowed the brief, phony salvation of sleep. My bed sheets were always soaked in the mornings from sweat, and I could barely manage to look at my children without breaking down. Moe's words of support and encouragement were the first actual parries of optimism against the advancing thrust of darkness and terror.

Let me just be frank. I could never have survived the coming months without him, or without my other friends and family, the ones who knew the real me, a person who didn't even remotely resemble the financial criminal and consigliere, the greedy and evil caricature of me that was being peddled by the government and being lapped up by the press.

"Tell me how it goes with Sommer, and keep your head up," Moe said as we concluded our meal together. "Call me anytime, no matter what. I might not be a prosecutor much longer anyway. When that change happens, we can *really* talk."

I looked at him quizzically. *Moe leave the public sector?* Given my friend's temperament, it seemed like a fantasy.

"Farin wants a third kid," Moe said, as if reading my thoughts. "It's awfully hard to raise three kids in New York City on a government salary. It might be time to test the waters of private practice."

"Well . . . welcome to the dark side." I said as we walked back outside. "I mean . . . I shouldn't have phrased it that way. You know what I mean. I'll call you after I meet with Sommer tomorrow."

"Please do," he said and gave me a hug. "After all, I owe you. All your buddies do. Compared to you, Mike, we're all in the running now for Husband of the Year."

I couldn't help but smile, because deep down, I knew this was true. And I thought again about Lisa, probably in bed, sobbing and afraid and pissed at me. I couldn't blame her. Being innocent didn't change the fact that I was responsible for our mess. With each passing hour it became increasingly clear that my choice of business partners and associates—in particular, the track-suited brothers (fucking Zvi!)—could have been a whole lot better. And now those choices might just land me in prison and disrupt my family in God knew what way.

Every marriage has its own private dynamics, with inevitable ups and downs. Don't believe the people who tell you it can ever be perfect. *Fight? Never. Fuck? Why of course: at least every other day, after fifteen years.* Nope. Sorry, but I don't buy it.

Lisa had a right to feel she might have made the mistake of her life in marrying me, and I knew it. Driving back to the house from my lunch, with Cam quickly falling into a doze in the back, I remembered when we'd first met, at Duke's on Park Avenue South. Moe, of all people, had organized a party there for the Lafayette-Lehigh game. It was fall of 1998.

I noticed her right away. Or perhaps I should say "remembered." When I'd been a senior, Lisa had been that hot redhead freshman dating a sophomore from our fraternity. Our frat brother was, for lack of a better word, already whipped. There was no doubt in hell who ran the show in *that* relationship. You could tell from a distance. At Duke's—perhaps forgetting this detail—I immediately decided that I was going to go talk to her. She was surprisingly receptive. I don't remember what we talked about, but I remember that when she laughed she blushed, and when she blushed she smoldered. I gave her my card, with SULLIVAN & CROMWELL emblazoned on it, and more importantly my cell phone number. I was heading back home to Los Angeles in a couple of days to see my family for Thanksgiving, but I asked her to call. She did. While I was there we talked on the phone several times. Long talks. This was back in the day when people still talked rather than texted. I had planned to stay in

LA for ten days, but I flew back early just to see Lisa. Our first date was at the Bank Café, and it was a total hit. We connected in a way I'd never experienced. I learned so much about this fascinating, gorgeous woman.

Lisa had been born in DC, where her father had served on the Council of Economic Advisers for the Nixon White House before being promoted to president of the Chicago Federal Reserve and serving in that post for twenty-odd years. He settled his family in an upscale suburb called Winnetka. It rivaled any town in Westchester or Fairfield County for privileged preppiness. She wasn't a spoiled rich girl, however—at least I didn't think she was, not really—although she was definitely accustomed to a certain level of comfort and style. It was clear to me that she expected her adult life would afford her similar circumstances. But Lisa wasn't waiting for anyone to hand things to her. She was ambitious in her own right. When we met, she was working for Martha Stewart. Lisa would go on to produce live cooking shows on the Food Network before starting her own catering business. And I instantly liked that about her, this strong entrepreneurial side.

As fate would have it, we also lived quite close to each other—she on 34th and 1st, while I was on 24th and 2nd. We moved in together in February of 1999, just two months after our first date. I waited till June to propose. Did it with a picnic dinner and a bottle of champagne at sunset, up on our rooftop. As you might imagine, planning a wedding with someone who produces live events for the Food Network can become a complicated process. Our planning dragged out for fourteen months, till we finally tied the knot at the Standard Club in Chicago. As newlyweds, we lived in the West Village. That changed after 9/11, when the sight of that tragic empty space down 7th Avenue, where the Twin Towers used to be—forever reminding us of friends we'd lost—led us out to the suburbs. First we tried Westport, Connecticut—full-on Martha Stewart territory—but the commute to the city was just too long, so we moved again and settled on quaint and quiet Larchmont. There, we soon welcomed Sylvie into our lives. Cam and Phinnie followed. The marriage was still far from perfect—our equally strong personalities often clashed—but we were in it for the long haul, come what may, and we both seemed to have a sense of that.

Now, however, I knew that everything between us was about to change. To really splinter and fray. Under the weight of charges from the federal government, the crack that once existed would soon become a canyon.

CHAPTER FOUR

INTO THE LAWYER'S DEN

I'VE ALWAYS BEEN AMBIVALENT ABOUT HOW I felt about lawyers, even after having been one myself for a while. Never in a million years did I think that my future—my entire life, really—would actually rest in a lawyer's hands.

Yet, suddenly, there I was, loitering outside the lobby of the Credit Agricole building at 1301 Avenue of the Americas, rubbing my sweaty palms together and trying to muster the will to walk inside.

The securities firm Wilson Sonsini occupied several floors of the building, along with the now-bankrupt Dewey Leboeuf and several other major banks. I was in the belly of the beast.

I knew the area fairly well. It was one block south of the Hilton Hotel that was my parents' preferred abode whenever they came to visit New York. When I gave my name to the receptionist on the fortieth floor, I was relieved that she didn't recoil. I felt like my name was all over the news.

I sat down to wait and read the *Wall Street Journal*. For the last twelve years, I had devoured this paper, consuming it whole every morning on the train as the starting point for my day's worth of research. Now, scanning the headlines, my only thought was that the content was totally meaningless to me now. All of it. There wasn't a single thing in here that impacted my life anymore. Not one iota. It was all entertainment. Business porn from a faraway world. My life was now simply down to the case before me—no more, no less. And the outcome would dictate whether my family would have enough money to live on, and whether my children would have a real father. It would decide if I would go to prison, and if so, for how long.

The *Journal* and its contents were irrelevant now.

Outside of the realm of my family and my lawyers, virtually nothing else mattered.

I tossed the *Journal* aside and gazed at the wall until my lawyer Michael Sommer came bounding up the stairs from the thirty-ninth floor to shake my hand. I wasn't sure what the appropriate expression was to wear, and no longer cared. His was the perfect mix of subdued confidence and deep concern. A solid, attractive man with a receding hairline and a high-end Italian suit, Michael knew this business cold. He had been a prosecutor in the Southern District of New York (SDNY). They had been the All Stars of the prosecution world for years. With its purview encompassing New York City, the Southern District drew a greater share of high-profile cases than any other district in the nation. The World Trade Center bombing, the Milken-Boesky insider trading cases, the Giuliani mob prosecutions—these cases and others like them had turned a few SDNY prosecutors into superstars and household names. If you were a talented and serious prosecutor, it was where you wanted to be. Since crossing over to the defense side, Michael had allegedly never lost a case, including the high-profile win in the Symbol accounting fraud case several years ago.

He escorted me to the aptly named Conference Room F, as in "Fucked," and sat down across an impressive dark wood table from me.

"Michael, let's take this from the top," he said. "I want to review the complaint with you and then we can discuss your options—that is, how best to proceed. I want to start by saying that I know this is the hardest thing you've ever gone through. I know it can feel terrifying and impossible to handle. But I want to tell you, while the *hardest* part may not be over, the *scariest* part probably is. I was on the other side of this as a prosecutor for a lot of years. I know the system, how it works. I know most if not all of the players. The shock, fear, and shame—that's bad, but it's over now, okay? The project now is to figure out whether there's anything we can do to get them to drop the case or at least defer prosecution. I'll be very frank. It's an uphill battle for something this well publicized. It's a lot easier to get the government to do the right thing when they haven't splashed your picture all over the news. For them to drop the charges now would require them to admit, in a very public fashion, that they were wrong. But I'm not saying it's impossible. Now if you were Zvi? Zero chance. That would be a career killer for them. But out of this group of nine that were arrested, your name is at the bottom. Prosecutors usually do these lists in order of culpability. Worst on top, least on bottom. I'd say you and David Plate, the ones at the bottom, are who the government aim to squeeze the most. Peripheral guys they expect to help them with the case, either through information or your testimony."

I heard Sommer's words loud and clear, but I couldn't really process them. After three days of the purest stress imaginable, Ambien-induced nightmare naps and an anti-anxiety trance had left me a zombie, a shell of my former self. Squeeze the most? Me?

"To be frank," Sommer continued, "I think it'll be impossible to get them to drop the case entirely. The next best thing is a deferred prosecution. A deferred prosecution, or DP, is when the government agrees not to move forward with the case and comes to an agreement with the defendant that if he can stay out of trouble for a set period of time—two years, three years, whatever—then they'll agree not to bring it to trial. That's a home run in this game. When you get back to your house later, Google a case I was hired on last year. Ramesh Chakrapani. He was a banker at Blackstone. I got the government to agree to defer his prosecution by illustrating that their view of the case, their view of his actions, was wrong. That it wasn't consistent with the evidence and that they would be making a mistake taking him to trial and trying to convict."

Here Sommer paused and leaned forward—possibly for dramatic effect, possibly just savoring the recollection of his previous victory.

"I hope to do the same in your case, Michael. You have to understand that this is a long shot, it'll be difficult, but it's not impossible, especially if there are key parts of the complaint or the government's theory that are wrong."

I exhaled a deep breath and offered a bland, "Okay."

I understood what he was saying, but at the same time I couldn't put any odds on it. As a trader, I'd always needed to know the chances of hitting worst-case scenario so I could mentally prepare myself. Here, though, the odds felt impossible to know.

Sommer was still speaking, leaning forward on his arms, and I didn't want to interrupt him. I was sure there would be plenty of time for questions later.

"You see," he went on, "the complaint is essentially the government's road-map of the case. In an abbreviated trial, this is what they would attempt to present and prove. But understand that this is baseline. Cases don't get weaker over time, they get stronger. Defendants become informants, additional witnesses come forward, an investigation turns up new evidence. So don't get your hopes up that this is it."

He held up the complaint and gestured with it.

"There will be more."

I nodded, trying to take it all in. I was hearing every sentence but each part brought up so many other thoughts and questions that Sommer was always three sentences past by the time my attention clicked back. I was scribbling notes ferociously.

"I'm telling you now," I warned, "I'm going to ask you to repeat things again and again. Whether it's stress or lack of sleep, I can't seem to remember things like I used to."

"Understood," my lawyer said, as if I were not to first client to have this problem. "Now let's look at the people. Give me a brief description or tell me about your background relationship with the people listed—Zvi and Nu and so forth. Start with the lawyer, Arthur Cutillo."

"Never heard of him. Never met him before the arrest."

"Never?"

"No. Never."

"What about Jason Jenkins?"

"Same. Never."

"Ok. What about David Plate?"

"Met him a handful of times. I think twice at this bar a lot of traders go to for happy hour. Then maybe one more time. I knew him really only as the guy who sat next to Zvi at Schottenfeld. He's a smart technology analyst that used to work for Mario Gabelli. But I don't really know him."

"Gautham Shankar."

"I think I spoke to him twice. Maybe three times. Barely know him. Same bar, same happy hour, small-talk chitchat and some macro market talk. I also vaguely remember interviewing him for a job. At some point he considered coming over to Incremental."

"Drimal."

"Less than a handful of times. He was an early passive investor in Incremental. He works at Galleon and is good friends with Zvi."

"So then it seems like out of the nine people listed in the complaint, the only ones you really know are Zvi and Nu?"

"Yes."

Sommer made a brief notation on his legal pad and then looked back up at me.

"Okay, let's look at the complaint now. They allege two counts. One is a 'substantive' count of insider trading, meaning you actually made a trade they deem illegal, and the other is 'conspiracy,' a catch-all prosecutors use to try to entangle someone. It's a very liberal, wide-net charge that covers an agreement between two or more people to potentially do something wrong. You don't need to actually commit the crime. You can be thinking about it or planning it. As long as you take a step toward committing the crime, you can be found guilty of conspiracy. You didn't have to make the trade or be successful. Just having an agreement to commit insider trading would be enough."

You can be convicted for your thoughts, I thought to myself. This was beginning to sound like a bad Orwellian dream, or a nightmarish science fiction from William Gibson or Philip K. Dick.

"That seems . . . ridiculous," I stammered. I was still in shock over the idea that I might be going to prison for insider trading, *without any actual trading*.

"It may. But conspiracy is very broad and an effective tool for prosecutors. It's how more than half the people in prison right now were convicted."

"So again, because I'm not sure I heard you right, I can be convicted of conspiracy to commit insider trading without actually making any trades?"

"Yes. I know it's hard to believe, but yes. You're hearing me right."

Stress, fear, shame, vodka—my brain cried out for and against each one. I thought, *If the government is Sauron, conspiracy is the One Ring.* The thing they can use to do whatever they want.

That was my first introduction to the concept of conspiracy. I would spend the next eighteen months debating my lawyers (and everyone else), trying to determine what it really meant and what it actually covered. When dozens of highly paid lawyers, defendants, prosecutors, and judges can't give you a firm and final answer, you realize it's nothing more than a magic hammer for prosecutors to smash defendants, suspects, and persons of interest into submission.

Insider trading without a trade. WTF?!

That overwhelming, almost suffocating feeling of dread that Moe had successfully dispelled over burgers with the kids was lunging back with an impressive counteroffensive.

"Now let's go back to the complaint again," Sommer continued. "The government alleges that on August 7th you, Zvi, Emanuel, Drimal, Shankar, and Plate all bought shares of 3Com while *knowingly* in possession of inside information. With regard to you, the complaint says you bought 10,000 shares while in possession of nonpublic information that was knowingly acquired from someone in breach of their fiduciary duty on that date. Do you remember buying shares that day?"

"Not really," I said. "But it's highly unlikely that I did."

"Why?"

"Because I was in DC, at the Federal Reserve, having lunch with my father-in-law."

"Was anyone else at lunch with you?"

"Yes. My wife . . . and Alan Greenspan and Ben Bernanke."

Sommer looked at me for several seconds without saying a word.

"Are you serious?" he finally managed to ask, even though his gut instinct was probably to shout: "Stop fucking around here. Your life is on the line and this isn't the time for jokes."

But I wasn't kidding.

I told Sommer that my father-in-law, formerly the president of the Chicago Federal Reserve, had his retirement luncheon in DC on that date.

"My wife and I sat at a table with Greenspan, Bernanke, my father-in-law, and a few other Fed Heads. Greenspan and my wife discussed which vegetables gave him gas pains, and Bernanke and my eight-year-old nephew had engaged in that timeless debate—Red Sox or Yankees."

Sommer was still staring straight at me. I'm sure he had a question or two, but with a new client the best approach is caution, until you find out what makes them tick.

"Oh . . . kay," he said. "I assume you have some sort of documentation to verify this?"

"Yup, I do. I checked before I came here and have credit card receipts of my hotel stay, flight itinerary . . . all the stuff like that."

"And you didn't have a laptop or anything with you, or have someone execute trades for you while you were there?"

"No," I said. "We were at the Fed and they were meeting on interest rates. There's a limit on what technology you can bring in when that's going on. They had a strict 'no laptops or cell phones' policy until after the decision was released. And, I mean, it's not like I knew the decision, but I do remember thinking if I could backdoor Bernanke into revealing it and find a carrier pigeon, I could make a lot of money. The Fed makes its decision around noon and then they embargo it until 2:15 p.m., when they disseminate it publicly to the markets."

"And you are absolutely positive that was August 7, 2007?" Sommer asked again. It seemed that he still did not fully believe what I was saying.

"Yes," I insisted.

"Well . . . I'll have to see that documentation," Sommer said, seeming to relent somewhat. "It's hard to believe the government would get that date wrong. That's the most essential part of this complaint. If that's wrong, it's a *serious* fuck-up. Very sloppy."

Sommer shook his head. He consulted the page before him. Then he began again.

"Do you remember trading 3Com *ever* around this time period?"

"Yes," I said. "I don't have my records from Quad Capital, where I was working at the time. But in my PA, my personal account, it shows that I traded 3Com on August 10th."

"August 10th," Sommer said with a smile "Three days later? Okay, that's good. Let's not get too excited here, because it may not be a big deal, but I like it. It breaks up their narrative that everyone traded on the same day. If they're wrong about something as simple as a date, they can be wrong about other things. But what about the quote in the complaint? The one where Zvi tells you, *'PF Chang's, print it all out'*?"

"I don't remember that," I said. "I know I traded Chang's. I know I lost money in it. If we were trading it, and it was more of an intermediate than a day trade, I'd probably have had a research file on it."

"OK. What about when you said, *'There's always a reason to be paranoid'*? What about that quote?"

They had obviously tapped phone lines or bugged us to get these quotes in the complaints. But at that moment, I didn't know which phone had been tapped, or which of my coworkers had been wired. If I had, it might have been easier to recall these conversations.

"Always a reason to be paranoid . . ." I slowly repeated, searching my brain for anything that felt familiar. "No idea. I don't know when I said that, or what it was regarding. That's my personality in business, though. I'm a paranoid guy. Or maybe that's not even totally the right word. I'm always nervously trying to divine what's next or where my weaknesses are. This is one of the riskiest, most regulated industries out there. You *need* to be skeptical and paranoid. Andy Grove, the CEO of Intel, even wrote a book called *Only the Paranoid Survive*. I'm not sure how paranoia is proof of a criminal mindset."

"And what about; 'Joked about it coming from a guy fixing a pothole'?"

"I kind of remember that one," I said. "Vaguely. I can recall Zvi, in a pitch meeting once, saying something about how he occasionally gets information from a construction worker. There was a guy outside our window, drilling a pothole for Con Ed. I made a joke about how that was the guy Zvi gets his information from. You had to be there, but it was a good joke. I think the whole room cracked up."

"Hmm, all right," said Sommer neutrally. "So here's the next step. I have a conversation with the government team prosecutors and the FBI lead case agent. I find out what they're thinking and then I come back to you. They may want you to do a *proffer*."

"What's that?"

"That's where we sit down in the same room with the Assistant US Attorneys, and maybe the FBI case agent, and they interrogate you."

"Sounds lovely," I said.

"My position on proffers is very simple," Sommer said. "I don't do them. They almost *never* help a defendant. More times than not, they get seriously hurt. It's irrelevant whether or not you're innocent. In a proffer, they can ask you vague questions and later say you didn't answer them fully. They can be sneaky and confusing about the dates, and then claim you answered incorrectly. Proffers are a way to cement a case if you're a prosecutor, because the prosecutor can almost always hit the defendant with a perjury or obstruction of justice charge afterwards. It's not just a 'material misstatement' they can get you for. Remember that. It's a 'material misstatement *or omission*.' So they can say that while you answered truthfully, you failed to mention X, and that was an omission. Welcome to obstruction of justice and perjury. I take it you've heard the phrase: *It's not the crime, it's the cover-up.*"

"Watergate."

I was well-versed in Nixonian lore.

"Proffers are designed to work that angle," Sommer told me. "There are a lot of people in jail who aren't there for any substantive crime, just perjury or obstruction. Look at Martha Stewart. It's the same reason you never answer questions or speak to an FBI agent when they arrest or approach you. They use your answers as the basis to bring additional charges. It's your word against theirs, and theirs always wins."

"I'm starting to agree it makes sense to turn down a proffer," I told him.

"Now . . ." Sommer said with a deep sigh. "We reach the part that I don't like talking about and I'm sure you won't either . . . money."

"Lay it out for me," I said, tightening my sphincter to prevent myself from flinching (or perhaps from actually soiling myself). I was praying the guy's fee would be in my ballpark. I really liked Sommer and wanted him to represent me for this.

"Well, there are two phases here," Sommer said, gently easing me into it. "We're going to try to get this dismissed or resolved *pre-indictment*. For the pre-indictment phase, I can *get by* with a retainer of only $100,000. That's just a retainer. If we use less, and the case gets dismissed or wraps up before then, you receive the balance of what hasn't been used. That is, you get some of your money back."

"Okay," I said, exhaling slowly through my nose.

I had a hundred grand.

It would hurt, sure, but if I could keep the costs there and we could get this thing dismissed or deferred, it wouldn't be fatal.

But just as the clouds seemed to be parting, Sommer's face fell. His expression told me that this rosy scenario was unlikely. I realized had to ask the big, scary question.

"What happens if I get indicted?"

"Then, again, you have three paths to choose from," Sommer explained. "You can plead guilty and cooperate, plead guilty and not cooperate, or go to trial. If you plead guilty right away and don't cooperate, it won't cost that much. Maybe another $100,000, maybe less; it depends on how long it takes to settle the SEC case and whatnot. If you cooperate, it will be more expensive, but you'll be looking at either no jail time or a significantly reduced jail sentence. Also, the SEC and DOJ will likely waive any financial penalties or fines, or at least hit you with a much smaller penalty."

I swallowed hard and asked about the granddaddy of them all. The mother lode. The big kahuna.

"What if I want to go to trial?"

"Hard to say," Sommer replied casually, like I'd asked if it would rain later. "It will depend on if there are multiple defendants and how complex the case is. A boost to those elements can make a trial last longer and become more expensive. If you're the only defendant, that would be less expensive."

I couldn't believe I had to press him on this. I swallowed again and forced myself to proceed.

"Look, I'm not going to hold you to a quote . . . but for planning, I'd like to have a ballpark figure."

"If you're the only defendant and it's a simple trial, it could be as little as $500,000," Sommer said. "If it's complex, with multiple defendants and witnesses, it will run into the millions."

Sommer said this so matter-of-fucking-factly that I felt myself reflexively grabbing the handles of my chair just to keep myself from sliding under the table. The sensation was physical, nauseating, and imparted a terrifying vertigo. Hitchcock had got it completely right. It was just like what you see in the movies. Endless, bottomless panic as you sink into the spinning abyss.

Sommer continued talking. Perhaps he did this to shake up my vertigo. Perhaps I was not the first client to have this reaction in front of him.

"It will also depend on you, Michael. You're a lawyer. If you do some of the work, you can alleviate some of the costs. For example, if there are multiple wiretaps, we can pay an associate $450 an hour to listen to those tapes and transcribe them. Or you can do it. I may need research done, or discovery and document review. You can cut your costs significantly if you are willing to do, and can do, the work."

He was offering a lifeline, but the rope still didn't seem long enough. *Millions* was a lot to defray in $450 chunks.

"I'm willing," I told him. "I mean, I'm an attorney who hasn't practiced law in ten years and doesn't know shit about criminal law. But sure, I can listen to tapes. Transcribe and review documents. I know the players and the lingo."

I decided to press my luck.

"Or what about a flat fee?" I asked. "Do you guys ever consider something like that?"

Sommer smiled like I was a precocious child.

"We do consider flat fees in certain exceptional cases," he replied. "But I have to ask . . . Are you financing your own defense? Do you have an employer or D&O insurance that will pay for it? Can Incremental pay for it?"

"Um, I am Incremental," I said. "It's my money and we don't have D&O insurance. Even if we did, I'm not sure it would cover a criminal charge. So it's all me. To be frank, I don't have a lot of money. I've got a big chunk of my savings frozen at Incremental. I do have some other funds, but not to take this to trial. So let's take it one step at a time."

"We will," Sommer assured me. "First things first, let's see what the government has to say and find out where the other defendants stand. I'll contact the Assistant US Attorneys on the case tomorrow and ask for the evidence in the case. Often they'll provide some discovery before indictment to induce the defendants to plead. So whatever they show us tomorrow, most likely, it'll be the best they've got."

I smiled, too bewildered to be reassured.

"Keep your head up," Sommer instructed. "You will get through this, Michael. I know it's overwhelming. But if you decide to retain me, I'll help you navigate everything. I'll help your family navigate the process and I'll get you to the other side, hopefully to the 'least worst' outcome. You'll survive this either way. And just as a small aside, I should let you know that when I was a prosecutor, I used to work together at the Southern District with Richard Sullivan, the judge assigned to your case. We still have a *very* good relationship."

Sommer stood. I realized the meeting was ending.

He said: "If you have any questions in the meantime, don't hesitate to call me."

Sommer is the friend of the judge in my case? I thought to myself.

That seemed to make it an easy decision. Maybe my luck was turning. The vertigo began to abate. I stood up, thanked Sommer sincerely, and shook his hand heartily. There was nothing about this case that seemed typical or ordinary. Nevertheless, by the time we were through, there would be several firsts and on more than one occasion I would hear Sommer say, after more than twenty years on the job, "I've never seen *that* before." If only I'd known that when I strolled out of that meeting room.

Back outside, I looked up and down Sixth Avenue. The city that used to make me smile, with its possibilities of riches and beautiful women and wild nights on the town, had vanished. I used to love Manhattan, heart and soul. Now all I could think was that it had kicked my ass, and even betrayed me. I would have been better off staying in LA. The grass wasn't any greener there; it just wasn't caked with scum and littered with my broken, bloodied limbs and shattered years. I tried to collect myself and prepare for what was yet to come.

CHAPTER FIVE

ENTER THE DATEK

———

THE IDEA OF BECOMING A LAWYER first struck me as a five-year-old, after a violent hairy beast named Baron, my best friend Matt Slavin's Germans shepherd, nearly ripped my face off. The threat of a lawsuit had been enough for them to have the thing banished from their family, something which delighted my father. Normally, my father couldn't stand lawyers. As an OB/GYN physician, he had to pay absurd amounts of money for medical malpractice insurance and deal with being sued by ambulance-chasing predators who liked to channel dead babies at trial. Ah, but to me, a young kid with eighty-five stitches across my face, to see Baron exiled forever from the neighborhood because "we don't want to get lawyers involved" had planted that first seed.

I also wanted to be a pro ball player—as a Jewish Dodgers fan, the next Sandy Koufax sounded just fine—but that dream faded in high school, where the caliber of players in Southern California was so strong, it was sobering. As an undergrad at Lafayette, I still played ball freshman year but knew it was my swan song. I found myself torn between business and law school. I'd never had a burning desire to be Clarence Darrow, and I was always good with numbers. I liked the inherent risks and tempting payoffs associated with finance, and had my first taste of it when I interned at Chemical Bank right after college, at 270 Park Avenue (today, the Bear Stearns mausoleum).

Still, law school struck me as more practical. You can always "learn" business out in the field, I told myself—most people in business don't have business degrees, anyway—but the law was different. A degree was required. Despite my best intentions, my grades were decent, even with a semester in Australia, where I traveled the continent rather than attend class, forcing me to lobby professors just for a gentleman's C. Even so, I crushed the LSAT. This seemed to offset my middling GPA and I soon found myself accepted at Emory, Georgetown, and USC. With no interest in diplomacy or politics, it was down to Emory and USC—and with my buddy Moe going to Emory it seemed like that would be the one. But I thought about it long and hard, and realized that Emory would be the better choice only if I wanted to practice in Atlanta—and I knew I didn't. All I knew of Atlanta was Ted Turner and the Braves. And like every other school or college choice, the bottom line is that you don't go for the knowledge—you can get that almost anywhere—but you go for the people. The *connections*. If I was going to stay in Los Angeles—and at that point in my life, that was my plan—then you had to go to law school in LA.

USC's Gould School of Law was the oldest law school in the entire southwest. It was a great place to study; plus, I got to live in South Central LA and Brentwood, just down the block from where Nicole Simpson was murdered by someone still at large. As graduation loomed, I thought about taking the bar in California, but the pull of Manhattan became too strong. The more I heard about it—the opportunities, the lifestyle—the more I liked. It proved hypnotic. The city's energy and women cast a genuine spell on me. Soon, I had arrived and planted my flag in New York City. I was living in a fifth floor walk-up on 28th and 3rd, a staggering 300 square feet, with a bathroom through the tiniest of kitchenettes, but still, it was mine.

The decision to accept an offer to go work for Sullivan & Cromwell in Manhattan was an easy one. I had interned there after my second year, living in pre-trendy Tribeca, where a 5,000 square foot loft cost an outrageous $1600 a month. I split the rent with my friend Sona, a fellow USC student, in order to defray the price (which, twenty years later, is, of course, about ten times higher). By my third year of law school I was putting in a meaty forty hours a week paid externship with the firm, and seemed a shoe-in for a job. A "non-offer" from your summer employer after second year of law school meant you were literally an "untouchable." Indian lepers in Bangalore had a better chance of employment next year than you did. Granted, it was a different economy and most people got offers, but not at Sullivan & Cromwell. Few law firms are as storied; and nowhere does the term "white shoe" fit quite so snugly. At Sullivan & Cromwell, the shoes were crafted by hand, by fabled Tuscan cobblers, and the color a brilliant and blinding snow white. Founded in 1879 by Algernon Sydney Sullivan and William Thomas Cromwell, the two worked closely with Thomas Edison as he created, in 1882, what would become General Electric. But their success and connections didn't stop there. The much older Sullivan soon retired, and it was the colorful Cromwell whose clients included J. P. Morgan (as in the bulbous-nosed banker himself, the legend) and Andrew Carnegie. Future partners would include a secretary of state (the stern Presbyterian, John Foster Dulles), a director of the CIA (John's roguish, pipe-smoking younger brother, Allen Dulles), and a chief justice of the Supreme Court (Harlan Fisk Stone).

The musty Puritan WASP factor still lingered in the hallways, in the austere oil portraits of the famous and powerful partners. Yet by the time I got there—me, a nice Jewish boy from Southern California—the country club anti-Semitism of the firm was a thing of the past. Women and minorities could climb the greasy pole to partnership, which was what we all strived for.

Office politics had certainly changed since the stuffy days of WASP ascendancy—and when it came to after hours, we definitely let our hair down. When you work *all* the time, your more basic needs tend to get filled around the office, so everything was on the table. And everyone. People understood this. I believe the firm's unofficial policy was to hire the oldest secretaries and administrative staff they could find with the hopes that it wouldn't turn into a hothouse full of a potential sexual harassment suits (still a new thing, then). Still, there were transgressions aplenty, like the senior litigation partner who took a fancy to a summer associate thirty years his junior who was also a friend of mine. At one happy hour that ran about five hours over its intended limit, she ended up blowing him in the lower level of a well-known Third Avenue bar behind a Golden Tee game (she confided that the game's announcer had prophetically shouted "Fore!" a half-second before he erupted in her mouth).

It was that kind of life. Always there. Always at work. Your colleagues practically your only choice when it came to socializing or antics.

Going through the motions at the firm, glued to my cellphone and my desk, my mind would occasionally drift elsewhere. Finance continued to rattle around in my head like a recurrent daydream. Stuck in Sullivan & Cromwell, this dream soon became a full-blown desire. I knew I had the temperament to run money, to be a trader, and that I could make snap decisions, often under excruciating pressure. Not everybody can do that.

By its very nature, finance was a poker game, one that would be open every day, with the stakes of my choosing. Perhaps playing poker for a living rather than editing documents wouldn't be everyone's choice, but I knew it would be mine in a heartbeat. Something told me I wouldn't be a lawyer for long.

When the fateful day came, I'd been at the office since 9 a.m. Sunday, reviewing a Valujet prospectus we had drafted for Goldman Sachs—our client—making sure they were "bulletproof" after one of Valujet's planes had fallen out of the sky. I had also just done an overnight stint at "the printers," the most useless, technology-deprived wasteland of a department I'd ever come across. There, teams of stern-faced lawyers went over drafts, going to battle over commas and colons, and every round of changes took over an hour for the typesetters to incorporate. At 10:30 on Monday morning, I was back once again at my office, which wasn't even mine alone. I shared the space with a Chinese national named Wu whose family supposedly had politburo connections back on the mainland. Wu had attended law school in China, which I'd always guessed involved little more than an extra semester of college. After all, how comprehensive could the legal curriculum be in a country where they can unilaterally censor all print and media, where the warning shots are chest high into protesting students, and where they can kidnap and indefinitely detain anyone they please? *Habeas what?*

Lurking behind my desk that morning were two extra suits (one navy blue, one medium gray), three indifferent dress shirts, a hive of discarded ties behind the door, the hypo-allergenic pillow on my bookcase that fit nicely under my desk, and the small wool LL Bean blanket (a gift from Mom) I used to cover my feet when I slept under the desk because the AC was always blasting.

Wu was just arriving as well, fresh from a weekend of drinking, eating, and gambling in Chinatown's finest establishments. His desk was typically immaculate, not a hint of paper, here in a world that lived on nothing but paper. I had no idea how he did that. The familiar red blinking message light that haunted me was nowhere to be seen at his desk, where he sat down and took out a Chinese book and started to read.

"You don't really do anything, do you?" I asked Wu.

I had wanted to ask this question for a long time. He turned to me and smiled.

"Onrey when dey need me," he said slowly, smiling an even bigger smile and returning to his book. (Wu talked like a bad Chinese stereotype from a 1930s movie. Would it be better for me to lie and say that he didn't? I assume you can handle the truth.)

Maybe once a day, Wu would disappear for thirty minutes to speak to a partner about some hypothetical matter, or on the rare occasion when a Chinese company wanted something. At this time, although China was a budding economic powerhouse, the tiger was still decidedly number two, and the majority of real "business" they were doing with overseas partners tended toward piracy. Wu was merely a small investment in the future on behalf of the Sullivan & Cromwell partnership, which hoped that one day he would return to China, do something productive, and engage our firm as his US counsel. In the meantime, I got to watch him roll in at 10 a.m. every damn day, enjoy a two-hour lunch, and jet at 4:59.

It was at that very moment, glaring at Wu and reflecting on the day I was supposed to spend with my parents that had vanished, that I decided to give something else a try. Something *very* different. I knew halfwits who were making much more money than I was, and working way fewer hours. The hard part would be to deviate from the all-important *Path*. At Sullivan & Cromwell, as with all major Manhattan law firms (no matter the color of their shoes), there was a safe yellow brick road that ended with the Pick Six on the Upper East Side, the beach house in the Hamptons, the uber-elitist private schools, membership in the right clubs, and all the trappings and accoutrements of modern financial and material success. The hard part wasn't so much the distance—typically eight-plus years for a partnership track. The hard part was looking at those in the Winner's Circle. Seeing a thirty-five-year-old partner who looks forty-five years old is disheartening enough. But a lot of them looked fifty-five. Thinning gray hair on the cusp of white; premature jowls; tired eyes with dark circles. And there were forty-five-year-old partners all over the firm who looked ready to start collecting Social Security. Where's the joy in having money if you're ready for a premature date with the Grim Reaper and you feel even worse than you look? Never mind the fact that these partners had no time in which to spend their money because they were still working *all the time*.

I looked at Wu and took a deep breath.

It was the late 90s, and opportunity was in the air, just outside my office window. The tech bubble was ballooning; bankers were minting money in the ongoing capital markets orgy; and there was an opening in those fields for persons who were smart and aggressive enough to write their own tickets. At the same time, of course, nobody knew that the Great and Powerful Greenspan had fallen asleep at the wheel. No one knew what loomed ahead. (The *real* tragedy, of course, was that no one was paying attention to a lanky, turban-sporting Saudi with a portable dialysis machine some eight thousand miles away, who was starting to broadcast infomercials promising death to the Great Satan. Instead we were focused on Y2K. The computer manufacturers were throwing napalm on the fire and pulling their hair out, yelling, "If you don't buy a new computer RIGHT NOW! your bank account will evaporate in a microsecond!" The software mitigation experts and consultants were warning that unless they were allowed to bless and re-bless everyone's programs, planes would fall out of the sky and Solitaire and Minesweeper wouldn't work. Blinded by green, the "expert industry" issued one big "or else" to corporate America. It meant imminent ruin, shareholder suits, bankruptcy, and criminal negligence. Not everyone bought into it, but in our litigation-centric oligopoly, if you didn't make the CYA moves, you'd be eaten for lunch by the lawyers.)

Greenspan was still smarting from the bad press and the lack of public love from the last time he'd exercised some modest monetary discipline back in 1994, and decided Y2K with its slick three letter acronym was as good a reason as any to jimmy the accelerator pedal to the floor of the Monetary Machine and then jump out of the rapidly accelerating car on autopilot as it headed straight for the cliff. Fortunately for everyone else, the man who destroyed the car would be waiting at the bottom of the cliff with unprecedentedly low interest rates, eager to inflate an even bigger bubble and goose the market with some extra cash *once again*. Just as a precaution, of course.

Faced with such an absurd world, I knew, then and there, at that moment, staring into Wu's face, that it was time for me to hit the eject button. The very next day, I answered the call of a persistent headhunter who cold-called me every other week.

"Get me in front of the Goldman or Bear Stearns risk arbitration people or stop calling," I told him and hung up.

It worked.

Less than a week later, I banged a successful first interview with one of the Managing Directors on the Bear Arb desk. They said they liked me from a personality and pedigree standpoint, but needed to know whether I was good, or *really* good, before committing to hire. Their suggestion: Go see a trial going on right now for the next two days and provide them with realtime updates and a memo on how I thought it would get adjudicated. It was a legitimate request, and a real-life test I might have demanded had our roles been reversed. (Later on at Incremental, when I was hiring traders, I pined for a beta test that would have allowed me to match a trader's purported background and skills with the market of today. Too many of the prospective candidates were superstars on paper, and never made a dime once they got behind a keyboard for me. The Bear request was at least a glorified paper trade. *You say you know M&A and you know trading? Great, what do I do in this situation? And tell me quicker and more accurately than anyone else.* This was just my cup of tea.)

There was only one problem. It was nearly impossible to work a hundred-hour work week at Sullivan & Cromwell and disappear for a day, or even a half day, sans cellphone, into the caverns of 500 Pearl Street. My waking day contained a constant undercurrent of mortal fear that my cellphone would miss a call, or that I would forget to check voicemail and find some senior associate breathing fire and demanding retribution in flesh. Being without my albatross in a downtown federal court for a solid block of time was the quickest, most surefire way I could imagine to get myself fired, or to have partners asking questions that I didn't want to answer. And even while I had made up my mind to do something else with my career, I was still, at heart, a cautious guy, and not even remotely capable of quitting or risk losing a job until I had another one, if not *two*, in my pocket. I thought seriously about a sick day. However, requests for sick days at S&C were typically greeted with condescension. For my employer, the sick days were an embarrassing artifact mandated by government regulation. After all, sickness was for those weak of body and mind. They were also a quick way to get weeded out from the partnership track.

Instead of claiming to have the flu, I approached a respected senior associate I was friendly with and put the scenario before him. His response was that doing something like that for Bear Stearns violated pretty much every

Sullivan & Cromwell rule on conducting outside business while working for the firm and probably violated about seventeen different New York State Bar Association rules of ethics and conflicts as well.

"So that's a 'No'?" I asked, just to double check.

"Nope. That's a go ahead, but if anyone finds out, you'll be fired on the spot and possibly brought up before the Bar on disciplinary charges."

The senior associate's response was enough to cool me out on the live interview and let my Bear courters know that they would have to find another route to test my competency. Disappointed, they wanted me to come in the following week for another round of interviews. We would have to do with a one hour set of hypotheticals instead of the real thing.

It was all for naught, however, because that Friday, I paid a fateful visit to one of my closest friends from college, Randy Oser. It was a testament to the overlords of the Sullivan & Cromwell salt mines that I hadn't met Randy for lunch or drinks even once since I had started working there almost two years before. Randy was at 50 Broad and I was at 125 Broad—so close, I could probably drop a Titleist into his lobby with my 8 iron. Yet still we had never met up. It wasn't all on me, though. Randy may have had it even worse. I had asked Randy to lunch once or twice, but he'd always demurred.

"I don't leave my desk for lunch."

"They don't let you leave for lunch?"

"Oh, they *let* me leave. I can leave whenever the hell I want. I *choose* not to."

"So . . . you spend all day at your desk staring at a computer screen."

"All day," he quipped.

"I guess it's not that bad. You go home at 5 p.m. I'm just pouring my third cup of coffee by then, because my day is only half over."

"I'm sure the Pharaoh appreciates your sacrifice."

"Rand, I'm sick and tired of being sick and tired. This place sticks a Dirt Devil vacuum in my ear every morning and sucks out my soul. It's pure torture."

"Hmmm," Randy grunted. I could tell the twenty seconds he'd allotted me had elapsed and he was already busy elsewhere. Calling Randy during market hours was like talking to an Alzheimer's patient; they heard the sound of your voice, they just didn't *listen*.

"All right, how about I come by tomorrow and bring you lunch?" I offered. "My treat."

"Huh? Sure, whatever. 11:30. 50 Broad. Eighth floor. Ask for me."

"Sounds good, I'll . . ." and click, he had hung up.

What kind of a horrid job doesn't let you leave for lunch, ever? Even more ter-rifying, what kind of a job makes an employee not want to leave for lunch? My first instinct was to flee my desk whenever possible. Sunlight and people-watch-ing, even of the highly stressed, degraded quality found in the bowels of the downtown financial district, were a respite and the holy rite of us overworked drones everywhere. Was there really a job that people enjoyed so much that they didn't want to go out for lunch?

"Sounds like a cult," I said to Wu, who acknowledged me with an emphatic grunt.

The following morning—it was the first of February, 1999—I told Linda, my secretary, that I was going out to lunch with Conly Chi. Conly was a fellow associate who was also stuck on a hideous long-term project, a project finance deal.

"I'll have my cellphone," I said, "but try to cover for me for an hour if you can. Do you want me to bring you anything back?"

She did not.

I walked from 125 Broad Street to 50 Broad Street with no inkling that this was the beginning of the end of everything I had worked for—and the first step toward what I was born to do. A quick pit stop at a crowded, innoc-uous deli for a couple of sandwiches, a turkey and avocado that should have done the honorable thing and committed *hara-kiri* to end its dullness, and a decidedly more tasty chicken parmesan. I would give Randy first pick, and surely get stuck with the healthy one. I strolled by the Dark Tower of Goldman Sachs at 85 Broad, with its giant eye of Sauron up top, and looked through the window of the Goldman-centric Starbucks next to the lobby, where male pat-tern baldness–infected alpha men and perfectly coiffed, intimidatingly intense females were stopping in for their caffeine jolts before being summoned back up to the mothership.

While Goldman's lobby at 85 Broad was marbled and immense, staffed with security burned out by years with Blackwater and giant potted palms flown in from the Amazon Delta, the lobby at 50 Broad had all the charm of the back of a Chevy Astro van. The overweight guard with an Errol Flynn mustache barely looked up from his *New York Post* as I entered and walked to the elevators. I pressed 8 and was soon outside of two glass doors that read *Datek Securities, A NASD Co.* The logo looked like it was written by some free Logo Maker software, and the glass itself—good God!—it was smeared and streaked, just begging for Windex. My already slumping spirits sank even further as a four-foot-eleven, 200-pound receptionist buzzed me in without a smile and stared at me for a few seconds before barking, "*YES???*"

"Uh, sorry. I'm here to see Randy Oser?"

She popped her gum in acknowledgement and whispered something into the phone.

"He'll be right out," she said, neither inviting nor instructing me to sit down.

After an awkward minute, Randy came bounding in.

"What's up?" he said, giving me a handshake and wrapping me up. "Come with me."

Randy led me through a frosted glass door and into the inner sanctum. Of absolute and utter crap.

As a lawyer, I had done work for nearly every major investment bank, and had spent a considerable amount of time near the Goldman trading floor. With its banks of monitors, high ceilings, lush expensive carpeting, under-stated artwork, dozens of Bloomberg terminals, Herman Miller Aeron chairs, and high tech turret phone—it was a vast football field of technology.

This, here, Datek?

It was not even on the same planet.

Datek's trading floor was so cheap-looking it literally made me wince. It had ripped industrial blue carpets, plain wood desks that should have had liquidation stickers on them, flimsy fold-out catering tables, and self-assembled polyester overstock chairs from Staples. There was a mish-mash of randomly placed monitors from different manufacturers, chipped light blue walls in desperate need of a paint job and devoid of any art or attempt at decoration, and low ceilings with lighting connected by exposed wires. An unsettling, insect-like humming permeated the entire space. Two columns of desks created a path for foot traffic through the middle of the room, with six rows of traders on both sides of the aisle stuffed five to a row, each inhabiting perhaps thirty-six inches of living space. The trading floor at Goldman had a subdued but energetic buzz. Here, the buzz was like someone had stuffed a microphone in a wasp's nest. Randy grabbed a dented plastic folding chair and sidled me up to his desk.

"Kind of loud in here, huh?" I asked.

"Loud?" Randy was genuinely surprised. "It's lunchtime. You should hear it at the Open and the Close. Multiply what you hear now by a factor of three."

I glanced around while Randy pulled the sandwiches and Diet Cokes out of the paper bag. I took in the other people around me. Mixed in were a few adults, or at least guys my age, but most of the traders were kids, right out of college or maybe with a couple of years under their belts. Jeans, T-shirts, sneakers, and baseball caps were the uniform of choice. Some guys opted for golf visors, and a select few wore homemade visors that were about the silliest looking damn things I'd ever seen: cardboard half circles duct-taped to a normal golf or volleyball visor, so that the six-inch bill was now sixteen inches or bigger, with the sides tempered down to block out any ambient light.

"Who's that maniac?" I asked, unable to suppress the urge to gesture toward a tall, skeletally thin geek wearing green-tinted John Lennon sunglasses and a visor the size of a tanning reflector.

"That's Brad Masters. He may not look like much, but he averages about $500K per month—his end," Randy said driving a verbal elbow into my Adam's apple.

"How much of that does he keep?" I asked, trying to keep my voice from cracking with envy.

"His end . . . meaning all of it. That's his net, Mike. His gross was at least double that."

Randy was doing his best to suppress a *"who's laughing now, fuckface"* smile.

My mind was spinning, craving oxygen as my blood flow headed south. This Brad character was a kid who would have gotten beaten up at my high school during lunch. In fact, I had an incomprehensible urge to pummel him right then and there for wearing that absurd mega-visor. Yet he was making multiples of what I and most lawyers were being paid annually . . . each month! Greed is like a leech, a silent, unseen deer tick that hooks its claws into you in a flash and never willingly lets go.

Maybe Brad was an aberration, a statistical freak.

"You're gonna catch a fly in that mouth, Mike," Randy sniped. He was right: my mouth was actually agape, my jaw had dropped, and I was almost drooling.

"But Brad's one of the best," he continued. "Those aren't typical numbers."

I was relieved. If those numbers had been the norm, I probably would have walked back to my office, resigned on the spot, and come back over to pledge my undying loyalty to whomever or whatever I had to.

"So how's work?" Randy asked.

"Work?" I recovered. "Oh, work is *GREAT*."

I oozed sarcasm.

"But forget about me; what've you got here?" I asked, pointing to the dizzying array of red, green, and blue numbers blinking across his twin screens.

For the next five minutes, Randy gave me an accelerated tutorial of his trading monitor. The three Level II boxes at the bottom of the screen gave an in-depth bid-ask of a stock. The Level II quotes showed every market maker and ECN lined up on the left (the bid side) at the price they were willing to buy stock, and their mirror quote on the right (the ask side) at the price they'd be willing to sell stock. Some stocks, like Dell or Microsoft, had a nice tight spread of no more than 1/8 of a dollar, while faster or thinner stocks like Inktomi or CMGI might be separated by as much as 1/2 dollar.

"And *what's* that?" I asked, as I pointed at a bolded green number on the right edge of an inversely highlighted horizontal bar down the middle of the screen.

"That's my P&L."

I knew enough about trading to know that P&L meant "Profit and Loss"—essentially the amount you were up or down for the day. The number on the screen read P&L 11696.

"Almost $117. Ok, not too shabby for what, two hours of work so far?"

Randy rotated my way, with the hint of a grin.

"Yeah, 117," he said, the grin starting to grow.

"Wait, come on. $11 . . . *thousand*?"

I turned back to the screen, to double-check if my eyes were playing tricks on me.

"Nice day," I said, my emotions pinging between disbelief and pure spite. Just prior to saying anything, I had run the numbers in my head. I doubled

$117 plus some for an end of day $300 gain. Multiplied by five days equals $1500 for the week, with fifty weeks getting him to $75,000. Nice, for sure, but nothing special. Still, a better deal than my gig, based on his forty-hour work week and the ability to sport flip flops and shorts to the office.

But $11,000, however, was a whole different ballgame. Now we were talking $55,000 for the week, which, multiplied by fifty, gets him to . . . $2,750,000 for the year.

What the fuck am I doing working one hundred hours a week and sleeping under my desk for $100,000?

This was suddenly a huge practical joke. I felt an intense anger brewing toward Randy, for not having opened my eyes sooner. A real friend would have grabbed me Neanderthal-style by the hair and dragged me from one end of Broad Street to the other.

"Is this an average day?" I asked, almost choking. "Great day? *Lousy* day? Give me some perspective."

He pulled out a busted-up blue spiral notebook with his "runs" for the previous three months. His daily averages were between $3 and $20 thousand. Monthlies were pivoting around $200,000. Holy shit. This was real. It was really real. I looked at Randy like he had just confessed to banging my fiancé, and I genuinely stammered while motioning to the rest of the room. "Ev-ev-everyone here?"

"No," Randy scoffed.

Whew. I didn't think so. Randy was a superb card player, a good golfer, and an engineer—sharp all around and disciplined. I didn't know if he would be tops in here—it sounded like that Brad Masters guy already was—but I knew he would be at least a top 20 percent type guy, and likely much higher.

"Probably a quarter of these guys make no money," Randy explained. "Then the top quarter, anywhere from $1 to $5 million. The middle 50 percent, anywhere from $100 to $500K, I'd say. That's all ballpark," he said, punching a few buttons and taking a bite of his chicken parmesan sandwich, as I saw his P&L change to 12014.

I sat there, gawking at the screen, but my brain was humming with possibilities.

"Who runs this place?"

"The boss is Erik Maschler. He's, uh . . . he's a special kind of animal."

"Introduce me to him. Can you get me a job here?"

Fuck the foreplay. I didn't want to beat around the bush. I was love-struck.

"Slow down," Randy said. "You've been here five minutes and you're ready to throw away three years of law school and a job at the best law firm in the world—just to sit here and play video games with a bunch of maniacs?"

"When you phrase it like that, Randy, I start feeling like maybe I should think about it," I said with a smile. "But also, my gut's saying 'What the fuck is there to think about?' If those numbers are real, then there's *nothing* to think about. I could make partner at S&C, putting in six more years of one hundred-hour work weeks, then I could earn $1 million or more a year and *still* work eighty to ninety-hour weeks, and never see my wife or kids."

"Wait? You've got kids? When did you even get married?"

"Not yet, but I'd like to. And I dig this girl I'm hanging with. Lisa."

"Jay's old girl?"

"Yes, Jay's old girl. Can we not refer to her that way?"

"Sorry, Mike. You mean Crazy Red?"

"Fuck you," I said. "I like her a lot. But I never get to see her because I work until eleven every night."

"Not *every* night, surely?"

"You're right," I said. "Some nights I work until midnight. I'm lucky if it's only 10 p.m. I'm tired of the salt mines, Randy. Of getting bossed around by people that live in mortal fear of our clients at the banks. I can't stand being ordered around by the senior associate, who gets ordered around by the partner, who gets ordered around by some twenty-nine-year-old douchebag at an investment bank. I want to *BE* the twenty-nine-year-old douchebag at the investment bank. You know I've always loved the markets, gambling, cards. Taking risks. I traded my way through law school, and that was on a bullshit E-Trade account. I had no idea there were tools like this."

"You would be good at it," Randy admitted, his eyes consulting the corners of their sockets as he mentally verified this. "It's one reason why I didn't want to tell you about it. I don't want to recruit you and be responsible for you throwing away a job at a marquee firm. Your life might be hard right now, but believe me, this is hard too. It burns people out. It's the only job where you can do all your homework and preparation, and they *still* can reach into your pocket and take your money away from you at the end of the day. And who knows how long the opportunities here will last. Because of the market, this can all disappear in a heartbeat."

"Exactly, which is why I should start now," I insisted. "Worst-case scenario? I do it for a year, the market crashes, or the laws change, and then I go back to work at S&C or some other law firm. What's the risk?"

I was playing innocent. There were risks, plural, and I knew that.

If I told my firm that I wanted to go be a visor-wearing day-trader, and then came crawling back in six or twelve months, they might give me a job again, but they'd make life hell for me and future opportunities would be few and far between.

That did not deter me. If some of these knuckleheads here in this weird room could make $250,000 a year—and the good ones were making seven figures—it was a no-brainer.

Randy sighed.

"You really want to do this? I'd have to stick my neck out for you. Erik's a bit . . . unpredictable. And 95 percent of these guys here are Ivy League. I was the first non-Ivy guy they hired. But because I did well, he's hired a few more. I think I can get him to take a chance on you, but you have to want to do it. No 'I'm thinking about it' or 'We'll see.'"

"Brother, I'll start today if he lets me. I'll fax my resignation back to S&C from here."

Randy laughed.

"You promise not to hold me responsible in any way whatsoever, that you are of sound mind and body and making this decision sober and with all your . . . faculties?" Randy checked one more time.

"Scout's honor," I said, holding up my hand.

"Then . . . you want to do this right now?" Randy asked. "We can see if he's got time."

My eyes went wide.

"Rock 'n' roll," I said, standing up and straightening my tie.

"First of all, take that off; you look fucking ridiculous," Randy said, pointing to my Hermes necktie. I glanced around the room. There were people with hats on backward, in shorts, or even barefoot—despite the February chill.

"Oh," I said. "I see your point."

"Wait here, and I'll go see if Erik's around," he said. "And whatever you do, don't fucking touch anything."

Five minutes later, Randy reappeared.

"He's in his office, down the aisle in the back. Says he'll meet with you. I put in the best word I could. Now it's all up to you."

"Thanks Rand. I owe you."

"You know I wouldn't recommend any of our other friends. But *you* . . . I think you've got the right mentality to do this. Just don't embarrass me."

"No more than usual," I said and walked across the trading floor and down the hallway. The door was open, and after double-checking the name on the plaque, I gave a light knock.

"Come in and shut the door," a voice commanded. I did as ordered, and Erik popped up from behind his desk. He had a large, pear-shaped belly and matching chubby red cheeks that seemed out of place on a kid that couldn't have been more than twenty-six years old. I tried to feel intimidated.

"So you're Randy's friend?"

"Yup. Mike Kimelman, thanks for taking the time to meet me."

I offered a thin smile and pumped his hand.

"Sooo, you're a *loy-yah*?" he said with a thick Staten Island accent.

"I am. Though hopefully, not for long."

Then he exploded.

"Ya know, loy-yuz are . . . *THE WORST FUCKING TRADERS I'VE EVER SEEN!*" he shouted, addressing the traders down the hall as much as me. He threw up his arms with the intensity of someone trying to scare off a bear. I wondered if he was being serious, and if I should try to respond. Then I realized he was just getting warmed up.

"*THEY CAN'T PULL THE FUCKIN' TRIGGER!*" he literally shouted. "*THEY OVERANALYZE EVERYTHING!* Ya know, if Randy hadn't made me so much fuckin' money, I wouldn't have even wasted five minutes to talk to one."

Okay, so it wasn't quite the interview style Latham or Davis Polk came at me with. Hell, even Skadden Arps hadn't been like this, and they were widely known as some of the meanest bastards in Big Law. As I was to learn later, Wall Street interviews are different. I'd heard of Goldman's thirty interviews, case studies, complex mathematical and brain puzzles—all that, sure. But this was something else entirely. I thought of the Monty Python skit where a guy comes in for an argument, and says, "Hey wait, this is just abuse."

My mind raced until it found the one place where this type of questioning had been routine. Based on the kids out there—out on the loud, crowded Datek trading floor—I thought I might have just understood something. Datek was a fraternity, and I was a potential pledge. At Phi Delt, our verbal abuse had been legendary. The hazing, the pranks, the psychological warfare. And now this guy Erik wanted to take his turn as an in-your-face drill sergeant, a sadistic pledge-master, a slob with the keys to a $250M a year cash machine.

Sensing familiar waters, I quickly moved to highlight my twin addictions of gambling and drinking.

"Randy is the best," I said. "But you can ask him about me and confirm everything I'm going to tell you here. I may be a lawyer, but I'm the farthest thing from a technical, four-eyed nerd. I played baseball in college and Randy and I used Atlantic City as our personal ATM in college. We clobbered people on the poker tables, and I can drink like a fish and play blackjack all night. I've been banned from Resorts International for counting cards and I still have a host at Trump Taj that will send me a car anywhere in the northeast on thirty minutes' notice."

Erik's face transformed into a curious stare that told me I had successfully changed the tenor of the conversation. He looked at me for a few more long seconds, slowly nodding his head to the internal monologue in his brain. He walked back to his chair and sat down. He reached under his desk and pulled out two huge notebooks labeled SERIES 7 and slammed them down.

"You gotta pass the Series 7. You think you can do that?" he growled. "I have to sponsor you . . . And if you fail, are you going to pay me back?"

That sounded an awful lot like a job offer, and the fastest one I'd ever gotten. I smiled. I didn't answer his question immediately, simply because I couldn't tell if he was being serious.

"I'm not asking you, guy, I'm telling you," he snapped before I could respond. "You fail, you pay for the test."

"Don't worry about that," I managed.

"Cocky bastard, aren't you?"

"Not really. When I commit to something, I *commit*. There's zero chance I will fail it."

I'd passed the New York Bar without breaking a sweat, and *nobody* is about to confuse the Series 7 for the Bar. I had seen enough of my knucklehead high school friends pass the Series 7 to not be scared of it.

"Consider it done," I continued. "What's the timetable?"

"You schedule the test yourself," he said. "Most people take about three months to study. After you pass, *if* you pass, you start a twelve-week training program here."

"Okay, I'll see you in two weeks," I said.

"Two weeks?" he scoffed. "You're nuts. The quickest anyone's done it here was a month. Don't shoot yourself in the foot. Take the time to know the material. You fail it, you're done. There's no second chances here."

"It was the same at my law firm. One shot at the Bar. I'll be fine. I appreciate the opportunity, Erik."

I walked over to his desk to shake his hand.

"Go see Barry next door in HR, and give him all your info," Erik barked. "He'll get you started on the paperwork."

After meeting Barry, the only bona fide adult in the place, I walked back out to Randy carrying my Series 7 books and drawing guarded looks from the other eighty traders in the room. Another mouth to feed. Another competitor. I strolled up to Randy with an ear-to-ear grin.

"What do you have there?" he asked, frowning.

"The Series 7 books. I'm starting in two weeks."

"You're not even going to think about it or talk to your firm?"

"It's time for a change, Rand. Plus, only a fool would turn down the type of numbers you're putting up. If I can make half or even a quarter of what you're doing, it'll be a home run. And that's just on the comp side. The hours are the real prize. I like this girl I've been hanging with. I don't get to see her enough. I don't get to read, work out, or do anything. Too many people who are less motivated than me are making coin and making moves. This is the wrong time to be a drone."

Randy looked me up and down—sensing, I think, my total determination—and shook his head.

"I know you're right, but I still feel responsible. I don't want you to throw away a promising career for . . ."

"We covered this already, bro. You're off the hook. Now shut up and give me a hug."

We hugged it out and Randy walked me back to the front door.

"What are you going to tell Sullivan & Cromwell?"

"I don't know yet," I said truthfully. "But I'm going to keep working there and wait until I pass the Seven for sure."

"You'll pass," he assured me. "I've seen guys pass it after a three-day coke and booze bender."

"They should probably *require* people to take it under those conditions; it better models the industry," I said with a grin, and departed.

When I got back to my office, I called the SIPC scheduling agent and booked the first available date for the Seven—three weeks away. It would still be a Datek speed record, and would give me more than enough time to study. When I hung up the phone, I saw Wu watching me closely. After a passing pang of paranoia, I figured that even if he understood, he couldn't care less.

Fuck it.

"That's right, Wu," I said. "It's time to make some real money. You're about to have your own private office, all to yourself."

Wu looked up.

"Fock dis place," he said with an agreeable nod, then buried his head back in his book.

CHAPTER SIX

THE TRADING GAME . . .

───────

I ACED THE SERIES 7 AND jumped headfirst into a brave new world. Randy and everyone else at Datek urged caution and patience, telling me that it would take anywhere from nine months to a year to learn the business, and that I should expect to see no paycheck above the de minimis $500 a week draw they paid traders in the training program. While $500 a week might work in some cities, in NYC you'd be lucky to cover a room in a flea-ridden hostel. At Sullivan & Cromwell, I'd been pulling several times that.

But after two weeks of intensive training and paper trading, under the guidance of a guy named Dan Balber, I was ready to go live. Within six months, I knew that I'd made the right decision. I was positive three out of five days and learning quickly to eliminate my mistakes and see the tape. Nine months in, I was making real money and taking home my first substantial paychecks. They weren't jaw-dropping, but they were consistent: anywhere between $25,000 and $75,000 for the firm each month, and approximately 40 percent in my end. My confidence was growing, steady and solid.

It had happened. I was hooked.

At Datek, the bosses who reaped the jaw-dropping bonuses were personal degenerates, but they knew how to get results from us. The key was competition. The first time someone made $10,000 in a day, it was only a matter of weeks before several other traders had pulled that in. Then the bar was raised to $50,000, then came $100,000—all in a day—and soon enough others matched those figures. With each new impossible milestone reached—$1,000,000 in a month!—the roar of greed, speculation, and success boomed louder and louder. Erik Maschler and his cronies were the Roman

Emperors, holding their thumbs up or down to whip a coliseum of financial gladiators into a frenzy of money-lust and one-upmanship.

Our emperors' weapon of choice for fomenting maximum competition was something called the Watcher trading software. At most firms back then, traders only saw their own P&Ls. The Watcher allowed any trader to pull up a list of the entire firm's daily P&Ls, laid out from top to bottom. You can imagine how it went.

Who's up $25K? Bastard. Who's gonna get ripped a new asshole for being $30K in the red? Ha, love it.

You could click "Top Losers" with your mouse and the Watcher would give your P&L in reverse order from worst to first. There were no secrets at Datek; and thus no bullshit lies after hours; and certainly no tenure. Poor performers could be fired at any time and there was no honeymoon period, no "take your time to settle in." Competitive pride was juiced even further by managers launching contests, handing out a few thousand in cold, crisp, impromptu cash for Best Week or Best Day.

Look at those jealous glares.

Those new Ben Franklins were often topped off with all-you-can-drink alcohol-infused parties at nearby bars. Movados, Tag Heuers, and Rolexes (bottom-of-the-line Rolexes, but still Rolexes) were handed out like party favors. Erik loved rewarding and praising his best, and vocally shaming his worst. Managers were given fat expense accounts to entertain traders at steak dinners across Manhattan. These meals were often followed by hours in strip clubs, and the jaunts occasionally concluded with trips to Asian massage parlors for a "happy ending" to the evening. These excesses infused loyalty into the trader ranks and ingrained that cash-money lifestyle into their blood. It didn't take much to get hooked. To fucking need it. The raw meat of cash gifts, of steak dinners followed by female flesh, and expensive watches tossed in for the fuck of it . . . it made the boys more loyal than they ever ought to have been.

The rewards were legendary, but so was the abuse. Erik was a plump Napoleon, prone to spittle-spraying verbal attacks. This was a jarring change for me. At Sullivan & Cromwell, the hallways were rarely louder than a whisper. If a partner or senior associate wanted to yell at you, he pulled you into his office, shut the door, and went for the jugular with soft-voiced sarcasm. (*"Here's a quarter, Mr. Kimelman. Go call your mother and tell her you'll never be a lawyer . . ."*) Datek was the opposite. Erik stalked the floor like a male lion before the morning's opening bell, waiting to pounce. There was palpable tension in the room—a real feeling that violence was a possibility—and God help the trader who dared to make eye contact.

Take the tale of Alex Perez. A quick-on-the-uptake trader, and one of the few guys who, like me, was over twenty-five. Alex had been a trader for Cantor Fitzgerald and Prudential before deciding, again like me, to join Datek because one of his boyhood buddies was printing money on an everyday basis. One day in late '98, with the futures way down, I glanced out from my protected corner (always have your back to the wall in such an environment) and saw Erik, hands clasped behind his back, high stepping through the aisles to inspect traders' pre-open rituals. Alex was at his desk, munching on a bagel smeared with cream cheese and punching up the charts of different stocks that piqued his curiosity. Erik walked right up beside him, hovering, and the next time Alex put the bagel in his mouth, Erik wound up and swiped an open hand as hard as he could into Alex's fingers, sending the bagel flying out of his mouth and across the room with a loud "thwack." (You wouldn't think bagels would be loud, but there you go.) Alex was in total shock. His mouth hung open. Before he could respond, Erik screamed, "You motherfucker, don't let me *EVER* catch you eating right before the open. This is game time! You want to stuff your fat face, go do it before 8:30, when the real traders do. Well, what do you have to say for yourself!?"

It wasn't even remotely a question.

"I'm . . . sorry?" Alex sputtered.

But Erik had moved on. Another trader, after four straight down days, was told that today would be a "big day" for him. The trader asked how.

"How big?" Erik growled. "Here's how big. If you're negative again today, you can either choose to be fired, or shave your head."

This wasn't a buzz-cut kid either. With blonde, wavy, enviable surfer hair, you could see his heart just sink. The kid did his best but still ended up losing a token amount that day. He chose to shave his head, and two other traders whipped out the clippers and took him to the bathroom to complete the sacrificial offering. When the shiny-scalped kid was negative the following day, Erik fired him anyway.

Pride? Why wouldn't you quit? Because you wanted, you *needed* to ride that gravy train. And where else were you going to make that kind of money, at that age?

That was life at Datek. Those who didn't earn were harassed until they either started making money or were weeded out and let go. Datek was like a trellis full of roses, and Erik the gardener with the sharp pruning shears—carefully cultivating his favorites and mercilessly removing everything else.

It was hard to convey to other people how absurd it was to work there. These were the true barbarians, the savage hordes plundering. For fifty years, the big banks had operated as a virtual oligopoly, with an iron-clad lock on the markets. Goldman, Merrill, Morgan, Lehman—functionally, they were little different than the Gambinos, the Genovese, and the Bonnanos, comprising and operating a ruthless cartel colluding toward a single end—fleecing the common man.

It wasn't until the mid-90s that technology allowed the day-trading firms like Datek to challenge these established powers. As a securities lawyer, I was intimately familiar with the SEC. Or *thought* I was. To the outside world, and according to its own press team, the SEC was the regulator of the markets—enforcing the rules and ensuring fairness. But at Datek, I received an eye-popping crash-course in the *real* role of the SEC.

It quickly became bracingly clear that they were the defenders of the established cartel—nothing more, nothing less. They were running a protection racket that smashed any upstart firms that in any way challenged the old banks' dominance. On occasion, an established banker or broker would fleece a retail client so egregiously, so sloppily, that the SEC would be *forced* to come in and slap a wrist, just to maintain the appearance that they were there to protect the public. But those cases were few and far between. The SEC existed, first and foremost, to protect the traditional Wall Street powerhouse banks from the public, and not the other way around. The overwhelming majority of the agency was staffed by mediocre, bottom-of-their-class bureaucrats who hadn't been able to cut it in the private sector. And for those few at the SEC who *were* competent, their allegiance was co-opted through the portal of corruption known as the Revolving Door, which ensured a future payoff in the form of a lucrative gig with the very banks they were supposed to be regulating. *Perfect Capture.*

In 1997, some of my buddies at Sullivan & Cromwell worked on a big class action settlement from a suit against the banks filed by the National Association of Securities Dealers, or NASD, and the SEC. Banker's Trust was our client, and their numerous derivatives blowups were keeping the firm's billables high. The talk of the firm was a $4 billion NASD settlement, the largest by the banks in history for artificially keeping spreads wide (in our parlance, "raping retail"). Here's how it worked. Traders would quote a stock, for instance, Microsoft (MSFT) at $25 by $25 1/2. If one of the banks on the offer decided to narrow the quote and make it $25 by $25 1/4, the rest of the banks would call that trader and raise bloody hell. Why did this matter? Simple: Because banks make markets, and by keeping the spread at 1/2, that meant that a retail client would pay a spread of fifty cents every time they wanted to buy or sell that stock. So 1,000 shares would mean an extra $500 profit for the banks right out of the retail client's pocket. Not bad, right? That's what happens when competition is artificially suppressed with the implicit blessing of the SEC. If there had been a real market, Microsoft might really have been trading at $25 by $25 1/16. That's a $62 profit, instead of $500—a savings of $438 to the retail client. When the original day-trading firms began impacting the artificially wide spreads maintained by the boys at the top of food chain, what do you think happened? I think you already know the answer. Rather than going after the big banks for illegally colluding to keep the spreads artificially high, the SEC targeted the day-trading firms any way they could.

Once we learned that the SEC were not, in fact, the good guys—but crooked cops protecting bankers—it was hard not to lose respect for them altogether. When the SEC gave the big banks a free pass on something like spread fixing, but then came after Datek for canceling orders,* it was hard to feel like you were working for a firm doing anything fundamentally wrong.

This all might sound like the Wild West, but it's important to understand day-trading firms like Datek were also a far cry from the seedier, mafia-infused boiler rooms that were operating at that time on Staten Island, Long Island, and even Manhattan, under the leadership of such "wolves" as Jordan Belfort.

---

* Traders could put in a large buy order in order to fool the robots or other traders into trying to front run the order and get them to pay the offer (where the trader might have stock for sale), and then cancel the same buy order before it was executed.

These firms—Belfort's babies, as we called them—weren't trading. They were stealing. How? They were selling stock that didn't exist. (Or if the stock *did* exist, it was manipulated penny stock garbage, artificially inflated.) Datek wasn't that kind of boiler room. We were a bare-bones trading floor, stacked with bright aggressive kids fresh out of the top colleges and universities—a generation of video gamers that had found the ultimate video game. Sure the people running the firms might have had some questionable backgrounds, but they were still light years from the boiler-room grifters.

Having said that, Datek was still the closest thing to an insane asylum I've ever been a part of. There was an "anything and everything goes" mentality that was hard to grasp until you saw it firsthand. But why not? It was the late '90s, Internet millionaires cropped up overnight, bank analysts were peddling profitless Internet stocks, IPOs were through the roof, and the president was too busy with his cigar and intern to care. All looked right with America.

On a weekly basis, we ran wild, taking our cue from the stellar moral leadership. When the original group of senior trading management departed to start a firm called Tradescape*, the management duties fell to the two managers, Scrappy and Anthony . . . and that's where the real frat boy degeneracy began. They'd host contests revolving around downing a whole gallon of milk, or eating two dozen saltine crackers in under five minutes, all for ridiculous stakes that would make jaws drop in flyover country.

My second week there, in the spring of '98, one of the traders sent me a link on AOL IM. (I'd quickly learned that email and phone were secondary, petty methods of communications—IM, instant message, was our go-to principal.) I clicked it and up opened a picture of a naked young woman on all fours, winking, which I quickly clicked off and looked around, hoping no one had noticed. The trader next to me had a huge shit-eating grin and offered a loud.

"Noiiiice! Bring that back up."

I gave him a rushed finger against my lips and shush.

"What?" he barked, laughing loudly.

I started to panic. At Sullivan & Cromwell, there were strict rules on Internet use. The Internet was still in its infancy, and in a law firm as stodgy

---

* Tradescape was eventually sold to ETrade for $200 million, in a deal that made AOL's $182 billion purchase of Time Warner look savvy.

as that, even a trip to harmless sites like ESPN or CNN was strictly verboten. Viewing dainty, Bob Guccione porn back then was the present-day equivalent of child porn: an immediate, no questions asked/no explanations accepted, 100 percent terminable offense, never encountered or discussed. Even a snapshot of Maria Bartiromo showing a little too much cleavage could get you a nasty drumming down from the folks at HR. I didn't know what the rule was at Datek, but I figured discretion was the better part of valor.

Shows how much I knew.

Suddenly another trader, Kwan Soo, piped in: "Come on, let's see that, or send it my way if you're gay."

"What's the deal here with . . . with this . . . *stuff*?" I asked with genuine innocence.

Kwan answered, "As long as it's not hardcore, it's fine. Just no hardcore."

"As long as it's not . . . *hardcore?* That's a real rule?"

It was.

Kwan pursed his lips and arched his eyebrows, as if this was the first time anyone had presented this question. "You know . . . fisting, anal, money shots, gang bangs . . . I guess anything with penetration. Or cocks. Definitely no cocks."

"No cocks is an actual rule?" I marveled.

"I mean, it's not like it's in the employee handbook, but ask Scrappy. He told me when I first started working here. *Playboy, Maxim*, that stuff is always safe."

There was a lot of nonsense working at Datek, and a lot of details that seemed unbelievable to outsiders, but the real unbelievable action was always in the work. The last three months of 1999 were just about the sickest thing I'd ever seen. It was an orgy, but I simply couldn't bring myself to buy a stock that was up $10, hoping it would go up $15, even though it was overvalued by $100. But by choosing to sit out most of the ramp, determined to wait for the inevitable implosion, I was the Greatest Fool of All, as those around me made mind-numbing profits, day after day. YHOO, AMZN and CMGI would gap $10 a day, immune to gravity as the Nazz, aka NASDAQ, ripped right past 3000 and didn't even blink rocketing past 4000. At the end of the year, the Nazz was up 83 percent, a far cry from the 5–7 percent stocks had returned historically. People were too busy celebrating and shouting "It's different this time" to realize such an adjustment was unsustainable. It's like a guy who averages five home runs a year suddenly hitting fifty. Something is not right in Mudville.

The end of the year at Datek meant big paychecks, fat bonuses, and off-the-charts celebrations, all capped off by the granddaddy of them all, the savage Christmas party, *aka* the Full Employment Act for Sex Workers and Unlicensed Pharmaceutical Dealers. That year's party was like nothing I'd ever seen in a corporate environment. Erik had rented out the main room in the Waldorf-Astoria Hotel and invited traders and their significant others to come and indulge. In keeping with our barbarians at the gate reputation, we ransacked the Waldorf like the Huns under Attila. Erik had negotiated a per person all you can drink/eat rate from the hotel, and whatever the Waldorf people may have budgeted for alcohol, you can be damn sure they underestimated. This was a crew where each of us could polish off a dozen shots, almost as many cocktails, and a twelve-pack of beer over the course of a night and still be emotionally devastated by those two loneliest words in the English language, "Last call." Additionally, many of the wives or significant others were good for a bottle of wine and a line or two each. The year before, Lisa and I had been at the Pierre for the Sullivan & Cromwell snoozefest. In 1999, we were present for a true balls-out blast.

The Monday morning post-Xmas party was always good for a laugh. There was a decadent roll-call, as Erik read a list of the party's highlights and passed out the gifts to the workers in the firm. He didn't even have to prepare a sheet, the Waldorf having done it for him.

"'We regret to inform that due to the following list of documented damages, management will be unable to return your security deposit from the night of December 15, 1999,'" he said to smiles and budding laughter.

"Seventeen broken glasses," he began, just warming up. "A cracked mirror in the Northwest powder room. A broken bathroom stall door in the men's room opposite the ballroom. Numerous complaints registered from the staff and other guests including rampant drug use, and several lewd and public acts performed in the balcony and throughout other public places in the hotel. If you have any questions, you may contact Donald Fortunato at the number above."

"I've got a question for you, Donald," Erik shouted as the crowd of traders roared with laughter and applause, "haven't you ever heard of a *par-tay*? And what does some chick showing her ass out on the balcony have to do with my security deposit? Care to put a number on that?"

"Put a number on, Donald!" someone yelled out, and Erik responded in kind. "Donald? Let's say $65K a year, if he's lucky! *WITH BENEFITS TOO!*" he shouted maliciously, the rest of the room erupting in laughter like drunken hyenas, even the ones still hungover from Saturday night.

Erik and his managers/minions would then soften the two-day hangovers by passing out our Christmas gifts. My first year, it was a high-end wood-grain humidor and a bottle of Johnnie Walker Blue Label scotch. The gifts, like the party the weekend before, seemed like a very big deal. But for Erik, who had probably made $250 million that past year, spending $500,000 for a party was certainly *no* big deal. The same was true for our gifts. He might have spent $1,000 total on each of us. With about seventy traders at the firm, he'd spent less than $100,000. To the traders, it was probably the nicest gift they'd ever been given and engendered tremendous loyalty. Meanwhile, Erik was raping us on tickets at $15 a trade (which eventually went up to $25, until the Tradescape rebellion—and to prevent much of the firm from walking out *en masse*, Erik had offered "deals" on tickets and payouts). I was spending $1,500 every day in commissions, or more than the cost of my "generous" holiday gift. But give me a beautiful wooden humidor stocked with a few contraband Cuban cigars and a bottle of Blue Label, and I was ready to give him a hug and apologize for calling him a "greedy troll" on at least a dozen distinct occasions.

It shouldn't have worked, but it did. Boy, did it ever.

CHAPTER SEVEN

A STAR IS BORN: THE ADVENT OF ZVI

I LASTED ANOTHER YEAR AT DATEK. A lot happened: The tech bubble burst, 9/11, my wedding day. Of these, 9/11 might have been the most impactful. The finance community was hit particularly hard. Everybody knew somebody. If it wasn't our immediate friends and family murdered (though for many of us, it was), it was at least someone we knew casually. In the weeks right after, baseball caps and flip flops at Datek were replaced by suits pulled from the back of our closets, as we attended the funerals of friends and colleagues who had done nothing more than kiss their kids and spouses goodbye one Tuesday morning and show up for work.

While several I knew were lost, I did have two close friends spared by what I can only describe as the hand of God. The first, my friend George, was on a golf trip with clients in New Jersey, instead of at his desk on the 102nd floor for Aon Insurance. Though 192 Aon employees perished that morning, it could have been 193. The other, my first cousin Brian, was taking a cigarette break outside on his perch at Morgan Stanley in the South Tower when the first plane hit. Security instructed him to go back upstairs until it could be sorted out, an order so preposterous in hindsight he luckily disobeyed it. Plane number two hit eighteen minutes later.

For me personally, 9/11 was emotionally devastating. Rather than seek professional help—as I would years later, after my arrest—I tried to chase the anger and sadness by smothering it with vodka. The emotional maelstrom and difficulty of that period wasn't helped by Lisa's work situation, either. She had been laid off the week before by Food Network. It turned out that while I was at work numb from grief and watching men in Hazmat suits scour our office's ledges and terraces for missing body parts, Lisa was dealing with things in her own way. I would come home, still in a state of mild shock, and find her and her Food Network friends carousing on the stoop of our West Village apartment, polishing off bottles of wine by the case and cooking up ornate hors d'oeuvres. Perhaps they were smothering sorrows in the best ways they knew how, but I couldn't relate on even the smallest level. I'd just trudge upstairs past them, barely able to say hello. Looking back, it feels like this was the first real gap of weirdness and disconnection that opened between my wife and me. Rather than address it, I chose to drown it—drinking for nights on end, occasionally with friends from work, but mostly alone in my living room.

In 2002, I moved from Datek to Schoenfeld Securities, where I lasted almost three years. By the spring of 2005, I was feeling antsy. I hadn't learned a goddamned thing in most of my time at Schoenfeld. The talent at the firm was thin. I was just grinding out a living day-to-day, not getting significantly better as a trader or improving my skillset. The stagnation allowed me to spend a lot of time with Lisa and Sylvie, who had just turned two, while finishing up my Chartered Financial Analyst degree. The CFA is a three-year degree. Candidates are required to pass one test each year to move on to the next level. I had just passed Level 3, the final stage of the degree, making me an official Chartered Financial Analyst, a member of a select group of individuals that had passed a mostly meaningless series of tests and obstacles for little more than bragging rights. And I knew that. Thousands of brilliant analysts weren't CFAs and, likewise, thousands of current CFAs couldn't make money armed with tomorrow's *Wall Street Journal*.

Even so, I still think Level 2 of the CFA exam just might be the hardest standardized test in existence. The fabled NY State Bar Exam, the bane of most new law school graduates and a four-time victor over JFK Jr., feels like third grade addition and subtraction by comparison. About 60 percent pass the NY Bar at their first go. The pass rate the year I took Level 2 of the CFA was less than 30 percent. Whatever the worth of the CFA, people who knew trading knew I had done something very hard. I wanted to use that to move up in the world. By the summer of 2005, I was trying to network my way into a new and better gig.

Every Wednesday night that summer, I played softball in Central Park. It was a real collection of misfits. Bryan Roth, my trading "partner" on the Schoenfeld desk, had recruited me to play for a slow pitch team composed mostly of former Datek traders. The only three guys I didn't know on the team were Yoon—my friend Kwan Soo Lee's K-town buddy—and two former Datek traders from a different floor. One was Joe Mancuso . . . and the other, this guy named Zvi.

Zvi's brother Nu was also on the team and worked at Datek back in the day, but I actually remembered him, since he sat near me for a couple of weeks just before I left for Schoenfeld. Nu offered a nearly flawless imitation of Andrew "Dice" Clay upon command. It took a little while, but I eventually realized this wasn't an imitation. Nu was actually a Dice Clay doppelgänger, who looked and sounded remarkably like the Brooklyn-born comic, so a dead-on impression wasn't a challenge at all; it was second nature. On Datek's trading floor, Nu was green, but showed potential. He was both fearless and disciplined, two of the toughest traits in the trader's arsenal to acquire, and two of the most essential to succeed. It may come as a surprise to most amateurs, but discipline can be learned a lot easier than fearlessness. The ability to step out of your comfort zone and size up a trade appropriately is one of the most difficult things to learn as a trader and almost impossible to teach. Nu showed early promise at both. Nu's compass pointed to softball, drinking, eating, and trading. I didn't know him well enough yet to discern what else made him tick, but clearly these were the staples. It was only after years of being friends with the guy that I realized that I had solved the enigma of Nu in the first few weeks: there really was nothing else. He was blessed with a disposition and mental capacity that enjoyed life and didn't ask too many questions. He operated at two distinct speeds, drunk and business, with the volume knob stuck on eleven for both of them. Whether it was a softball field, trading floor, or bar, within seconds Nu made his presence known. With an unmistakable permanent "outdoor voice" peppered by booming belly guffaws and an ever-present beer super-glued to his hand, Nu walked the earth like a tenth-century Viking reincarnated in the body of a twenty-first-century elephantine Jewish simpleton from Brooklyn.

To this day, I'd be surprised if Nu had made a single adult decision in his entire life without first consulting his brother, including his eventual decision to get married and have two children.

After losing two of our first three games, our team began to properly click. We reeled off eight wins in a row to make the playoffs, and then dismantled three straight "unbeatable" teams to win the Central Park B Team championship (the A League being comprised of semi-pros—seriously, they were mostly mustachioed mercenaries bused in from Milwaukee, or journeymen minor leaguers). Friendships were accelerated by the joy of winning, and cemented during customary post-game binge drinking at Blondie's West Side, on 88th and Amsterdam. We'd start at 7 p.m. and practically shut the place down. One of the owners was a friend and granted us most favored nation status with reduced pricing, bottled beers for $4 and shots for $6—and that's in New York City. Yet somehow we still managed to run up a $1,000 bar tab nearly every time.

When it came to business, it wasn't until near the end of our championship season that the newcomer Zvi laid his cards on the table. The best salesman is one who is selling you without your realizing it. I didn't really notice when he was doing it. For a twenty-eight-year-old kid, he was a goddamned natural. Zvi gradually shared that for the past six months he had been working on launching a new proprietary trading firm backed by a very well-known and respected hedge fund manager, Rob Koltun. Rob was the founder of RNK Capital, a sizable hedge fund specializing in carbon and energy credits, a sexy new field. Rob was one of the earliest entrants into the carbon credit business, and the respect he enjoyed was more a result of his being an early mover in the space than for any stellar performance. Rob was looking to start a complementary hedge fund specializing in energy equities, the stocks of energy companies. Apparently, Rob planned to use this equities platform to launch a synergistic prop trading firm that Zvi and his other partner, John Deignan, were going to run. Zvi raved about Deignan, characterizing him as an aggressive trading veteran with connections all over the Street.

"You need to sit down with Rob and Deigs," Zvi insisted one evening, waving his hand as if to dismiss any other potential opportunity I might be inclined to pursue. "It's the best possible career move you can make right now."

I was tempted.

With Schoenfeld a boring grind, if Zvi's new baby was even one quarter of the things he said it was, I felt prepared to give it a shot. I explained to Zvi I was more interested in working for Rob as an analyst or trader for the hedge fund, rather than the prop trading firm. I had "done prop," and was eager to try something new, something challenging. Zvi assured me he could get me a meeting with Rob and that I'd be a good fit with the hedge fund.

And so, one hot late afternoon in June, just after the market had closed, Zvi and I walked from his offices in the Radio City Music Hall building on 51st and 6th over to meet Rob at 44th and Lexington, home of the proprietary trading firm they were calling Remsenberg Capital. It had been named after Rob's beach house in the town of the same name, albeit spelled incorrectly. (It was actually Remsen*burg*.) The space on 44th Street was huge, and the plan was to move Rob's hedge fund there as well. But for the time being, Rob was still working out of offices on 54th and Madison in a hedge fund hotel seeded by Sanders Morris Harris and operated by a guy named Mike Rosen.

During our walk over, Zvi explained that Rob was going to move his operations to 44th and Lexington, and that Zvi and his current boss, Gregg Ettin at Carlin Financial, would be joining the floor in the near future. On the elevator ride up, Zvi let me know that Rob was a "casual guy" and might not be what I expected. The stereotype of the hedge fund honcho has become fairly recognizable in NYC over the past decade: Fit (courtesy of a $3,000 a month personal trainer), well-groomed ($150 haircut and manicure every other week), in a hand-tailored suit, hand-crafted brogues, a platinum Swiss timepiece, chic wire-rimmed glasses, and an attitude that said "Not only am I better than you, but consider yourself incredibly fortunate to even be in the same room with me having this conversation."

We passed through a small reception area with *Remsenberg* plastered on a frosted pane window, then made our way into a spartan yet sizable trading floor shaped like an "L." A few traders typing on keyboards glanced up at us for a few seconds before returning to their screens. Somebody came strolling out of one of the executive offices in the back. Based on Zvi's advance warning, I assumed this was Rob, a short, round figure with graying straight hair that could use a trim and that looked to be allergic both to both comb and brush. He wore tan khakis and a generic lemon yellow polo shirt that was splattered with what appeared to be several ounces worth of a chocolate milkshake. A large pair of unisex eyeglasses usually seen only among the elderly of Palm Springs or Palm Beach was perched on his large, bumpy nose. On his feet, a pair of tattered, filthy Stan Smith tennis shoes with the laces untied. The sneakers looked so old, Stan Smith himself might have worn them. I honestly thought that I was being punked. Was this for real? The guy was a mess, a hybrid of MIT Media Lab and homeless chic. Zvi made the introductions and we shook hands, both of us all smiles, mine slightly bigger than his, despite my best efforts.

"I've heard a lot about you," Rob said, and gave a laugh that was three seconds of an escalating, falsetto whine. He had the most peculiar quirk of awkwardly chuckling in the most bizarre manner after most everything he said. Words can't really do it justice, but people who didn't know him, or who met him for the first time, would look at each other with furrowed brows as if to say, "What the fuck is *that*? Is he not aware that he is doing that?"

I cloaked my surprise by forcing myself to say, "Likewise, nearly all of it good."

He walked me around the trading floor and then we spoke about my background and trading style. I explained my voodoo and my approach to trading, and asked him about his plans.

"We're going to build the best damn prop shop we can, from the ground up, and I want to fill the seats with guys exactly like you," Rob said matter-of-factly.

"You had me at hello, Rob." I smiled, shaking his hand again when I realized I had the job.

Naturally, there were details to work out, but it was happening. Even though Rob was a little odd, I was impressed by what I had heard and seen. Also important to me was that the location was a mere block from Grand Central and the Metro-North commuter train I hopped to and from Larchmont every day. You couldn't find a more convenient location. That was it. I gave notice at Schoenfeld and less than two weeks later, I was at Remsenberg programming my screens and software.

But all did not go as forecasted.

After a few months, I noticed that two out of the three people Zvi had told me were going to come onboard never really arrived. Most bizarrely of all, that included Zvi himself. I tried to convince myself that this was irrelevant; I liked the location, the setup, and was learning and developing a good trading rapport with Deignan, or JD as we called him. It would still be a good place to work. Only in my few idle moments did I wonder whether Zvi's plans had been altered by changing circumstances, if they had been bullshitting me the whole time for some reason, or what?

One day, my curiosity got the better of me, and I called Zvi to ask when he was planning on moving over.

"My boss still needs to work out a few details with regard to our current space," was all he would say.

When I broached the question again, months later, the answer was more definitive.

"It doesn't look like it's going to happen. There are some issues surrounding whether I can still be a partner at Remsenberg. Conflicts. I'm probably going to end up selling my shares back to Rob, and giving some to Joe Mancuso as well. I'll still be able to have a say in the management and the firm through Joe, but it's best for everyone if I'm not on paper."

At the time, it made sense to me.

Zvi's boss was Greg Ettin, a well-established execution broker at Carlin Financial, handling order flow for mutual funds. That this created conflicts was obvious. Even the big Wall Street firms pretended to separate execution business for clients, or brokerage from the banks' own proprietary in-house trading. What was less obvious to me was that Rob and his financial partner Ian Behar had already settled with Zvi weeks ago, giving him back his startup capital in exchange for his shares. That had nothing to do with conflicts, but solely with Zvi's non-performance. After I was firmly in the door, Rob and Ian would comfortably badmouth Zvi behind his back.

Apparently, other than me, Zvi had only able to bring in a handful of pikers who didn't move the needle at all, although he had promised Rob twenty good traders by mid-year, and fifty able bodies in the six months after that. And so they quietly came to an agreement: Zvi would get his startup capital back, and then he would quietly go away. It might have been the last quiet thing Zvi did in his life.

I should have been so lucky.

At the same time, I don't think Rob ever planned to sit at 44th Street and run his fund from there. Weeks passed, and I hadn't seen Rob in a while, so after the market closed one day in late September, I walked up the ten blocks to 54th Street to see him. The second I entered that office, I realized there was zero chance Rob would *ever* leave. Decorated luxuriously, with enormous glass windows providing a view of majestic Madison Avenue, it looked like an Aston Martin DB8 compared to the Honda Civic we were driving. Other than keeping trader morale up, a marquee location and expensive furnishings were meaningless on the prop side. However, hedge funds are primarily asset gatherers at heart, and to gather assets you have to impress clients. These clients tend to be extremely wealthy people who won't invest capital in a business that looks "poor" or somehow shoddy. Nothing says you're doing something right like Carrara marble floors and original artworks by the likes of Julian Schnabel.

Prop, on the other hand, typically has partner capital or one or two investors and a younger trader base that's less influenced by appearances. Take the notable trading firm First New York. They were based in offices on 47th and 3rd Ave. that had stained carpets from ten years ago, paint peeling off the walls, and cheap chipped wooden Staples desks cobbled together with duct tape where people sat and traded hundreds of millions of dollars. It had all the markings of a telemarketing center in Bangalore, but for the fact that many of the traders were routinely taking home seven-figure paychecks.

That was our world. That was just how it went.

Anyhow, I eventually saw Zvi again.

At a Remsenberg poker tournament in early June of 2006, I found myself seated at table next to Zvi. We passed the time trading stories from our Datek days and polishing off a twelve-pack of beer between us. We both advanced to the next table through a combination of luck and conservative play. In poker, as in trading, you can win sometimes (or at least be ahead) simply by doing nothing. And that's what we did for the first hour, a whole lot of nothing. We talked trading styles and stocks. I told him about a few things I was trading and then keyed him into a company that I had put a lot of work into, Imergent, IIG. It was a god-awful piece of a garbage company, *but* its price reflected that, with a healthy discount. The company sold "do it yourself websites" for several thousand dollars, a business that had a shelf life of a few years at most. That technology was getting cheaper all the time, and major players were moving into the space. Its stock had been cruising along at $30 until Stock Lemon, a website run by a notorious cabal of short sellers, got their hooks into it. Stock

Lemon and its insiders (i.e. those lucky enough to get the heads-up that a nasty editorial piece was imminent) had thoroughly crushed the stock and slandered management. A bear raid *nonpareil* that quickly followed left the company in convulsions, bleeding like a deer that had just been run over by a twelve-wheel rig. The tactical execution was a thing of beauty to watch, except I found myself long and wrong as I tried to catch a bottom. It was an absolute feeding frenzy for shorts and they shredded the stock from $30 to a single-digit midget in a matter of weeks.

Now it was on life support at $4 and some change, yet absolutely nothing had changed in terms of its core business. Sure, there were a few lawsuits from the attorneys general of two states, charging that IIG had misled customers and demanding that they refund money. Still, even if it did refund the money of every person owed in those two states, the company still had enough free cash flow in the other forty-eight that the stock deserved to be trading around $15. My friend's fund was a major shareholder and had done significant work on the company. The fund spoke to management, who assured them their capital was more than adequate, their business opportunities still prolific, and their regulatory issues mostly behind them. Companies will often lie to your face about these things, which is why stocks like IIG need to be purchased at a discount. At the current discount, the worst-case scenario was all but fully priced in . . . and one piece of good news would likely send shorts scrambling.

I broke it all down for Zvi and laid out the exhausting due diligence I had performed on the company. The clincher was the Amex had just started trading options with a $5 strike price. Sentiment was so bad, that you could buy $5 calls out to November for a mere .50. If the stock goes to zero, you know your damage or exposure is capped at fifty cents. If they release decent earnings and force the shorts to cover, there could be a stampede to $10 in a hurry. Clearly the market makers at Amex misunderstood the backstory and the amount of volatility in the stock. I had started buying shares at $8 and had been adding at intervals on the way down, convinced the worst was behind the company. Limited downside, significant upside, short squeeze potential—Zvi loved it and thanked me profusely, telling me he was going to put it on tomorrow and then do some research on the company. Not wanting to take without some give, he took a pen from his pocket and wrote the ticker symbol JAMS on the cocktail napkin next to me.

"Just be there," he said with a measured glance to his left, then his right. "I'll talk to you more about it when we're alone."

From the look on his face I knew he was serious. That's why you play poker, to network and talk to people in the business. I had been to countless dinners, happy hours, industry conferences, and events. A lot of them were miserable affairs, but one good idea can make it all worth it. You never know who you're going to meet or what you might learn.

"You long a nice amount?" I asked.

Zvi smiled.

"Nice doesn't even begin to describe it, buddy," he said, nodding his head and pretending to push his entire stack of chips forward, mouthing the words "All in."

I had just spent the better part of fifteen minutes giving him a comprehensive bottoms-up analysis of a company based on sweeping diligence, yet with a mere four letters on a napkin Zvi had me salivating. I was ready to take off my IIG position and plow the proceeds into JAMS—something I had never even heard of. Ah, the power of hidden allure. A dollar and a dream, indeed.

Later that week at Remsenberg, I approached Zvi's brother Nu and asked him if we could talk privately. We went to the soda machine in the kitchen alcove. I told him what his brother had said during the poker game. I asked Nu how much he thought I should buy, or was that a question for his brother? His immediate response was "Ask Zvi," but then he also volunteered that he was long 200,000 shares for now.

"*200K*?" I said. "Wow. Okay."

I was genuinely surprised, and worried that my inflection had exposed me as a piker. Sure, it was only a $1.50 stock, but 200,000 shares was still a nice chunk and significantly bigger than any other position he had. I figured I'd buy 150,000. I didn't know the whole story and Zvi hadn't given me any other details.

Anyhow, for the next month, the stock yo-yoed between $1.40 and $1.60. Even after several conversations with Zvi, I *still* wasn't sure what the play was or where it was coming from, other than the fact that there were "friends of friends" involved. A broker from Saratoga Capital was apparently instrumental somehow, and even Rony Seikaly, the former center for the Miami Heat and Syracuse Orangemen, had made a cameo appearance in Zvi's tale. He was a known companion (known by whom? I wanted to ask) of several apparently connected guys (connected to what, Zvi?) and was coming in, possibly as a capital (or drinking) partner to one of the principals affiliated with an investment group that was circling. This was like the financial version of the game Clue, except instead of Colonel Mustard in the living room with a candlestick, I already had a feeling that the only one about to get murdered was me. It wasn't a pure flyer though. I could verify that JAMS owned a portfolio of extended-stay apartments and cheap hotels. The rampaging value of American real estate made the ground the hotels were built on worth more than the company as an operating business. Kmart and numerous other companies were looking to monetize the fair market value of their real estate assets by selling or spinning them off. The fundamentals of the company supported a higher stock price, and this was 2005; every expert and his mother knew real estate would continue to double every four years into perpetuity.

JAMS seemed to relish being in a tight trading until a week later, when Nu was in Hawaii for his honeymoon. Nu had already lived and died for almost two months with this piece of garbage, and the stock seemed to enjoy Nu's absence as a chance to engage in a little opportunistic volatility. On Monday, it broke its range on the downside and started to bleed . . . $1.30 . . . $1.20. By Tuesday we were looking at $1.10. On Thursday morning, Nu's assistant Eric was fielding an angry, panicked call from Hawaii. Eric had to check twice to make sure that he had heard Nu correctly: "You want me to blow out of the entire position right now?"

I typed it up on my trading screen and readied myself for fireworks. As the first large prints began to come through and the stock started ticking violently downward for no apparent reason, I whispered "foot in the aisle" to the guys in my row and starting putting in my buy orders lower. JAMS was a relatively thin trading stock, and Nu's 200,000-share "out-in-a-hurry" market sale smashed it. When the $1 level broke, additional stop losses were triggered and the stock traded down to 90 cents in a heartbeat. As soon as $1 broke, I was bidding and bidding, scooping Nu's puke and then buying back up to $1 when it started bouncing. I unloaded the entire position at $1.30 a week later, to break even overall in the trade. It was nice to be on the receiving end of a panic trade for a change.

I felt slightly bad for Nu, certain that the JAMS implosion and call to Eric would remain the primary memory of his honeymoon. I had seen this movie before. In fact, I had starred in the original*. But my sympathy was tempered when I waited, and waited, and waited even more for a follow-up call from Zvi, Nu, or Eric to say that these guys had hit the eject button and I was flying solo. It eventually came days later, but too late to be of any use whatsoever. As I would slowly but surely learn, after a few weeks in a stock, Zvi would typically become disillusioned and snap if you asked him a follow-up question. Ostensibly, this type of reaction was a manifestation of his frustration and hypersensitivity with the underperformance of the position.

A cliché in the trading business is that there's always another train leaving the station. The challenge, however, was always to find the one that was going to reach its intended destination before it derailed. I was learning that, in Zvi's mind, such an action was an admission of *defeat*. I thought that was nuts. There were no "sure things" in this game (at least not for people at our level). Everyone that's been in the industry for more than a few years knows that the timeless admonition of *caveat emptor* reigns supreme. We're all adults. You swim at your own risk. Zvi was learning by trial and error. Mostly error, but he was on the right path and just had a little growing up to do—all part of the learning curve.

I privately decided that if he could ever learn or be taught to distinguish between a nugget of gold from a nugget of fool's gold, he had the potential to be the real thing. And with this little bit of maturing and molding on my part, we would get there together.

Fast forward to our next softball season. I'd been working at Remsenberg for several months. We were back at Blondie's on the Upper West Side after a game. It was after my seventh shot and seventh beer, following a big victory against a team from Price Waterhouse, when Zvi leaned in and started telling me how he would soon be running a billion-dollar hedge fund. I listened politely—drunk and under the impression I was being bullshitted—with one eye on the Yankee game in the background. Zvi wanted to raise his own fund. He complained

---

* During the tech meltdown in 2000, I had shorted SUNW, the last tech soldier standing, and done so relentlessly, only to cover the day before my wedding/honeymoon. SUNW proceeded to drop 25 percent in the next two weeks, which would have paid for several dozen honeymoons had I still been short.

that his current boss was taking every one of his ideas and passing them off to their clients as his own. To listen to Zvi, it sounded like David Winters and Bob Jaffe were putting up impressive numbers solely because some unknown broker's assistant's assistant was feeding them *his* brilliant ideas. Yet it wasn't entirely implausible. It had happened before.

I got bored and said: "I'm going to lighten on ATYT."

"Why?" Zvi asked. He appeared not to mind having his tale derailed, but also suddenly seemed worried. This was because Zvi had been the genesis of the "get long on ATYT" idea a month before, a call buttressed by JD and his contacts at hedge fund SAC.

"Garrett is concerned how one-sided our firm is in it," I said invoking Remsenberg's risk manager. "I'm also hesitant because the rumors are *so* pronounced and the stock price hasn't ticked up at all."

For weeks, ATYT had been the subject of wide-eyed tales of takeover.

"Don't you think if someone was kicking the tires, the stock price would be climbing higher?" I added dismissively. "This thing is on its ass still."

"Don't sell a share," Zvi said, and took a long sip of his beer.

When all I did was raise an eyebrow, he began to fill the silence.

"What I'm about to tell you can't go to anyone else," he said softly.

"If you tell me not to tell anyone else, I don't tell anyone else," I assured him, and thank God I didn't. JAMS, BGO, TWX, HD, KGC, ALEX, BMHC . . . the list of stocks where he told me to "load the boat" went on and on—a long shortlist. Indeed, if I had told anyone else about these "high conviction calls" from Zvi there'd be a lynch mob out after me, with torches and pitchforks. I almost laughed at the dichotomy between the caliber he ascribed to himself and his information and the objective reality of his actual performance.

"So last week, one of my Galleon guys calls me," Zvi said, still *sotto voce*. "Long story short, this is the guy who originally told me about ATYT, and he knew about it because he sits near Raj's execution trader. During lunch, he overheard Raj's trader on the phone say, 'He wants 500 thousand more ATYT?' in a really surprised voice. My guy asked him what was up, and the guy told my guy he didn't know anything except that that Raj was buying ATYT for size again. It's now one of Galleon's biggest positions."

Zvi took another long sip from his Amstel. It seemed as though the oracle had spoken.

"Um, okay. Cool. Thanks, man," I managed, trying to flag down the waitress for another round.

"Idiot, that's not the story."

"Oh? Then what is?"

"Later, my guy is taking a piss next to Raj in the men's room . . . And Raj asks him what he's doing today. My guy says to Raj, 'Please don't ever talk to me when I've got my dick in my hand!' which Raj thinks is hysterical and practically pisses all over himself. Then my buddy says he's only kidding and asks Raj if he saw the article in *Light Reading* on ATYT."

Light Reading was an industry rag focusing on networking.

"Raj said he hadn't, and asked him to send it over to Ian, his trader," Zvi continued. "My guy then says 'What do you think of the name here?' to which Raj replies with a devilish smile, 'Buy it. This one is for your kids' IRA.' Your *KIDS' IRA! FOR YOUR KIDS' IRA!*"

Zvi was shouting and people at the bar were looking over.

"Do you know what that means?" he continued, wide-eyed.

I actually didn't, and not just because the number of beers I'd consumed was nearing double digits. I had no fucking clue what it meant. The phrasing was familiar, though. I had heard people describe high conviction ideas as "Buy it for your retirement fund," or "Buy it in your IRA." Retirement funds are supposed to be the safest, most conservative investments, so the connection was that if you were buying it in your IRA it was a safe, high conviction play. "Buy it for your kid's college fund" was another one, meaning essentially the same thing. But buy it for your *kids' IRA*? Was this an investment Minotaur, some mythological, rare, ultimate hybrid of safety and return, or just some Sri Lankan mogul with piss on his hands confusing the investment lexicon?

"Are kids even allowed to have IRAs?" I asked with a wiseass smile. "I've never heard of that."

Zvi looked at me like I'd suddenly grown a second nose one my face.

"Are you fucking retarded? Who *cares* if kids are allowed to have IRAs? This is the King saying he was buying it for *his kids'* IRA."

"Wait, wait, wait," I said drunkenly. "You told me he told your friend to buy it for *his* kids' IRA, *not* that Raj was buying it for *his* kids' IRA."

"*WHAT FUCKING DIFFERENCE DOES THAT MAKE?*" Zvi exploded, slamming his beer bottle onto the table and sending foam billowing.

"I'm just trying to get the story straight," I said trying not to smile. He stared at me like he was deciding whether to put me in a headlock, smash his beer over my head, or maybe—just maybe—keep talking.

"You're missing the point," he said, finally lowering his voice again. "You're missing the point because you're drunk, Michael. The King is saying 'Be there.' Do you realize how rare it is to get that type of edge in a stock? This is Raj. He makes more money in a day than you and your whole fucking family have made their *entire* lives; he is the best tech investor in the game. Period. You ignore a call like that at your own peril. I'm going to be there for size."

A lot of what Zvi was saying was true, or at least close to it.

At the time, Raj's reputation was pure gold. Universally considered one of the smartest guys in the tech space, Raj had built Galleon from $10 million to $7 billion in less than a decade. He was friends and partners with a *Who's Who* of investors and contacts throughout the industry. I was debating telling Zvi that my daughter Sylvie was now two, and maybe I *should* actually check into opening up an IRA for her. Zvi's teeth were grinding in frustration and the jaw muscle in his right upper cheekbone was popping in and out like a golf ball with a heartbeat.

A core trait of Zvi's was that he lacked all patience with other people's questions or perspectives. After a certain point, Zvi would simply shut down, and any subsequent comment or argument would only enrage him. It was like dealing with the Incredible Hulk. In fact, according to Nu, Zvi even had a nine-inch foam action doll of the Hulk on his desk. (That bothered me. Not just because the Hulk was an irrational beast brimming with violence, and Zvi seemed to embody some of these characteristics, but because I loved the Hulk and felt an emotional connection to him. Growing up, I'd bonded with the big green monster. He was my favorite superhero. That he should have any connection to a guy like Zvi was always somehow disheartening.)

Anyhow, I left the bar before Zvi could turn green and smash the place up.

The next day, the tension at Remsenberg rivaled Kennedy's blockade of Cuba, with the potential for full-scale global thermonuclear war.

Nu had tried to buy another 10,000 shares each of ATYT and RBAK, as Zvi had hinted he should the night before. But the orders were rejected by the system, flashing him a message that he had exceeded his intraday buying power. Nu went to discuss the situation with Garrett and was told that he couldn't be leveraged more than 6 to 1. That meant if Nu had $100,000 on deposit, he could purchase only $600,000 worth of stock. After Nu growled for a few seconds, Garrett turned spineless and immediately pointed the finger at JD. Two critical traits for a risk manager are (1) forewarned consistency, so traders know what is expected of them, and (2) a sturdy, healthy spine. Remsenberg's risk parameters were ad hoc at best, and Garrett's spine was never featured on the back of a milk carton because he never had one in the first place.

Nu went to the conference room to fill in Zvi on the situation via conference call. I imagined that from Zvi's point of view, this was no less a declaration of war than the Japanese bombing Pearl Harbor. There had been an hour of back and forth shuttling to and from Garrett's room, the conference room, and a furious barrage of IMs between Zvi, Mancuso, JD, Garrett, and Nu. The end result was me (*how'd I get dragged into this?*) and everyone in the conference room, *sans* JD, with Joe frantically telling us that Zvi was coming down to the firm "to break JD's legs."

I laughed out loud when Joe said this. The rest of the people in the room looked at me like I was out of my mind. This, it seemed, was serious business. I thought it was pure bluster, but my colleagues Nu, Joe, Eric, and Garrett were all guzzling the Zvi Kool-Aid. As if it were prophesied and already written, Garrett instructed us that the only chance JD had of saving his legs was for this determined Fellowship of the Conference Room to intervene somehow on his behalf. I still didn't know Zvi that well and was unabashedly eager to see what kind of a person breaks another guy's legs over proper financial risk management. I had intended to go out and grab a sandwich for lunch, but now I was prepared to stay and go hungry just to see how it would all play out.

Actual fights on trading floors are extremely rare. There had been one wrestling match back at Datek, but that had been over issues of religious jingoism. A Pakistani trader had referred to Rediff, an Indian software company, as "pig shit." An Indian trader had taken exception and offered a few choice words about the relative attractiveness of the Indian stock market compared to Pakistan's. A few seconds later, one of them—I forget which—went all-in and brought up the disputed region of Kashmir. That was it. They ended up wrestling on the floor to the wild cheers of the rest of the traders.

Ever the peacemaker, I went to the group with an idea. I proposed that if Nu bought puts on the position, we should really only calculate the exposure based on the part that was unhedged. This meant that if ATYT was trading at $15 and Nu bought puts with a strike price of $10, he really would only have $5 of exposure, because if the stock traded under $10, he would be protected from all further losses by the puts. The group seemed to like my solution and murmured their approval. Perhaps my proposal was the difference—perhaps not—but either way Joe intercepted a fuming Zvi on the street and cooler heads prevailed.

Regrettably, my compromise may have avoided short term pain for JD, but it enhanced the myth of Zvi the Hulk. In retrospect, it would have been better to instruct Joe to stand down and let Zvi rage. Had Zvi's bluff been called then, Zvi might have been much easier to deal with in the future. Instead, the threat of violence, which is always much more effective than actual violence, was left unchecked. And in the future, Zvi would use it to get his way.

You won't like me when I'm angry, Hulk would say. I tended to believe Zvi was telling the truth.

Chapter Eight

HERE TODAY, IN LIMBO

———

AMERICA IS AN ADD NATION. WE want things right now—from food to sex to entertainment. Americans will complain if a movie goes over two hours. Our parents and grandparents gladly sat through *Gone With the Wind*, *Ben Hur*, and *Lawrence of Arabia*. When it comes to courtroom dramas, we want our results lightning fast. Every movie goes from arrest to trial to resolution lickety split. On TV shows like *Law & Order*, they do it in forty minutes, if you don't count commercials.

The reality of a legal proceeding could not feel or smell or taste more different.

Days meld into weeks, weeks into months, and so on, *ad infinitum*, as you weigh your options and seek solace in meds, booze, and denial. For me, in the months after my arrest, I consulted regularly with Moe and Sommer, with my parents, with a very select group of friends, and of course with Lisa. It was never easy, with any of them. I had my pick of options and scenarios for my future—from the sublime to the terrifying. There was also a new, surreal, unsettlingly routine to our daily lives. It was like walking through a nightmare. I had a genuine sense that at any point I might just wake up and it would all be over with. With one abrupt snapping awake, life as I knew it, and wanted it, would return. Of course that never happened. The nightmare was very real indeed. And it seemed to become even more real when I realized that I was still under observation.

Sunday morning was traditionally my "me and the kids time," which allowed Lisa to sleep late. But on one given Sunday during this period, Lisa got up early and we all decided to head to the Rye Bagel Shop, one town over from Larchmont.

We drove to the restaurant; Lisa and our four-year-old, Cam, secured a table in front. With eleven-month-old Phinnie in my arms, Sylvie and I juggled an order for five that included the all-powerful aromatherapy of fresh black coffee and a garlic bagel for me, and other assorted bagels, cream cheese, and juices for the rest of the gang. I scooped up Phin like a running back gripping a football, balancing a crowded tray in my free hand, with Syl doing her best with the juices. Then, as we duck-walked back to the table in the front, I saw a man watching us. He was in his late thirties, with short black hair and a pock-marked face. His gaze was intense, unblinking. He also looked slightly familiar. The tendon in my left bicep was close to snapping, as little Phinnie continued to wriggle and squirm. I got to the table and began unloading bagels and cream cheeses and juices. I strapped Phin into the wooden high chair and sat down, eager to put some food and caffeine in my system. I took a bite of the bagel and looked up: the pockmarked man was still there, chatting to the cashier and handing over a bill in exchange for a cup of coffee. He turned and stared me right in the face. *Where the hell do I know this guy from?* I wondered. I had seen him before, I was certain, but couldn't place it. He was *not* smiling as if he knew me. Rather, it was a strange, blank expression. He got his change, took another long look right at me—right through me—and turned around and walked out.

"Hello, hun—are you here with us?" Lisa called playfully.

"That guy who's leaving, do we know him from somewhere?" I pointed him out to Lisa. She swiveled around just as he departed.

"That guy? I can't really see his face from here. Phinnie, *NO!*"

Our toddler was intentionally dribbling juice out of his mouth, to the giggling delight of his older brother and sister.

We were seated by the window and I had a clear view of Purchase Street. Twenty yards away, the pockmarked guy was crossing the road. As he did, he glanced back over his shoulder at us once more. Something about his walk . . . and then it hit me. It was David Makol, the lead FBI agent on my case. My interaction with him the day of my arrest had been brief. While in the booking tank, he had ripped the cell out of my hand while I was on the phone with Matt Subilia, Incremental's CFO, trying to get him to dump our positions, fully aware of the inevitable bloodbath once word of our arrests hit the wire (little did I know that we were already on the CNBC loop, and Goldman had pulled the plug).

"That's the end of that," Makol had barked, snatching the phone from me in mid-sentence, and asked if I wanted to talk. I didn't. He tried one last attempt to coerce me into cooperating by stating with a mocking smile, "You know your friend Dave Plate is down the hall coming clean on everyone." The fact that he thought Dave Plate and I were friends confused me even further but I opted not to correct him. And that had been it between the two of us.

Now here he was again. It was the same man. The trauma of that day had blurred his face into my memory, like he was some ghoul in a nightmare.

Was this a coincidence? Was there some chance that he lived around here and was out for a bagel himself? No. The world did not work that way. Especially the world of FBI agents.

I stood up and started to move to the door, but he was already in his car and driving away. My first reaction was anger. *Stalk my family? Follow me here and menace me in front of my wife and little kids?* But soon the adrenaline and anger slowed and I could feel my twin sensations, fear and nausea, returning to their familiar positions at the fore.

So this was what it was going to be. The implication was clear. They could follow me anywhere, harass me and my family. And it would not stop unless I cooperated or pled out.

"Are you all right?" Lisa asked. "Who was it?"

I had my best poker face on, but the frustration was hard to hide. My stomach felt like it was bubbling and burning, and my hand was shaking.

"No one," I lied. "Thought it was someone else."

Lisa stared right at me—I didn't fool her for a second—but she clearly did not want to dig any deeper in front of the kids. I sat back down, looked at my children, and tried to hold back the waves of fear.

In mid-December, just over a month after my arrest, we hesitantly headed to a holiday party hosted by our friends the Wilcotts in Purchase, New York. With the exception of a Larchmont Temple fundraiser in November, it was the first real party we'd attended since my name and face had been plastered across the newspapers. The Temple fundraiser only partially counted, because Lisa catered the event. It was a gig. She spent most of the time managing the kitchen staff and tasting the hors d'oeuvres as they came out of the oven, not mingling. I'd been left to stumble around solo, in a vodka-induced daze, an accidental celebrity regarded with a mix of curiosity and pity by those who didn't know me—and with genuine concern by those who did.

The Wilcott holiday party would be the first *real* party since it had all happened. Lisa was nervous, to say the least, and I knew the floor of her closet would resemble backstage at the end of a fashion show by the time she had found something suitable to wear. In anticipation, I had "edited" her calendar to a 7 p.m. start time, buying us an extra hour for cursing and crying during the *"I have no good clothes"* portion of the evening. I was comfortably numb, courtesy of the half a Klonopin I had chewed earlier. The general effects had worn off, but my emotional nerve endings were still pleasantly dulled. My hope was for Vitamin K's "flattening" effect to last until I could tap my good buddy, vodka, to take over and escort me for the night's heavy lifting. Fortunately, the guest list was a benign mix of strangers that didn't know me and good college friends that really knew me.

We arrived at the big and beautiful house in Purchase. Once through the door I made sure Lisa's coat was hung up before informing her that I was planning on blitzkrieging the bar. I asked if I could get her something.

"Diet Coke," she called.

I made my way to the bar, through a bevy of thin, perfectly dressed young women, and a mix of preppy and scruffy men. Everyone was in their thirties like us. Everyone seemed placid, content with the place they had found in life. This was the self-satisfied celebrating their satisfaction.

I bumped into George Gettleman, a friend from Lafayette a few years younger than me. We said hello. A little small talk later, and he was going straight for my case.

"Mike, come on, man!" he said, shaking his head. "Don't you watch *The Wire*? What the fuck?"

He thought I was a fool for having failed to notice the noose tightening.

"Saw an early episode or two, loved it, but never sat down and watched the whole thing."

"It's so fucking good," he said. Would've made a helluva lesson for you. First season DVD for $49.99 would have saved you, what, $500K you had to put up for bail."

"Actually, it was $250K for bail, George, but when you're right, you're right."

It was the best, most direct piece of advice I would receive all night.

I spent the rest of the night parrying and dodging that peculiarly American cocktail party question, "So, what do you do?"

"Do? Me? I'm awaiting trial on a federal securities fraud case."

"No, really?"

I also had "I'm unemployed." Or "I'm retired." Or "I'm in between things."

It was late 2009, so the unemployed/in-between gigs line didn't even draw a measure of surprise or sympathy. The stigma of losing one's job had been erased. Even the chosen, the I-bankers and the biglaw lawyers, had felt the blade. For the first time in generations, the guarantee that so many at this kind of cocktail party felt, of being rich and beautiful (or at least rich) for life, had been voided.

"I'm retired" got the best responses. "Best" meaning, of course, funniest for me. Coming from a thirty-seven-year-old male, it usually engendered a brief hint of shock, followed by some degree of anger and jealousy. For the men especially, it came off as a challenge to their manhood that I might have already reached the finish line. The flustered couple, politely excusing themselves, would promptly seek out our host and hostess and ask for the straight talk about me. When they found out the truth, that I was actually heading towards an extended federal vacation, their features visibly softened with genuine relief.

I tired quickly, however, of talking about myself. And I was certainly not interested in anyone else's life. Hey, mine was shit—and nothing was going to change that at this point—but I didn't need to know about anybody else's. So mostly, I just kept drinking.

Toward the end of the night, I wasn't quite numb, but had finally reached a comfortable state in which I could mentally watch the rest of the party from afar. My bed started calling. I hoped we would leave soon, and that Lisa would count it a small but meaningful psychic victory for the two of us. A return to normalcy. I hoped she had been able to talk to the friends she hadn't spoken to in a while, and relegate, if only for a few hours, the sick scent of depression that seemed to dominate every waking moment in our house. (She was still busy with work, but I was starting to notice she was making excuses not to leave the house. This concerned me. I could understand that it felt safer at home—far from the unsmiling neighbors and questions, no matter how well-intentioned—but it was also not hard to see how staying indoors all the time could lead to a very bad place.)

I wandered over to the fireplace—it was in a small den right next to the main gathering—and looked at some of the pictures on the mantel. Family photos of beautiful children. Perfect teeth, even. An embarrassing surplus of smiles. Happiness blazed from left to right on top of our friends' fireplace. It seemed real. It did not feel fake. This pictures might actually be who those people were, I thought. And how the fuck should that make someone like me feel? I had photos of smiling kids inside my house too. But what did I have to be happy about?

My college buddy Dino wandered in. Dino and I had been through dozens of adventures together, both in college and after. One year during spring break in Jamaica, he was kidnapped after a Ziggy Marley concert. In a brazen act of drunken stupidity, I pursued the snatch car down a dark, muddy road with my friend Keith. When it stopped for a moment, I opened the back door, threw a beer in the face of the driver, and pulled Dino out while punching the passenger that was holding onto him.

Dino was one of my closest friends, knew me better than most. I liked, if not loved him.

"How ya doing, man?" he asked with a forced smile. I could tell that he was trying to keep the mood light, but also that he wanted to know where my head was. This wasn't bullshit. Dino cared.

"Great," I told him with my best Nicholson circa *The Shining* smile. "Can you keep a secret?"

"Yeah, of course," he said, bracing, not knowing quite what to expect.

"I'm going to kill myself tonight," I deadpanned.

"Really?" he said.

"No," I said.

He broke out in laughter—deep, Viking-like bellows—and I couldn't help but join him. It felt good to laugh. Cathartic. I *wasn't* actually going to kill myself. There were, actually, worse things. That elusive truth revealed itself, if only for the tiniest of instants.

"I love you, man," Dino said and gave me a hug.

Lisa and I left soon thereafter. We said a quick goodbye to the hosts and our friends and quietly walked out the front door, the celebration still raging loudly behind us. After the thumping tunes of the party, the silent, cold walk to the car felt vastly magnified by the widening gulf between us.

The party had been pure fiction. This stark winter chill was our reality. Everyone else's lives around us were progressing; promotions and bonuses, kids' milestones and achievements, five-star vacations and romantic getaways. But Lisa and I were stuck in neutral, with a sword dangling inches above our heads. Two people stuck together at the hip, yet as if we were moving further and further apart. Instead of leaning on one other for support, there was only blame and anger, disappointment with our present condition, and fear for our future.

We went to Lisa's dad's place in Florida for Christmas. I thought the Sunshine State might offer an escape from feeling hunted, but I was sorely mistaken. When you're a finance guy and your father-in-law is Michael Moskow, he knows what's up with you before you do.

And he wasn't the only one. Marc Bender from Millennium was there with his in-laws. Marc, with the wavy black hair, nerdy build, and the fastest fingers ever to touch a Blackberry, narrowly dodged a bullet by not giving us money. Izzy Englender would have served his head on a platter had Millennium's name been dragged into this after their mutual find timing scandal a few years earlier. Marc's face registered shock when he laid eyes on me. Rather than play social dodgeball for a week, I decided to walk right over and say a very polite hello. He glanced around nervously—as if looking for FBI agents on my tail—as we exchanged strained pleasantries. Marc asked only the minimum required:

"How are you?" and "Who do you know here?"

I responded with a diplomatic, "I'm doing okay, all things considered."

He wished me a halting good luck.

I understood, then, that I was toxic. Cursed. Anyone who worked anywhere near my industry would not want to be seen associating with me. Whatever I had, they thought they might catch it.

As I left Marc and walked out of the room, I fought the urge to lift my shirt and proclaim: "Look, ma! No wire!"

My nights were still spent drunk, alone, and despondent. During the days, I promised not to let my depression affect the kids' vacation, and we played like crazy, filling our time with sports, swimming, and sandcastle-building. I was acutely aware that these memories might have to last me a while.

While I was in Florida, Sommer had a second meeting with Brodsky and Fish, the Assistant US Attorneys, to try to convince them, once again, that I was an extra in this case—a dolphin roped in to the Fed's enormous and indiscriminate tuna net. His pitch was: Why not let the SEC put him before a jury and try him? It's a lower standard of conviction because it's civil (pre-ponderance of the evidence, i.e. 51 percent, versus beyond a reasonable doubt for criminal—think 85 to 90 percent). It made perfect sense to me, but it was a pipe dream. The US Attorney's Office would never voluntarily sacrifice the limelight and kick a high profile case over to the SEC. Additionally, they would never risk the SEC compromising their larger case against Zvi and Raj. It might have produced a more equitable outcome, but careers and, more importantly, prospects for glory were on the line here, so you couldn't expect much.

The day of Sommer's meeting, I must have checked my phone more than a hundred times. The call finally came as we were pulling up in the driveway after a day of swimming and fishing. My heart was in my throat. Would I get a rose from the Bachelorette?

"Can you talk?" Sommer asked.

Was he serious?

No, I'm busy watching Kim and Kourtney take NY. Call me back in an hour.

I wanted to scream in the phone: "Of course I can fucking talk! I've been holding my breath for five fucking hours!"

Instead, I took a long, deep breath.

"Yeah, I can talk. How'd it go?"

"Now these things are never definitive," Sommer said. "It's more about interpretation . . . reading the other side. Even if they were convinced that we made a compelling case that you don't belong here, they would still have to go 'up the chain,' so to speak, and run this by their supervisors . . . who would then eventually have to go up to the head of the criminal division and to the US Attorney, Preet Bharara himself. In a case this high profile, these guys at the bottom, the guys prosecuting the case, can't make a move without check-ing all the way up the line."

Holy shit, was I going free? Was Sommer actually telling me he thought he'd convinced them not to indict and now they have to go talk to their bosses?

"It works the same the other way as well," he continued.

Okay, there was the caveat.

You idiot! I wanted to shout at myself. Why allow yourself to get excited, even for a moment?

"How's that?" I asked.

"Well, if Brodsky and Fish are resistant, I am going to let them know that WE intend to go up the chain, and WE will want to make the same pitch to their supervisor, a man named Marc Berger, head of the financial crimes division. If he's not willing to listen, then we go to Ray Lauria, head of the entire criminal division. And finally, to Preet himself."

"So these guys weren't listening?" I darted to the conclusion. Enough foreplay, I'm about to explode here. Let me know what the fuck happened.

"I didn't say that," Sommers countered, a slight crack in his voice. "I'm just setting the table for you to understand how the process works. I was a little more forward today. I didn't want them to just sit back like they did last time and not offer a word. This is a give and take. You know this helps them make their case, if they decide to take you to trial, because we're giving them a preview of the defense strategy we plan on utilizing at trial. Without the element of surprise, they can spend the next nine months trying to find witnesses and tasking investigators to debunk our approach."

"I gotcha. We're opening the kimono."

"A little bit, yes," Sommer said. "So you'll recall that at the last meeting, we laid out our story and they basically took notes. This meeting, I started by asking them their thoughts about the last meeting. What did their superiors say about it, and so forth? They said they went over all the evidence, everything we told them last time, and while they agreed that your case was *dramatically* different from all of the others involved, they still felt they had enough evidence, even if some of it is circumstantial."

"*SOME* of it?" I shouted, struggling to keep my voice below a bellow. "Give me one piece that's not circumstantial! What direct evidence do they have?"

"That was the very question I posed to them," Sommer replied. "I said, 'Guys, if you can give me one piece of *direct* evidence that my client had Material Non-Public Information when he traded 3Com, I will get up from this meeting, stop wasting your time, and leave right now. One piece, and we're through today. You won't hear peep from me about a DP or dropping the case again.'"

"Right, so what did they say?" I asked.

I liked that Sommer was finally—finally!—putting their feet to the fire. Took a deep breath, wondering what they had done next.

"It was *crickets*, Mike. They didn't say a word. I have to say, even I was surprised. Now, before you get too excited, this doesn't mean that they don't have direct evidence."

"They don't. I'm telling you."

"I know. But with all due respect, Mike, I would rather hear it from the US Attorneys prosecuting the case than from you. *They're* the ones that have to make this case and meet the burden of proof. We don't have to prove you are innocent; *they* have to prove, beyond a reasonable doubt, mind you, that you are guilty. And either they don't have it, or the other more troubling option is, they are not disclosing whatever they have . . . keeping their kimono closed, so to speak."

"Nice give and take. We give. They take."

"Sometimes that's how it works, Mike. Anyway, again, either they don't have any direct evidence or they are not sharing what they have. It might be the latter. They did say there are other witnesses and more discovery they plan on producing next week. Any idea who that might be?"

"Another witness? A cooperator? No idea. Could be anyone. I didn't know most of these guys so there could be others."

"Remember, Mike. Even if they don't have direct evidence, they can still make a successful case on *circumstantial* evidence. That's the way some insider trading cases were made in the '80s."

"Right," I said. "But doesn't it say something when you have two years of body wires and wiretaps and the best you can say is '*circumstantially* they traded around the same?' And every other person in this case has massive, *direct* wiretap evidence against them?"

I was pacing now, heart racing, head swirling.

"To me it does," Sommer answered soberly. "Clearly, it means something to you as well. And if we were forced to go to trial down the line, we would make those very powerful arguments. But remember that to laymen, circumstantial evidence can be convincing. How many times have you heard someone say, 'I don't believe in coincidence'? You be surprised how many people think that way. And that can put a rope around your neck. Uh . . . pardon the terminology."

"What's our next step?" I asked anxiously.

"Nothing," Sommer said. "We wait to hear back from them. They're going to discuss what they've heard today with their supervisors and with the head of the criminal division. If they come back to us and it's clear they haven't seen the light, then we continue to work our way up the ladder. All in all, Mike, this was a fairly positive meeting. There were no surprises."

"I'm starting to think that you purposely waited until I was in Florida to hold this meeting, so you could be confident I wouldn't show up at 26 Federal Plaza and give them an earful."

"I can't say the thought didn't cross my mind," he answered. "But no, the timing just happened to work out that way."

Right. No surprises today.

Those wouldn't come for another few weeks.

Our return home from Florida to Larchmont was a return to an inherently unknowable future. This was made painfully clear as soon as we got back. I was in the kitchen, playing with Phin and making him a bottle, when I heard Lisa yelling from her office.

"What do you mean they didn't get paid? I don't understand."

That didn't sound good.

Lisa's catering business was always dancing from one catastrophe to another. I can't tell you the number of times I'd had to deliver a last-minute tray of hand-rolled canapés or a vat of mojito mix to a McMansion in Greenwich, sometimes with our kids in the car. Usually we were able to pull everything off seamlessly. Somehow, in front of the green curtain, the clients were never the wiser that their pricey, beautifully executed party had come within a hair of potential disaster.

I was keeping Phin busy in his bouncy harness by offering him various dolls, which he would quickly toss off the tray and laugh. I would try to catch the dolls before they hit the ground. Lisa burst out of the office, breathing fire, tears of anger in her eyes. She motioned me into the living room, so we could talk.

"Mike," she seethed. "None of my vendors have been paid, and I've had three servers call in the last hour to tell me their checks bounced."

"What happened?"

"Why don't *you* tell *me*?" she snapped.

"Me? What does this have to do with me?"

"I called the bank and they told me the account is frozen and in the process of being closed!" Lisa shouted. "THEY WON'T TELL ME WHY."

"I don't understand."

"It has something to do with *you*," Lisa sobbed. "She wouldn't give me any details over the phone, but it was Rosie, the teller we always see, and she said it was because of you."

I felt like collapsing.

Now they were dragging Lisa's business down? For what? Why?

"I don't get it," I said.

"Is your account or the joint account working?" she demanded.

We had a joint account, and I also had my own personal account that I never got rid of when we married.

"I dunno. I haven't gotten money out recently. I didn't have a problem last week. I'll go check."

As soon as I logged in on my bank's website, I faced a strange red warning that hovered over the "Accounts" page. It notified me that my account was indeed suspended, and said to please call customer service. I nearly vomited. I discovered the same notification when I tried to log into our joint account too.

"This is crazy," I said, struggling to keep my voice at an even keel—Phin was right nearby—but Lisa lost it, screaming,

"What are we going to do, Mike? WE HAVE NO MONEY! YOUR SHIT IS FUCKING WITH MY BUSINESS NOW, MIKE!"

Her normally green eyes turned red, bloodshot with rage and pain.

"How could I do this? What did *I* do? Lisa, I didn't do this. Let me call the bank. Maybe they"ll talk to me."

After waiting on hold for ten minutes, they finally patched me through to the manager.

"I'm not at liberty to say, sir. The only thing I can tell you is there is an ongoing investigation for a suspicious transaction."

"What transaction?"

"I can't say, sir."

"Well what's suspicious about it?"

"I can't tell you that either, sir."

"So, what *can* you tell me?"

"I can give you the number of corporate. Perhaps they can give you more information. I'm very sorry."

I called, but it was a Saturday, and the recording said they were closed until Monday.

I hung up, defeated.

"*WHAT ARE WE GOING TO DO?*" Lisa screamed again, now starting to cry.

I reached over to comfort her but she pushed me away.

"*NO!* You did this to us. You put us all in danger. Everything. How could you?"

She bolted up the stairs.

I wanted to follow but knew nothing good could come of it. I knew Lisa. She needed time to calm down. Frankly, so did I. I stepped out to the front porch to catch my breath and put on the happy face for the kids. I had a sinking feeling that this was only an opening salvo.

As it turned out, I was right. Over the next week, all the dominoes began to tumble. My credit cards were declined, one by one, and then canceled. I received a vicious runaround from my bank's corporate and local offices. They refused to provide a concrete reason, other than to tell me a "suspicious transaction" had taken place in my account. Finally, one senior customer service rep took pity on me and called me back on her cell phone, presumably to avoid the call being recorded internally, and told me that according to their system, I had been red flagged as a potential money launderer, and that there was no specific transaction. Someone in the government had sent my bank a little heads-up. I was sure that had to be it.

This made me furious.

There was even less evidence that I was a money launderer than that I'd traded 3Com on inside information. Yet, as I was later to learn, despite not presenting a single shred of evidence, the government had no problem convincing a magistrate judge to sign off on the money laundering charge in the complaint.

Imagine what that did to me. Try living day-to-day in our society with no bank account or credit cards. Try paying your mortgage every month with a money order from CVS. That was bad, but by far, the worst of it was the damage the government's hardball tactics inflicted on Lisa's catering business. Her checks to vendors bounced, she couldn't pay staff, and she wasted countless hours trying unfreeze her accounts and credit cards. It severely damaged her business. At the time, her business was the only thing putting food on our table.

The government was trying to get me to cooperate or to plead out. Putting me on the equivalent of a financial no-fly list was just another tactic to that end. The damage to my wife and her business was acceptable collateral damage—as far as they were concerned—in their mission to get me to cop a plea.

I figured if I could absorb these blows and play rope-a-dope until the government had finished with discovery and the dirty tricks, then it would be our turn to go on the offensive. Little did I know that these were also pipe dreams. It was about to get even worse.

CHAPTER NINE

LEAP OF FAITH

———

To REALLY UNDERSTAND HOW WE ARRIVED at this point in our lives, it's necessary to return to the past, to three years earlier. Almost a decade had passed since I had escaped the uptight legal world of Sullivan & Cromwell, the hundred-hour work week, and sleeping under my desk. Throughout my subsequent time as a trader—despite the assholes and the backstabbers—not a day went by that I regretted the decision to hang up my lawyer's hat. The ride had never been dull. Hanging out at a bar and downing Ketel Ones among friends, even in the aftermath of the market, still seemed light years better than the suffocating sobriety of Sullivan & Cromwell. I probably could have coasted along like that indefinitely, allowing Lisa to spend a small fortune remodeling our kitchen, taking family vacations, and squirreling away a comfortable nest egg.

But then things started to unravel at Remsenberg. I left for greener pastures, but it soon became clear that they were never going to be as green as they should be. The only real way to get where I wanted, where I felt I *needed* to be, would require a gamble. It would be the biggest yet of my life. I would branch out and start my own firm.

Prop trading, potentially viewed, is a form of gambling. We on the Street prefer the term "speculation," and realistically it is much more akin to a game of skill than chance (think poker vs. roulette), but there are still elements of chance to it. When the firm is yours, you become the house—and with that small fee on every trade tacked on, the house does always win . . . if only to a certain degree. If the traders are losing, and profits tumble, those small fees won't save you.

I had made it easy—perhaps too easy—for the Goffer brothers to tempt me away from Quad Capital, where I had gone with Jon Deigan (JD) after the meltdown at Remsenberg. Incremental Capital (ICAP) had been my idea to begin with, so I was itching to go. I had done the legwork and the research. I knew what we needed, and it was exactly what we had. JD had the charisma; I would be the operational and trading brains. My biggest mistake, in retrospect, was planting the Incremental seed early in the Goffers' minds, back when JD and I had collaborated on first marketing the Incremental concept.

The name said it all in terms of our goal. We'd be coupling a transactional model of commissions—just like the rake* in poker—while betting on talented traders taking small calculated risks. *Incremental profits, bit by bit.* But before I knew what was happening, JD had dropped out and Zvi was onboard.

I tried to adjust. Maybe it wouldn't be so bad. I figured that with Zvi and Nu's capital and connections, they would be okay minority partners for the fund. When JD fell out of the picture, any obstacle to their joining the firm went with him. In retrospect, of course, leaving was the smartest move JD ever made. His gut instinct about Zvi—that he was all talk and full of shit—was the correct one. And he never forgot Zvi's physical threats back at Remsenberg.

While still at Remsenberg, I'd once broached the possibility of bringing aboard the Brothers Goffer to JD.

"I know you're gonna hate the idea, but what if we just bring over Zvi and Nu and give them a tiny piece? These guys can recruit like mad and they're good traders. Zvi has a lot of connections. Granted, a lot of them are bullshit, but he's tight with a couple of these Galleon guys that are real hitters."

"You know, you're right," JD said, and paused to stroke his chin before pointing a finger at me. "I do hate the idea. He's a fucking retard and his brother is half that smart. That guy blows smoke, *that's all.* Remember when he was going to break my legs for asking Nu to rein in his risk? And I saved the firm because of that. If those guys had been here for the Cypress

---

* **Rake** is the scaled commission fee taken by a cardroom operating a poker game. It is generally 2.5 to 10 percent of the pot in each poker hand, up to a predetermined maximum amount.

disaster (CY:NYSE)* they'd have been down another $750K+. They're no-talent Brooklyn knuckleheads. And that's the *generous* assessment."

I knew JD was right about a lot. They were inexperienced. But they were also fast learners and absolute animals when it came to making connections. And Zvi was also the #1 performer at Schottenfeld, a respected prop firm with a lot of great traders. You don't get to be the top trader at a firm like that by accident.

For Zvi, running his own firm was a necessity. His personality made it inevitable that no matter where he went, he would eventually clash with management and be fired or quit—unless, that is, he became the manager himself. His attitude was, "I know more than you, so why the hell are you telling me what to do?" Oddly enough, on this particular issue, I saw his power wars with management as somewhat legitimate because he was right most of the time. This was not because Zvi was a genius, but because the typical managers were even dumber than he was. The reality is, most people running prop trading firms were absolute morons at that time. Capital was king, and if you had access to capital then you could open up a shop. *Anybody* with capital could. The formula was simple—capital, plus talent, plus a diligent risk management framework and you had an almost certain money maker. Capital was easy (or was before the financial world imploded in 2008). Risk management required finding the sweet and narrow middle ground. The so-called piker firms like Trillium or Schoenfeld Securities erred on the side of caution and produced small trading profits (but lots of commissions), and the so-called "cowboy firms" had no risk matrix whatsoever and were essentially ticking time bombs. You had to be in the tightrope's middle, the sweet spot that reined in the shooters and the cowboys, but gave some leeway to traders with talent making smart, calculated bets.

As we began, I was anointed the brains of our operation, doing most of the legwork required to build the firm literally from scratch. Nu, I would quickly discover, was a first-class alcoholic, interested in little other than getting ripped. It was decided early on that his primary responsibility would be

---

* At Remsenberg, Zvi was hearing "imminent takeover" of CY and spread the word far and wide so half the firm was long CY. When no deal materialized, the stock dropped precipitously, causing significant losses and nearly putting the firm out of business.

training a crew of young traders, and entertaining the more seasoned traders at Sutton Place, our local midtown-Manhattan watering hole. We had our spot unofficially reserved on the balcony overlooking the Second Avenue, and a regular set of bartenders who scrupulously attended to our every need.

I had heard enough about Zvi from people within the proprietary trading business to know that he should come equipped with warning lights. Zvi had made and lost a fortune at the Schottenfeld Group, along the way earning a reputation for being plugged in to the "smart money" pipeline. The "made a fortune" part was oft broadcast and widely known. The "lost a fortune" part was always concealed to the best of Zvi's ability. Zvi often bragged about being the first trader at Schottenfeld to make over a half-million dollars in one day, for which he'd been rewarded with five bottles of Dom Perignon, delivered to his trading desk by the buxom receptionist. Zvi's desk looked like a Dom tasting room, with dozens of bottles stacked neatly on top and underneath the desk, each courtesy of a $100K+ trading day. On his desk, Zvi had a red Staples "That Was Easy" button that he gleefully pressed every time he made a hugely profitable trade. Trading came easy for Zvi Goffer. Or so it seemed.

It was no secret that Zvi had left Schottenfeld to work directly for Raj Rajaratnam at the Galleon Group as a portfolio manager. It's impossible to over-emphasize the importance of this. It was important to our success at Incremental, but also one of the reasons Incremental got dubbed "Baby Galleon."

The Galleon Group was a highly successful hedge fund. More than that, everyone in the business knew it was the epicenter of information on the Street. Not illegal insider information, *per se* (though later it turned out that Raj had a great deal of that as well*), but superb research and impeccable street connections—those most invaluable commodities in the trading game. Zvi also had excellent inside contacts at that motherlode of all hedge funds, Stevie Cohen's SAC Capital. Because of these connections, with Zvi onboard, Incremental would ultimately raise $200 million to trade with, and our firm would be off to the races.

We were in the right place at the right time. Portfolio managers were being downsized by cost-cutting investment banks like Goldman Sachs, or fired

---

* *The Billionaire's Apprentice*, by Anita Raghavan (2013), remains the single best account of the rise and fall of Raj and Galleon, along with that of Rajiv Gupta, who ran McKinsey.

from hedge funds. By the fall of 2009, Incremental Capital had hired more than fifty traders, mostly Ivy League graduates with outstanding track records. We also had a laundry list of some of the biggest names in the business—SAC Capital, Millennium Partners, Todd Deutsch—breaking down our doors to invest.

Working with Zvi, I learned more of his weird quirks. He shuffled his feet constantly under his desk, and would bite his nails until they literally bled. Quirks aside, I continued to feel I was in a good place with a good partner. Once, when I brought Zvi to a Minyanville charity event during Incremental's earliest days, Rick Schottenfeld came up to Zvi and pronounced, "I never should have let you go. You might very well be the next Stevie Cohen." Cohen, at the time, was widely recognized as the most successful trader in history.

So I was hardly alone in seeing the talent and ability in Zvi, despite his flaws. I made the Faustian bargain. I took the risk. I told myself I could easily suffer through Zvi's mania and irrationality. I chose to see whatever Raj and Schottenfeld saw in him. I was determined to play four corner defense, until I could gain more control, and then, as soon as all was right and I was correctly positioned, I planned to just sell the damn thing. That thing being Incremental. From the word go, I knew we were less than two years from monetizing it.

What I didn't know was that there were already informants among us, wearing wires.

But I'm getting ahead of myself.

Our first serious backer at Incremental was Whitney Quillen, of W. Quillen Securities, as good a guy as there could be. An old-school gent whose family were proprietors of horses, manses, and superior jawlines, Whitney sublet us space at a very reasonable rate at 145 East 57th Street, right next door to Hammacher Schlemmer and Le Colonial. The latter had a French-Vietnamese themed bar upstairs that reminded me of what it must have been like in Saigon before the shit hit the fan. The Gerber Group also had offices in our building, which meant we kept our eyes open for Gerber's wife, Cindy Crawford. Whitney was enamored of Zvi after their first meeting. In exchange for a sweetheart deal on rent, he asked Zvi to make some trades through his desk. We had a "friend" on the desk anyway in Adam Weinstein (not his real name), who had put the final nail in Remsenberg not too long ago after perpetually playing Ahab to the white whale of Steve Jobs's Apple.

Around this time I had a brilliant idea that I would revisit later with another trader. Algo trading, or computerized program trading, was just starting to make a big splash on Wall Street. My idea was to build a black box that would take the trades of certain designated traders and "flip" them on the back end so that buys become sells and sells become buys. You could apply it to a trader like "Adam," who loses large sums of money most of the time, and mirror his executions without his knowing. So if Adam is down $5K, he'd actually be up $5K. The Algo would turn a trader with an abysmally low win ratio into a gold mine by doing the exact opposite of what he was doing. It worked for George Costanza, why couldn't it work for "Adam Weinstein"?

We would never let Adam have any discretionary authority on trading, but as far as pushing a buy button when we told him to? Well, even Adam couldn't fuck that up. It was easy business for Adam, and Whitney gave us a healthy discount on the rent.

When it came time to start raising money for Incremental, Whitney always told us he wanted to be a part of it. And it was Whitney's interest that forced us to wrap our heads around what we were worth, when we had basically nothing.

I went to Zvi about it.

"How do we come up with a number? What are we worth? What's even the mechanism for determining it?"

"Tell Whitney that for $200K, we'll give him 1 percent, or 5 percent for a million."

I laughed out loud. "So we're only valuing ourselves at $20 million?"

"Is that the math?" Zvi asked. "Sounds fair. Generic-Carlin sold that worthless chunk of shit firm to RBC for $100 million."

"Look, there's potential, and then there's reality," I cautioned. "Do I think we could be worth that at some point? Yes, of course. I wouldn't be here if I didn't. But right now it's just me and your brother and a few junior traders. A $1,000,000 valuation would be generous."

"I work for Raj, the King of all Kings," Zvi said mystically. "Franz is going to recruit some hedge-fund level A-talent for us. You were the top trader at the last two firms you've been at and know more about this business than anyone

I've ever met. That's not worth $1 million. That's worth ten today, and it's a steal at that."

I liked being flattered, but I still thought the number was ridiculous. There was no real revenue yet, and we were currently trading out of a glorified walk-in closet with leaking ceilings. But then again, finance always contains that hint of fantasy, of mystery, of what might be. Companies without profits go public all the time. Remember Yahoo? Early stage conceptual companies raise millions in venture capital money every year without even having a prototype. So-called "value" in a market is ultimately nothing more than what one side is willing to pay for it. It's all about perception.

Zvi suddenly decided to compromise: "Look, start at $15 mil. If he negotiates, fine. We can settle at ten."

"Sorry, Zvi," I replied. "There's no way I can ask for $15 million with a straight face. No way in hell. Some things don't need to be negotiated from a bullshit number first. When you do that, you lose credibility, which you can't get back. I'd rather set a real price."

"I'm not accepting less than ten," Zvi said, adamant.

"'You're not *accepting*? You're not a partner of this firm. Don't tell me what you'll accept."

"Well, my brother won't accept it. So there's no difference."

It was becoming increasingly clear that this was the reality I had bought into. Zvi wasn't technically a partner. But Nu was his puppet. Nu had probably never disagreed with Zvi a day in his life, even about what to wear to school. If Zvi said oil was at $120 a barrel because the Bush family wanted it there, then that was what Nu thought too.

"You go ask him then," I responded, doing my best not to lose my temper. "If you're not willing to accept less than $10 million, then you go ask. I don't want to create a situation where I ask for ten, he's willing to do $7.5, and I go to say yes, but then I can't because I remember—oh wait, Zvi's got some science-fiction number in his head."

"I *can't* ask because I'm not a partner," Zvi said with a smile. "I don't even know how it would work, the mechanics and all that."

"Think about it," I said. "Once you sell to one guy, it's always easier to sell to another using that as a baseline. Say Whitney bought X and we only had seven traders. That will be the floor. It can only go up from there."

"Fine," Zvi said dejectedly. By the tone in his voice and the look on his face, you would have thought that I had just forced him into involuntary bankruptcy.

"It doesn't matter. He's not going to do anything over $5. We're not going to have to worry about it."

"Anything less than $10 and I'm not doing another fucking share through his firm," Zvi barked. Then he barged out of the room and headed for the elevator. This was a bad omen. Up until this point I had argued with Zvi, sure, but mostly about shit I didn't care about. We had worked for separate firms. We'd no money, accounts, or interests intertwined. So if he loved something, but I didn't love it, I just didn't buy it. There was no interdependency. Now, we were getting joined at the hip. He was a part of key decisions about money. After all, it was his money.

I'd recently found out that he and Nu split everything.

Zvi had said he'd lost lost over $1 million in the AMD mess*. One time I asked him how.

"Oh, it was Nu actually," Zvi responded. "He and I split everything up and down, always."

Now that was a fact I would have preferred to learn before having gone into business with Nu. Because it meant that I was really in business with Zvi.

None of that mattered now. The doors were open and there was nothing but promise ahead of us. We had fought, sweated, cried, and bled to get to this point. I didn't want the assurance of success. I just wanted the opportunity. We had finally arrived at the waterline; it was now sink or swim time. I was ready.

I thought.

---

* Zvi, presumably via Drimal or one of his other Galleon contacts, was trumpeting AMD hearing that Raj was "all in" on the name and that he was going to piggyback the play for size.

CHAPTER TEN

MILLION DOLLAR CHECKS

I HAD CAUGHT THE 1:40 A.M. train home—the last one of the night—almost passing out mid-journey, which would have meant a devastating 3:00 a.m. last stop arrival at Stamford or Westport, Connecticut and a $100 taxi ride home. I stumbled out of the train, squinted at my twelve-year-old beige Lexus GS300, and kept walking, marking the first responsible decision of the night.

By the time I got home, I was desperate to water our front yard, even though it was the middle of winter. Oh, the primordial joy of urinating outdoors. Inside, I squinted at the glowing alarm keypad like it was the final question on *Who Wants to Be a Millionaire?* and disarmed the four-digit code, cooing like a baby when the light went red to green. I trudged upstairs, discarded my clothes, brushed my teeth, and crawled into bed. Lisa protested softly, either in the dream she was having, or at me, then rolled over and went back to sleep. I set the alarm for 5:30 a.m., which meant a solid three hours of shut-eye. I closed my eyes and tried to command my brain to halt the spinning, the music, and the ticker tape cycling through it.

When it came, 5:30 a.m. felt like the end of the world.

Why do I do this to myself? What's the point?

For the hundredth time that year, I swore to myself I would cut back. I was still drunk. Pain coursed through my body like a hot shot of liquid agony. The true hangover was just beginning. Dehydration, pounding head. I looked around briefly for the cat that must have crawled onto my face while I slept and crapped in my mouth, only to remember that we didn't have a fucking cat. Automaton time. Become a robot. That'll work.

Water, Advil, toothbrush, hot shower, heavy clothes, car keys.

Where the hell are my keys? A wave of panic rushed over me.

We had an important investor meeting at 7:15. That meant a 6:14 train to make sure I had time to grab coffee and navigate the swelling, heaving sea of humanity that was Grand Central Station and midtown Manhattan. It was almost 6:00. I was cutting it way too close if I wanted to grab Starbucks before the train. *I'll just use the valet key. Where the hell's my car?! My car's been stolen!* And then I remembered that I had sensibly left it at the train station. But it was 6:01 now and a mile to the station, which meant running. Over-the-shoulder duffel bag, wearing a suit and dress shoes, still drunk and burping up whatever garbage I'd eaten the night before to try to line my stomach. (I'd eaten *several* things. Breaded chicken strips with a spicy garlic mayo sauce. Calamari rings. Nachos covered in processed cheese, with jalapenos and bits of black olives.) Another burp.

Kill me now, please.

The train was just pulling up as I sprinted across Chatsworth Avenue and bounded down the steps toward the station. The conductor, in a rare act of sympathy (after all, one of the job perks must be the angry faces of entitled suburbanites as he shuts the door in their faces and pulls away), waited for an elderly gentleman with a cane. I used him as a human shield and slipped on right behind him. The thirty-minute ride without coffee or water was pure torture, but we pulled into Grand Central at 6:50, giving me a few minutes to grab a large Starbucks, a bottle of water, and a Turbo-chefed fake egg sandwich. I asked the barista to drop some ice into the coffee and consumed all three on the walk up to Michael Wilen's offices on 49th Street. 7:03. Zvi was waiting outside the building for me, sucking back a coffee and looking quite pained himself.

"What are you wearing?" I asked.

Zvi was in dark brown dress slacks, a collared white shirt, and a light brown houndstooth sweater. I'd never seen him wear a sweater before, and it looked ridiculous.

"Why are you late?" he returned with a grin.

Then Zvi asked me to push him in front of an approaching M60 line bus to end the pain. I commiserated. The six Advil and Venti redeye had done little to dent the thudding in my brain.

"So listen," Zvi said. "Nu's wife works for this guy. He likes her. So let me do the talking."

"Gladly," I groaned, dipping into the retail storefront for a couple of iced coffees for our foreheads.

Inside the law firm of Wilens & Co., Michael Wilens intercepted us at reception before the attractive secretary could seat us in the waiting area. Pushing forty, short and well-groomed, with an engaging smile, he vigorously shook our hands while asking the receptionist which conference rooms were available. A sudden morning influx of meetings had removed all the vacancies, so he apologized profusely as he led us to a very small but empty associate's office and positioned himself behind the desk, with the two of us in sleek Herman Miller Aeron chairs on the other side. Zvi and Wilens exchanged small talk about Nu's wife Jill and the state of the wildly fluctuating markets for a few minutes. Then Wilens went into his highlight reel of what the firm did.

Basically, they had secured the rights to every conceivable 1-800-LEGAL suffix: 1-800-IMMIGRATION, 1-800-DIVORCE and 1-800-BANKRUPTCY. The numbers were so popular and the leads they turned over so voluminous that Wilens' father had quickly—and correctly—figured out their firm wasn't suited to handle the onslaught of business they created. Rather than turning customers away, they'd reinvented themselves as a kind of third party marketing outfit that referred business to other law firms that could handle the customers, in exchange for generous referral/participation fees, of course.

This was an absolute monster moneymaker. Zvi was doing his best to appear interested, but the delay was killing him. Zvi's eyes were bloodshot, and his manic energy was manifested in leg tapping and scratching that houndstooth abomination on his chest. It might have been my imagination, but I thought could still smell the pheromone mix of perfume, tobacco, and alcohol that was the calling card of most city bars on his hair and clothes. The first time Wilens paused in the telling of the the Wilens & Co. autobiographical audio book, Zvi pounced—even though Wilens was still essentially mid-chapter.

"That's pretty incredible. This is really *some* business you guys have managed to build. Based on what you've told me and what Jill has told us, it seems clear that you're interested in exploring investments that aren't directly tied into your business or legal operations, in order to diversify your investment stream."

"Exactly," Wilens said enthusiastically.

"Traditionally, real estate would offer someone in your position an excellent way to diversify," Zvi said.

"Okay."

"There's only one problem with that approach right now," Zvi went on, changing his tone. "Real estate is finished. If you haven't bought it already, you can't buy it now. And if you have it and haven't *sold* it already, you're probably stuck with it. We've spent the last few months looking for office space and what we're seeing is the start of a serious downtrend that will last for years."

"I agree. Businesses are laying off people and breaking leases. Rents are collapsing."

"Precisely," Zvi said with a solemn nod. "So what we can offer is a business that is totally uncorrelated with the real estate collapse, and which can be a perfect complement to the more economically sensitive investments you already have."

"Your business itself is in a rather nice anti-recessionary space," I chimed in. "Divorce, bankruptcy. I imagine those are both perfectly countercyclical offsets to your other corporate work, which is more dependent on the economy."

"Yes, precisely," Wilens responded, enthusiastically pointing at me to say I'd got it right.

"I know you already know what a hedge fund is and have contacts in that industry," Zvi added.

"Have you heard the name Rich Grodin?" Wilens asked with a twinkle.

We both nodded. It hurt to nod.

"He's a good friend of mine. I know a lot of those ex-SAC guys and we've put some money to work in various funds. But I'm looking for something a little more substantive—something where I can have some input on the business and that's a little more early-stage. That's why I was excited to hear about you guys from Jill."

"Let me tell you a little bit more about us, and then we can talk about some of the ways we might be able to do something together," Zvi said.

He reeled off a ten-minute pitch covering who we were, where we came from, why we were much more conservative than a typical hedge fund, and how we'd make money no matter what way the market moved. He talked about how we were the casino—the house—and how we'd take a piece of every trader's transaction, but with enough upside on profits that the returns could be significantly higher than at most hedge funds. Around halfway through Zvi's pitch, which I also knew by heart, I picked up on a deep basso sound that, at first, I thought was Zvi's stomach rumbling. Yet soon it became clear that it was Dr. Dre's "The Next Episode" from *2001*. Where it was coming from, I couldn't precisely tell. I tried to tune back in for the conclusion of Zvi's pitch.

". . . a ground floor opportunity to help finance the growth. We're going to pick up guys like Grodin, plus a bunch of guys that used to work for SAC and Galleon, where I'm close to the King himself. Those are the ponds we're fishing in now. Top drawer all the way."

When Zvi finished, Wilens pulled out a checkbook from his jacket pocket. It caught both of us totally unprepared. A lawyer wasn't the ideal partner, but money was money. The only problem was, as our initial disagreement over what percentage to give Whitney for his $100,000 investment had shown, we really didn't have a set solution for how to value the firm or what we were willing to give up.

"Count me in," Wilens said, not missing a beat. "Here's a check for . . . a million dollars." He signed his name with a flourish, ripping the check from the checkbook and placing it on the edge of the desk in front of us.

My adrenaline started pumping as I realized this wasn't going to be an introductory "We'll get back to you" meeting, but that real decisions had to be made, here and now, hungover. The Dr. Dre tune had ended and led to "Warning Shot" by the Notorious B.I.G. I laughed inwardly for a quick second, thinking what an odd coincidence it was that both those songs were on my iPod, until I suddenly realized that it actually *was* my iPod playing in my jacket, hung up on the chair behind me. I decided that it would be worse to acknowledge it and turn it off rather than let it play on and pretend it didn't exist. Wilens might not have even heard the music, and even if he did, he might have assumed that it was coming from an adjacent office.

Wilens slid the check toward us, so we could count all the zeroes on it and confirm that it was signed.

"What . . . uh, what are you looking for?" Zvi stammered, and looked to me for help. I offered a single insipid nod. Punting it back to Wilens wasn't the worst option here. Although, as the son of the founder of a law firm worth nine figures, he had surely learned a thing or two and wasn't about to start negotiating against himself.

"You tell me. What does something like that, on the spot, get me?"

Zvi looked my way for me to take the lead, so I took it: "Well, we just did a minority investment with Whitney Quillen. Do you know the name?"

"Sounds familiar," Wilens lied.

"He's the founder of Quillen Capital," I continued. "His brother, Parker Quillen, is a very well-known hedge fund manager. A few months back he gave us $100,000 for 1 percent of the company. We've landed several good traders since then and might have found a great deal on space, so arguably the firm's position has only improved. But because because you may be able to introduce us to other investors or traders from your contact list, I'm comfortable making a deal for the same valuation. So your one million gets you 10 percent of the firm."

Wilens leaned back, thinking, which gave Zvi the opening to jump in.

"In reality, Michael, we gave Whitney that deal because of his connections. He knows traders, he knows money management, and he even has a platform that we might be able to use to garner a better rate with Goldman. So it's a little bit of a different situation. His strategic ties are extremely strong. I don't think I'd make that deal today for someone not in the industry. He's not going to be passive in the least."

Zvi was inadvertently helping close Wilens on the valuation I had put out there, but I instantly understood that his real motivation was to get Wilens to go higher. To Zvi, if the guy committed to a $10 million val, he could always come back trumpeting to Nu to veto and try to get him to $15 million.

Wilens put his elbows on the table.

"I'm not planning on being passive either. And while Whitney may have a different background, I know plenty of guys in finance. And with my legal *and* real estate skills, I can save us money on legal fees, documents, a new office, lease negotiations, and a dozen other ways. Not to mention I've got some very deep-pocketed friends in my Rolodex looking exactly for situations like this."

The guy was good. I'd give him 10 percent for that one million dollars sitting in front of me, no problem. But there *was* a problem.

"You see," Wilens said, "I'm looking for a bigger percentage. I'm willing to give you that million today without even looking at the firm's books." He paused, and to let me know that the next words out of his mouth would mark him as either a lunatic or a savvy player.

"But I want 25 percent of the company for it."

Wilens had effectively called our bluff. If we needed the money bad enough, we might snatch it. He could always come back if we said no and ask to see the books, noting that they might justify the $10 million valuation we were seeking. "Warning Shot" rolled into tracks from Ice Cube's *Death Certificate*, a fitting end for the meeting. I knew Zvi was thinking higher valuation than $10 million, not lower, but to his credit he responded very deftly.

"Well, obviously I'll put the offer in front of Nu, but we've got several other offers out there on par with the $10 million valuation, from individuals we respect as well. We'd love to do something with you, but at that number, it's frankly not going to happen. Come see the space we're looking at, meet some of the traders, and we can sit down again with you, but the numbers we discussed today are not going to get a deal done. Again, between Raj and Gary Rosenbach at Galleon, I can get a check for $5 to $10 million, but we'd have to give up half our firm. You see, we want to retain control. We're the ones out recruiting every night. We're the ones putting up the eye-popping P&L numbers during the day. And we're the ones that are going to work eighteen hours a day for the next three years to turn our operation into the next First New York. And you know what Stevie Cohen offered to buy them for last year?"

"What was the number?" Wilens eagerly asked.

"$400 million . . . and they said *no thanks!*" Zvi finished with a smirking flourish.

"Hmm. Okay. Well, I'm still interested in continuing the conversation. Talk to Nu and come back to me. In the meantime, I appreciate you guys dropping by. It was great to put a face to the 'famous Zvi' name. Your brother talks about you more than he talks about his wife, that's for sure."

"That's because I'm more interesting. But I bet you realized that three minutes into this meeting."

Zvi flashed a Cheshire grin, pulling down his horrible houndstooth sweater and standing to shake Wilens' hand. I followed suit, and we walked back to reception and took the elevator to the lobby, to the soundtrack playing in my jacket pocket.

In the end we never did business with Wilens. In hindsight, his potential business was not the important part of our meeting. Instead, it was what became clear to me because of it. Namely, that by hook or by crook Zvi was going to take on the role he wanted for himself, whether you liked it or not. I saw this again and again in the investor pitches we made in all the weeks that followed.

Zvi could sell you a Hummer when gas was $5 a gallon. His only problem was he had no idea how to close. Part of closing is actually signing a contract, getting that money in the bank. To get to that part you have to have a contract. And contract terms were where Zvi would become unhinged. There was a dictatorial streak to him, a Castro-like cult of personality that made it all but impossible to come to a realistic deal. To him business, trading, life in general—all of it was *war*, and you either destroyed your opponent or you got destroyed. I don't know if this was borne from the Israeli in him, that mentality of "You are always surrounded by hostile nations and you must fight for your life," or if this attitude was simply writ large in his DNA. Only later, much later, would I get a clear answer to that question. For now, here was this smart kid who came through the working-class public school system of Canarsie, Brooklyn, where survival for a smart white kid on Flatlands Avenue was damn remarkable.

Zvi's glasses weren't rose colored; they were hypnotic. If the other side wanted to look at trailing twelve months, Zvi wanted to look at the future twelve months. That, actually, made sense to me. After all, with respect to Incremental, it started out as semi-conceptual, and it was the future potential that mattered from an investment point of view. We had not only survived the greatest financial collapse since 1929, but had doubled our employees and been solidly profitable for every month, including up a blowout 3 percent the same month that Lehman Brothers exploded. We were doing *something* right.

Zvi was able to weave a brilliant interlocking combination of hard and soft sell. The soft was "Hey, I'm from Brooklyn, raised dirt poor, made more money last month than my parents made in their lifetimes. I'm comfortable, and if this all goes away tomorrow, I've got no regrets, so I really don't need or want your money. I'm just doing you a favor because Greg Ettin or Craig Drimal said you were a friend and spoke highly of you. Look, if you weren't friends with him, I wouldn't even be here."

Zvi was able to make you feel that by giving him money, *he* was actually doing *you* the ultimate favor.

"I'm only here because of you-know-who, and that's the only reason you're even in a position to have this opportunity to give us money, but since I am here and now you've seen it—this . . . 'machine' of ours that rivals anything the Bellagio or Stardust can put out on the casino floor—you know you'd have to be crazy not to take advantage of it."

We would put skeptics and ballbusters in their places by comparing the young hyper-growth returns of Incremental to whatever business or field the guy we were pitching was in. Most of these guys were megamillionaires who had plateaued with whatever they were doing and got a hard-on contemplating returns in the mid-teens. Anything in the 20s and they were salivating. We were offering 30s and 40s, or, if Zvi thought the guy wanted 40s, then 50s was our target. If he wanted 50s, Zvi would say that triple digits were not out of the question. He was never going to be underbid and there was no ceiling. We were selling futures. It wasn't unlike stock analysts who came up with any number their investment banking brethren needed to win the beauty contest to get the IPO business of young companies.

Things got so bad in the 1990s and early 2000s that the analysts had to make up new "metrics" altogether. Ratios which had been exhaustively vetted and used for decades and were the valuation gold standard suddenly became quaint. Granted it's hard for a company to have a P/E* when there is no fore-seeable E. But they just made stuff up. Eyeballs or number of people in the world divided by people that own or want to own a computer times $100. It was nonsense. Not even creative nonsense. Just run-of-the-mill nonsense. They were pulling magical numbers out of a hat to pad their bonus checks.

But that's the job of an analyst: to determine, or at least make a justifiable, defensible estimate. Show me the E or the sales or the revenue at some future date to justify a price today of $X. Instead, they just made stuff up. There was (and still is) almost disbelief when some analyst is told that retail traders actually relied on or used his research and analysis as the justification to purchase a stock. They most likely have to cover their mouth to suppress a giggle (I'm actually laughing now as I write this).

---

* Price to Earnings ratio, the conventional way to value stocks.

This should be shocking only if you have an altruistic view of Wall Street. And there aren't many of those left. And what reason could you possibly have for that? If you look at Wall Street's two original missions—first, to allocate capital formation efficiently, and second, to fleece Main Street—much of what we've witnessed and tsk-tsked these last twenty years becomes expected and consistent, rather than the "ugly, rogue" elements as it's been spun.

Zvi was a rainmaker. He sold dreams. He sold wild things that felt as though they could not possibly be true.

But what if they were?

That was the question now. For him, me, our investors. Everyone.

What if they were?

CHAPTER ELEVEN

FITTY

WHITNEY AND WILENS WERE ONE TYPE of investor, the predictable kind. But we were ready to talk to almost anyone. One the more unique pitches came courtesy of Franz Tudor, another man I would entirely misread. Franz, whom we took a chance on at Incremental, was a trader with a colorful and checkered past. He had worked for Raj Rajaratnam at Galleon, Art Samberg at Pequot Capital, and even Stevie Cohen at SAC Capital*. Franz came with a number of ace connections in the healthcare industry. While working at a proprietary trading firm called the Schottenfeld Group from 2006–2007, Franz had become their go-to healthcare guy. In the spring of 2007, he was white-hot, having given Schottenfeld's traders several very profitable tips. One well-timed tip involving Medimmune (MEDI), the maker of FluMist, made the firm a fortune when AstraZeneca bought the Maryland-based company for $15.2 billion. Nobody at Schottenfeld knew exactly why Franz was so confident about a MEDI acquisition, and nobody dared to ask. They just bought stock. Others throughout the hedge fund industry did the same. In the weeks leading up to the acquisition, SAC Capital increased its Medimmune holdings from about 150,000 shares to about 800,000 shares. Shortly after the deal was announced, SAC sold nearly its entire stake. Perhaps not coincidentally, the SEC opened an investigation into SAC Capital for potential insider trading before the Medimmune acquisition. The Schottenfeld partners bought Franz a black Cadillac Escalade as a "bonus" for Medimmune. Several Schottenfeld traders could have bought houses with their profits from this trade. Then, a few

---

* Later, all three "legends" would be investigated or prosecuted for insider trading.

months down the road, Franz got ice cold and started losing the firm money. The partners demanded that Franz return the Escalade and, adding insult to injury, famously made Franz prepay for parking when he returned the car. Janet Jackson may have recorded "What Have You Done for Me Lately" way back in 1986, but it was Wall Street's longstanding anthem going back to the Gilded Age.

After Franz "blew up" at Schottenfeld, we hired him. While not a great trader, we figured that he could help us raise some money, and perhaps give us a few good ideas. The key for us would be limiting his downside risk. Given how he had fallen from his lofty perch, it was understood that Franzie owed us big time for this job. After all, we were giving him another chance—a rare chance—to produce profits.

I was surprised one afternoon when he said he might be able to secure us some significant capital. The source of this potential bounty was not a bank or a bored trust-fund banker, but a musician. It turned out that when he wasn't trading stocks, Franz moonlighted as a hip-hop record promoter. Through some confluence of music industry connections and good luck, he said he'd gotten us a meeting with Curtis James Jackson III, aka rapper 50 Cent ("Fitty"). A few weeks earlier, Franzie had run into Fitty at a midtown Manhattan recording studio, where Franz was working on the production of a new track for his client Pittsburgh Slim, an Eminem wannabe with ties to Jay-Z and Def Jam Recordings.

Despite several debriefings, I still wasn't sure what Franz had told Fitty about Incremental, and I was suspicious of his motives. I was assuming this meeting was probably just a chit, a way for Franz to demonstrate his good faith or thank us for taking a shot on him. Either way, it would be interesting to see how a baller like Fitty rolled. Zvi, Nu, Franz, and I all came along to Fitty's recording studio in Chelsea. We went dressed to the nines. Even Franz had put away his pale blue Sean John sweatsuit and thrown on a dark blue three-button suit and a red Hermes tie. We gave each other a quick once-over and wiped the smirks off our faces. We were ready for business.

"Franz, we'll follow your lead," I said.

I knew we had a difficult pitch ahead of us, my instincts telling me that this was just a "feeler" meeting. After all, this was 50 Cent, a world-renowned music icon with insane talent, deep pockets, and financial acumen that belied his humble origins.

The eight Advil and Venti "blackeye" were doing all they could to alleviate the pounding headache. I'd spent another long night partying before this meeting. I looked at Nu, always a good gauge of relative hangovers.

"You feel as awful as you look?" I asked.

His thick neck was spilling over his starched white collar like a muffin top, and beads of sweat were rafting steadily down his forehead, temples, and cheeks, despite the frigid February air. Nu could only offer a guttural grunt. By bringing Nu, I knew that we had broken one of our cardinal Incremental commandments: *Thou shall not allow Nu in any important meetings.*

Yet there was simply no way to keep him out of a meet-and-greet with 50 Cent.

I stared at the heavily reinforced steel door to the studio. It was a little intimidating. I had no idea what to expect inside. Maybe having Nu here wasn't such a bad idea after all. Like Mary's mentally disabled brother in *There's Something About Mary*, Nu had a unique brand of strength he could summon in extreme situations. He used to brag about honing his fighting skills in his modest Brooklyn home, fighting gladiator style in the living room with Zvi and their dad.

We gingerly approached the steel caged elevator on the lobby floor, where we were greeted by a sinister looking guard, wearing all black, accentuated by a black sidearm. Black was Fitty's color of choice.

"Can I please see your IDs, gentlemen?"

I wondered how much they were paying this human shield, and whether he had a kill switch for the elevator if things got heated.

We rode the elevator up. The motif here was steel, the architect's likely inspiration being a post-apocalyptic octagonal dystopia. We looked at each other with a quizzical "What the fuck?" expression, and were led to Fitty's office by yet another strong man in black. When we reached the office entrance, the defense became even more impenetrable. The door was grenade-proof, the glass bullet-proof, and the entrance protected by an enormous brother wearing a baggy, dark denim outfit that could have housed a family of refugees.

Franz took the lead.

"Hi, Franz Tudor. I'm here with the partners of Incremental Capital. We have an appointment with Fitty."

I had to give him credit; he made it sound as if meeting between us and Fitty happened regularly.

We were admitted. Inside, the denim giant gave us a TSA-style pat down and an attractive office assistant offered us water and led us to the waiting room with its framed wall posters, platinum album covers, and a slew of magazines with 50 Cent gracing the covers. We soaked in testimonials to his genius and wealth for a few moments before Mr. Cent himself sauntered in.

"Fitty," Franz said, a note of relief in his voice. "Hey, man."

They exchanged pleasantries and an arm bump. Fitty wore a Yankee cap and was dressed down in jeans and a sweatshirt. But the guy shadowing him was wearing enough jewelry to qualify as a Diamond District satellite office. Franz then introduced us.

Fitty smiled.

"Hey, fellas. This is my main man, Sha, and that's my girl Ashley. You can call her Ash. Y'all gotta get through Ash in order to get to me. She'll take care of y'all. Let me get with Sha. A'ight now."

And with that, he was gone.

"That's Sha Money right there," Franz said, pointing through the bullet-proof glass to the guy talking with Fitty. "He's the real deal. Fitty's business manager. Handles all his investments."

Sha's real name was Michael Clervoix III, but in this world he was known as "Sha Money, XL." I guess if you made enough money in hip-hop you got your own Roman numerals. Or maybe it just meant "extra-large."

I was impressed by the surroundings, but still essentially skeptical. Maybe Sha Money did handle deals, promotions, and endorsements on the music side, but a guy as rich as Fitty had to also have an outside Wall Street financial team. Sha looked like a street gangster, even though he wore diamonds worth more than I would take home this year.

But it was Ashley, not Sha, with whom we would speak.

Ashley was short and attractive in three-inch pumps, a respectable length cream skirt and blouse, and her hair pulled back in a tight bun. Her assistant, Marcus, an eager to please young black man in an argyle V-neck sweater and Gucci eyeglasses, escorted us into a large conference room with a distinctly modern feel. The layout could have been borrowed from Sullivan & Cromwell, or any other buttoned-down midtown law firm.

Zvi and I entered the conference room first, and I whispered: "Feeler meeting, or do Franz a favor?"

We didn't plan this shit until the last minute sometimes.

"Feeler, get to know you," Zvi immediately answered. His cocksure response didn't surprise me one bit. Zvi operated in two modes; confident and over-confident. It was a refreshing counterpoint to my own personality, which rotated between cynicism and anxiety.

I took a look around and asked Zvi if he thought Fitty sending Ashley and Marcus to meet with us was comparable to our sending Nu to meet with potential investors. He shot me a dirty look. We'd been down this road before, having recently had a number of heated arguments about it already over drinks at Sutton Place. Zvi was keenly aware of his brother's weaknesses, but would never publicly acknowledge them. After exchanging names and handshakes, Franzie gave Ashley the two-minute explanation of who, what, and why.

"So, you're a hedge fund." Ashley's tone was perfectly neutral, more of a statement than a question.

"Not technically, Ashley," I said. "We're similar to a hedge fund, but we have a different structure. It's actually a much more advantageous structure for you, the investor. If a hedge fund loses half of your money, they still get their 2 percent. We don't take any management fee. If we don't make money, you don't pay us a dime."

I let that sink in for a second. At this point, a typical finance guy would zero in on this "free option" and start asking questions. But Ashley was anything but typical Wall Street. When she did not immediately respond, I broke out the Las Vegas analogy: "Think of the proprietary trading shop as being like 'the house' in Vegas. We're like the Bellagio. Would Fitty prefer to bankroll the high roller, or be the Bellagio? Let me answer that for you. He wants to be the Bellagio. The odds are always in the house's favor, and they also take a piece of every transaction. The 'rake' in poker, the 'vig' in sports betting, 'insurance' in blackjack, and roulette's 'zero/double zero'—these are just some of the ways the house takes your money when you gamble. At Incremental, we back our traders using our capital and appropriate leverage, and they generate a daily profit or loss. We carefully monitor their risk, both individually and collectively, and quickly get rid of those who underperform. Most of our traders run what we call a 'balanced book,' hedging out long positions with short positions to mitigate risk. Our advantage, or 'house edge,' is that we have enormous amounts of research and information flowing through our firm, cultivated from our relationships on the Street—but more importantly, we take a piece of every transaction, or trade. This is called the commission. That's our buffer, if you will, against a trader's losses."

An image of Willi Cicci testifying before the Senate in *The Godfather, Part II* flashed in my mind: "*Right, yeah, a buffer. The Family had a lot of buffers.*"

Ashley looked confused, and it felt possible that I was losing her entirely. Marcus's blank stare reinforced my original view that this meeting was just a favor to Franz. There was no interest. Desperate, I changed directions yet again.

"Listen, Ashley."

She abruptly cut in, "Please, Mike, call me Ash. Only Fifty and my dad call me Ashley."

At least she was listening.

"I'm sorry. Ash, we're fully aware of Fitty's tremendous talent and incredible brand. The Dubai deal you guys just negotiated. That was beyond brilliant. In my opinion, it was maybe the single most impressive promotion deal ever done."

Ash was smiling now. I was making progress. And I wasn't even throwing out total bullshit. Fitty got a $10 million promotion fee for appearing *one night* at a club in Dubai, and licensing his name on the door. It was shocking, and by my math perhaps the highest per-hour fee ever for an appearance/promotion deal. Clooney or Depp might get $10 million to make a movie, but you're talking about hundreds of hours of real work. This was simply: hop a private jet to Dubai, party like a rap star for a night, and fly back to New York. Voila, your net worth just increased by $10 million.

Eighteen hour flight; add two hours for transportation and security; so that's twenty hours each way. Let's be generous and say ten hours on the ground in Dubai. Fifty hours (there's that number again), divided by $10 million gives you $200k an hour. Holy shit! Bill Clinton only averages about $250K per speech . . . and he's the former President of the United States. Not bad, Fitty. Not bad at all.

"Ash, we want to take that $10 million fee and put it to work."

Ash was gazing at me now, and I felt like I had her locked in.

"Let me explain the buffer a little more. We hire traders to manage money for us, and charge them a commission for every trade they do. We get a rate for processing and clearing the trades of $1 per 1000 shares from Goldman Sachs. We then take that rate and mark it up to $10 for our traders. This is standard practice on the Street."

I forced my brain to shut down the part that always wanted to scream: 1000 percent markup? What were we doing? Making meth? Smuggling poppies out of Kandahar? God bless this industry.

"Through commissions alone," I continued, "we expect to make $700 thousand a month initially, and $1 million a month by the end of this year. That gives us a huge cushion. Our traders have to be down close to 10 percent on their books before we would lose $1 of the money you invest. No hedge fund in the world has that deal. Think about it, Ash. We're the casino, the house."

"And the house always wins," Zvi chipped in on cue. Now there were smiles all around the table. I waited a few seconds.

Ash was still stone faced and silent. I continued to jabber.

"Historically, proprietary trading firm returns have been in the 30 percent range, and we feel that due to the violent and unprecedented financial collapse, the current investment environment is a once-in-a-generation opportunity. In our business, volatility is a trader's best friend, and the equity markets are as volatile as they've ever been. With the talent we've assembled, a 40–50 percent return on investment is not unrealistic."

The lawyer in me knew that this was where you were supposed to explain that past returns were, of course, not guarantees of future performance, and that there were risks associated with this type of investment.

Ash seemed to be right there with me.

"Michael, can you guarantee us that we won't lose any money?" she asked.

Outsiders only cared about making money all the time, and not how remarkably they might be doing compared to the rest of the market. When it was their money on the line, the last thing they wanted to hear was that the S&P 500 index was down 40 percent, but their portfolio was *only* down 30 percent. That type of performance might be acceptable in mutual fund land, but in a lot of other places it meant you were out of business and most likely getting sued. In Little Italy, you'd probably end up with a shovel on a Queens waterfront, digging your own grave.

I was honest.

"Just as whales on a hot streak can occasionally hurt a casino, our traders will *sometimes* lose money. Even the Bellagio has a bad month. But most of the time, it does great. Legally, I can't say you'd never lose money if we have an off month. Securities laws don't allow us to make any such guarantees. This is not a Treasury bond."

"But really that's just a technicality," Zvi chimed in, still trying to close the deal. "We may not be *legally* able to guarantee it, but we can tell you that the absolute return on your investment *will be* 20 percent, and probably twice that much. Between you and me . . . that's what its going to be."

Well *this* was pure Zvi doublespeak, I thought with a smile. We *can't* guarantee, but we *are* guaranteeing. In an instant, Zvi had changed a plain-vanilla investment pitch into a tightrope walk. Spew that bullshit in a meeting with real Wall Street financial guys and you'd get laughed out of the room. Zvi thought he knew his audience, and was preying on what he presumed was her naiveté and unfamiliarity with the proprietary trading business. Ash leaned back in her chair and smiled at Marcus. I could see her thinking about what Zvi had promised.

"So it is safe to assume that we would earn at least a 10 percent return on our investment?" Ash asked.

"Yes," Zvi said, once again without a shadow of doubt.

This may have been my fault. I'd been trying to teach Zvi the virtue of knowing when to stop talking. I'd realized I needed to do this after several disastrous capital raising meetings in which Zvi had talked our way out of deals. (*"Don't fill the void with babble and obvious lies. It's not so hard, Zvi."*) He was a good study, and with the benefit of my tricks from the legal world, had become a very solid negotiator. But there was more to it with him. Zvi drove a hard bargain because he couldn't care less if he lost. Whatever happened, it had to be under his terms. *That* was what he cared about. He cared about dominating and winning. The Wikipedia entry for the expression "My way or the highway" should have a picture of Zvi flipping a double bird.

Zvi's over-the-top negotiating style did occasionally work. Investors and traders on the Street feared missing out on the next big thing more than they worried about cutting a bad deal for themselves. In the right light, Zvi could prey on this.

I flashed back to a scene in Scorsese's *Casino,* where the bank president tells Joe Pesci's character, "Listen, Nicky, there's a possibility you might have to take some kind of loss." Nicky responds with that sinister smile, "Tomorrow morning, I'll get up nice and early, take a walk down over to the bank, and if you don't have my money, I'll crack your fucking head wide open in front of everybody in the bank. And just about the time that I'm coming out of jail, hopefully, you'll be coming out of your coma . . . I'll split your fucking head open again."

A bloody vision danced in my head, and suddenly it wasn't Nicky I was worried about. It was the giant by the front door, or some other friend of Fitty's paying me a late-night visit. Zvi was just lying now. To people who you don't want to do that to.

When my business deals go bad, I want a pinstriped lawyer coming after me with a Montblanc pen, not a gangster with a Glock 9. Fitty had been shot nine times! 50 Cent divided by 9, that's almost 5.5 cents per bullet. That's not the kind of person I wanted to bang it out with. When I was twelve, my brother shot me in the ass with a BB gun and I cried for an hour.

"Let me clarify something here," I interjected, earning a harsh stare from Zvi.

By this point, Nu looked as if he needed a scorecard to figure who was playing, and Franz was fidgeting with his Hermes tie. I could sense that Franz was having second thoughts, knowing that Fitty and his crew would hold him responsible if they invested with us and lost money.

"Let's be very clear," I said. "We are better than a hedge fund because we have a buffer. We're the house, and we have an edge. But we do have risk, betting on our traders. If our traders lose money, those losses may be in excess of the buffer. As I said, while we expect to generate a 30 percent return on investment this year, we can't guarantee that. We also can't guarantee that you won't lose money. But we can say, based on past returns and realistic internal projections which we are happy to provide you, that we hope to return 30 percent."

I immediately felt the air come out of the room. Ash sat back in her seat and put her pen in her mouth.

Zvi was livid and tried to kick-save the meeting.

"We're *very* confident," he added. He gave her a knowing smirk that functioned as a wink. I let him get away with that.

"Okay, gentlemen," said Ash. "Thank you very much. We'll talk to Fifty and Sha and get back to you."

We said goodbye and filtered out of the room. The denim giant gave us a serious stare-down as we got in the elevator. I knew we would never get a $10 million investment from 50 Cent, as much as I knew that Zvi would explode the minute we got outside. Sure enough, he went ballistic right as we got out to Fifth Avenue.

"What the fuck was that, dude?" he raged at me.

"Zvi, we don't want that kind of money. It's too dangerous. They don't understand our business. You guarantee something to them and the collateral is your life. You can't come back in a year and say we lost 20 percent. What do you think they will say? No problem, fellas, thanks for trying? No, they'll say that we guaranteed them a 10 percent return, and the losses are our problem."

"Fuck you, pay me," Nu added, in his best Pesci voice, his first notable contribution of the day.

"Fuck *them*," Zvi shot back. "Fitty's easily worth $500 million. You think he's gonna sweat us over a few mil? Come on!"

"Remember *Casino*?" I replayed the familiar Pesci-banker scene for them, and a light went off in Nu's head. He smiled and nodded in agreement.

"You let me worry about Fitty," Zvi said.

"It's not Fitty that I'm worried about. It's the rest of the G-Unit soldiers that would put a bullet in our heads for around $2 grand and be thankful for the opportunity."

Zvi shook his head and laughed out loud.

"You've seen too many movies, dude."

It was funny hearing that from him, of all people. Zvi and Nu were gangster movie addicts. There wasn't a Pesci or DeNiro scene that the Brothers Goffer couldn't recite verbatim on demand. The Scorsese film library was their King James Bible.

Was I any different? I wondered. We had been inside for barely thirty minutes and my two key points of reference were *The Godfather* and *Casino*.

But yes, I quickly realized. I fucking was. Namely, because I realized that movies were entertainment, and this was real life. I was not prepared to do business with people who might kill us if or when we made a single bad trade on their behalf. For Zvi, this was not even an issue. A cold chill went up my spine as we climbed back into the car and headed away from Fitty's recording bunker. If Zvi would make these kind of promises to a literal gangster, then what else was he capable of?

CHAPTER TWELVE

THE UNDISCOVERED COUNTRY

———————

"MIKE, IT'S GARRETT," THE VOICE ON the other end breathed into the receiver with urgency that was only partly concealed.

"To what do I owe the honor?" I asked.

After Remsenberg had blown up, I'd given my friend Garrett Marquis a "temporary" $10,000 loan to "save his marriage" and keep a roof over his head. I found out later he'd hit Nu up for the same amount and God knows who else. This short-term "I owe you my life loan" was now going on three years, and it had survived Garrett's extravagant wedding, a new condo purchase, and a Mercedes ("it's only leased, Mike"). He was that kind of guy.

"You know my uncle is at Bear Stearns, right? Well, he says things are so bad over there that he thinks they'll get bought. Some bank from Sweden or something."

"I think that's kind of in the market already," I said as though Garrett were a small child who had conjectured that man might one day reach the moon. "Everybody knows Bear is in trouble. There was an article in this morning's *Times*, for goodness sake."

After a small pause to calculate why exactly Garrett was telling me this (like maybe "Hey man, you made $10 thousand on that Bear Stearns short, can we net out my debt?"), I asked him: "Do you want me to tell Zvi?"

"Please do. I gotta run."

I called Zvi.

"Yo, you know the spot where Garrett's uncle works?" I asked him, careful not to mention the name of the firm as the eyes and ears on the desk were always roving for action.

"Yeah?"

"Well he thinks something *really* might happen. Apparently it's a shitshow over there."

"Can I call Garrett direct and press him?" Zvi asked excitedly.

"Be my guest," I told him, well aware he'd call irrespective of what I said.

I hung up the phone and started punching up BSC charts on my Bloomie.

Zvi called Garrett, then hung up and dialed Joe Mancuso immediately.

"You know Garrett's uncle's company?"

"I think so, what's the symbol?"

"Brian Smells Clammy," Zvi whispered.

"What about them?"

"I think they get bought by Swiss. Swiss Cheese."

"Date and time? Wait, we'll talk more later face to face."

"We don't know anything. If it dips more you should put some on."

After calling Drimal and a handful of other contacts, Zvi circled back to his brother.

"Does your whole group have it on?" Zvi asked Nu.

"Yeah. Good size in the common and a smattering of near term calls. Did you tell Mike about this one?"

"Yeah. Joe too and a few others. Alright, if everyone's got it on. I'm going to walk it into the Big Guy."

Zvi let Nu know he was referring to Raj.

"Be ready to let some go, you know the Fat Man stampedes in like a fuckin' elephant."

"Roger that, Chief," Nu responded and cued up some more Bear Stearns sell orders.

We were trading in and out of Bear Stearns for a week, only making small coin. The stock was trending downward. Most of us stopped ourselves out when it triggered our initial entry point of $81, and now it was sitting precariously in the mid $50s, having shed the last $10 quicker than Marion Barry in a crack-house. Then something changed.

"What's going on with Bear Stearns!?" I shouted, as I noticed it ticking up violently from $55 to $59, leaping dollars like rungs of a ladder. Then it was through $60.

"Anything on the tape?" Paul barked as we checked our news services and fired off instant messages to other traders on the Street that might have some insight into the sudden ramp-up. Futures were gapping up now. Someone apparently knew that a *break-the-glass* scenario was off the table.

"Maybe it's a merger," I theorized. "Or some kind of an outside capital injection? Probably not a merger, but it could be a partnership? Is there anything on the web? Come on. What the fuck is the news? Goddamn Bear Stearns. Goddamn criminals!"

I cursed the buyers out there who were trading on information that the rest of us down the food chain weren't yet aware of. Somebody clearly knew something but it certainly wasn't me. The SEC examiners who had been auditing Whitney's firm for the last three months were seated in the conference room directly next to us. They gingerly stuck their heads out and looked around. I guess hearing me shout was decidedly more interesting than whatever they were parsing in there.

A few more seconds passed, and the news finally hit Bloomberg: *"Bear Stearns Bailout Keeps Firm Afloat."*

Embattled firm will tap emergency funding from JPMorgan and N.Y. Fed in effort to fend off collapse.

"This is huge!" Franz yelled across the floor.

A few traders immediately bought stock off the headline, and put it up higher.

"Huge!" I agreed. "But what the fuck does it mean? And what did Bear have to give up in exchange for this?"

I stared hard at my glowing green screen.

The full press release was just now hitting the Bloomberg wire and other news services would soon pick it up:

Battered Wall Street brokerage Bear Stearns said Friday that it is receiving short-term emergency funding to prevent its collapse. JPMorgan

Chase & Co. and the Federal Reserve Bank of New York said they would provide Bear Stearns funding for up to 28 days, with the Fed providing the money to JPMorgan through its discount window.

To help facilitate the deal, the Federal Reserve is taking the extraordinary step of providing as much as $30 billion in financing for Bear Stearns's less-liquid assets, such as mortgage securities that the firm has been unable to sell, in what is believed to be the largest Fed advance on record to a single company. Fed officials wouldn't describe the exact financing terms or assets involved. But if those assets decline in value, the Fed would bear any loss, not JP Morgan.

"What the hell is going on?" all of us seemed to say at once.

The last time the Fed had played capital-raise matchmaker had been back in 1998. Global markets had been melting down, and the object of the Fed's affections, Long Term Capital Management, had been literally self-destructing. And that had been but a $3 billion salvage operation to "save the world." This was $30 billion? Could things at Bear really be ten times as bad as they were at LTCM?

"Mike, any thoughts here?" Nu yelled across the floor as we all braced at our terminals like fighter pilots caught in a sudden hurricane. I didn't have anything to add. Not yet. I was still trying to digest the press release. If they really *were* just backstopping Bear Stearns in the interest of beneficent capitalism—or just injecting some short-term confidence to stop the liquidity panic—then the stock should probably be bought. It was trading at $60, and it had been over $90 a share only two weeks ago.

But this still didn't make sense. Why would the Fed and JPM be doing this? Did JPM have exposure to Bear's toxic assets? Were they opportunistically positioning for a buyout? Everyone knew Jamie Dimon was a pretty shrewd guy. Perhaps this was even being *forced* upon Bear.

I only knew one thing for sure. If Bear was doomed to become a carcass—which I thought probably it was—then $60 wasn't even remotely cheap. And any first year PR hack knows that you don't put "collapse" in a financial news release unless you want to set off a thermite grenade in a movie theater with the doors glued shut. Something was definitely happening. There were simply way too many unanswered questions for the press release to be credited at face value.

The confusion running through my head was of no benefit to anyone else, but it did keep my hand frozen on top of the mouse and prevented me from buying or selling any shares. The answer to Nu's question was "E" on the multiple choice grid: "Not Enough Information."

"I don't know," I finally said. "We don't know the full story. Watch the share price—it'll tell you whether the market likes it or not, and whether it's a good deal for Bear. Feels bearish to me."

We watched. All of us.

The stock continued ticking up to $63 . . . and then, ever so slowly, like a wave cresting, began ticking off.

"Fuck!" Paul yelled, as he tried to sell the stock he had just bought moments earlier for a slim profit. "Nice goddamn execution. Order at $62.50 and they filled me deep in the hole."

Filled in the hole. The clearest signal that there is supply and demand imbalance. The flip side holds true as well. If I were to put in a market order to buy when the stock was trading at $61.10, I'd rather be filled at $61.15 than $61.10. The higher fill tells me that I am competing with other buyers out there and the stock should head higher. Get filled at $61.05, and you know it's going lower.

Once Bear ticked back through $60, it started peeling off dollars. $59, $58, $57, $56, it sounded like a New Year's Eve countdown in Times Square. But instead of the ball dropping, it was a financial bomb aimed at global capitalism, the result of a decade of leverage, greed, and extremely bad policy decisions by our so-called leaders in Washington.

The war at $55 per share was ferocious. This was the proverbial line in the sand because it was the price at which the stock had closed the day before. Traders often refer to such a price as the "Armageddon Level."

If the stock went negative again today, after absorbing this news and after having been down almost 30 percent for the week, it meant that Bear was in much bigger trouble than anyone imagined, and half the Street would have a foot in the aisle, ready to hit eject.

"God, I hope Raj is flat Bear," I said to myself.

A few weeks earlier, Zvi had talked Raj into taking a position based upon the likelihood of an imminent takeover. If Raj was still long, Zvi's head would soon have an apple in its mouth, and our biggest ticket to investment Easy Street might well be lost. Raj had recently agreed to provide us investment capital, and being backed by a billionaire was bliss. But now we faced the reality that Raj would surely renege on his commitment if Zvi continued to lose Raj money. My only hope was that Raj had been smart enough to treat Zvi's "get long Bear Stearns now" *whisper wink* with the appropriate amount of skepticism, or that if Raj *had* bought it, that he'd punched the eject button long before today's news.

When the stock finally knifed through to $55, I looked up and noticed that the Spooz (S&P futures contracts) were still up fifteen points from their open, an obvious mispricing considering the catalyst for the entire bounce was the purportedly good news for Bear Stearns. I stared into my screen like a deer caught in the headlights. Even though my gut told me it was a bigtime short, I was terrified that some other news would come out and propel it higher.

Buying puts was the obvious route, but they were now too damn expensive. The volatility in Bear and the market in general had jacked option premiums. I had little doubt that the market was going lower, and so I shorted about $3 million of SPYs (the stock equivalent of the Spooz).

"Shorting SPYS!" I yelled to the room. "Gonna trade them off Bear Stearns. As long as Bear keeps going down, I'm staying short! Cover and flip long if Bear goes green."

Now that I had let everyone know my game plan, they were on their own.

"Look at the puts!" Eric shrieked. Murmurs of "Jesus," "Holy shit," and the more secular "Oh, fuck" filled the room. Someone had backed up the proverbial truck and was buying a ton of the March $40 puts! And the $30s?

"*WHAT SICK FUCK IS BUYING THE MARCH $10s?*" someone cried at the top of his lungs.

With the stock trading in the low $50s, traders were purchasing the $30 puts, the $20 puts, and now the $10 puts hand over fist. Never in Bear's 100-year history had the stock moved even 1/10 as much as traders were now predicting it would move in the next few days.

Were these buyers hedging hemorrhaging long positions in the stock or buying relatively cheap insurance against a Black Swan? Or did someone *know something*? There. There the darkest possibility. A flashback to President Nixon, but the question now for traders and later for regulators: "What did these Bear Stearns put buyers *know*, and *when* did they know?"

Bear continued to tumble as the afternoon passed and the market finally, blessedly closed for the day. We understood, however, that this was not the end. This was a short, temporary armistice in what was going to be a war for Bear's future, and maybe the future of the Street itself.

"No, *No, NO!*" she screamed, each shriek successively louder and more desperate than the last. Most husbands would have jumped at these escalating cries. I just shook my head because I knew exactly what was coming. I could hear the calm, sedated voice of a National Geographic narrator, *The female primate shows her frustration by yelling and banging on the butcher block in a show of force.* These weren't cries for help, just exasperation.

"April fucked this up! How could she? There's only one tray! Where's my *second* tray of mini-cheesecakes?"

I tried to ignore my wife and focus on my more immediate problem.

"Where the hell did I put that diaper bag?" I asked myself, as I tore apart our mudroom looking for the navy blue and white canvas bag. The only bag I could find was a Lily Pulitzer bag, hot pink with green trim and green and white polka dot handles. There was not a chance in hell I was carrying that thing, especially since my wife had just informed me, ten minutes before our scheduled departure, that due to a "work emergency," she didn't think she could come with us to Sylvie's friend Patrick's fourth birthday party.

A sign I once saw above a school administrator's desk flashed through my head: "Poor planning on your part *DOES NOT* constitute an emergency on my part." I kept that one to myself. My vodka-centric diet hadn't yet totally destroyed my self-preservation instinct.

It wasn't the fact that I was flying solo that annoyed me. That was the ordinary course of business. Lisa worked most weekends, so I usually had the kids all to myself. It was the timing, and the fact that she had already raised Sylvie's expectations that she'd be joining us. Had I known that an entire tray of mini-cheesecakes would vanish into thin air, I would have politely requested that she check "No Thanks" on that RSVP box.

While things were hectic at home, they were even crazier at work. I was encountering Class 5 rapids, trying to navigate the nastiest financial crisis in anyone's lifetime in a kayak. Or maybe a secondhand canoe. I was also building a business from scratch, pretty much on my own, and attempting to raise capital when the "smart money" was being put under the mattress, shotgun sales were soaring, and a few people upstate were literally locking themselves in the house with enough food and ammo to last six months. Every day a new crisis roiled the markets and interrupted my plan to expand the firm. I longed for a day to simply take a breath, to wind down, and decompress.

Today was clearly *not* going to be that day.

My daughter Sylvie was extraordinarily shy, to say the least. Even a neighborhood birthday party with her regular group of schoolmates had the potential to be a traumatic experience for her. Syl much preferred reading a book alone in her bedroom to interacting with groups of people. And the situation was worse now that Lisa would be working, and my attention would be divided because her younger brother Cam was gonna have to tag along.

Cam hadn't been properly invited, but bringing him wasn't a total faux pas. It was acceptable for the younger sibling to show up at a party *sans invite* at that age, especially if he didn't consume a lot of cake, juice, bathroom time, or party favors.

I was perfectly capable of handling both of them, at least enough to guarantee no permanent injuries or scars would occur. Besides, I was capable of exploiting the "Single Dad" phenomenon, and knew that I could expect to have a little help from my wife's friends. There was a bit of social sexism at work at these things, and I sure as hell was happy to use it to my advantage. A mother showing up to a birthday party without her husband was expected to have her shit *together* on all fronts—on time, well dressed, hair perfect, armed with a fully stocked diaper bag, anticipating any and all contingencies and mishaps. Throw a single dad alone into the same party, and the other mothers would inevitably find it adorable that he's "trying," and prove eager to lend a helping hand. It was a double standard and I knew it, but with everything in my life seeming ready to go to hell at any moment, I was going to take what I could get. "Come on, this bag has to be here—I just saw it!" I yelled at the room, knowing full well that "just saw" to my stress and Ketel-addled brain could mean days or months ago. I knew it was here though. In fact, we had a few of them lying around. The LL Bean, long handle, extra large canvas bag with a monogrammed name was my go-to baby gift. I would have patented it had the girl at the Trademark Office been willing to play ball. It wasn't just the practicality of the bag, it was the wondrous efficiency of the whole damn process. Receive a baby announcement in the mail? Go immediately to the LL Bean website. XL long handles? Check. Boy? Navy. Girl? Pink. Block small capital letter monogramming and free shipping courtesy of our LL Bean Visa card. All I needed was a name and an address, and in under five minutes I could knock off one of society's more painful rituals—the finding, purchasing, and delivering of an appropriate baby gift for proud new parents who wanted for naught.

After several years of enjoying a personal monopoly on the LL Bean gift bag, a few recipients decided they liked my idea, or that turnabout was fair play. When Cam was born, we received three of the bags back our way. It one of these "regifts" of my trusty navy canvas gift bag that I was desperately searching for.

"These are *YOUR* friends, sweetheart!" I yelled, knowing full well that Lisa couldn't hear me over the furious hum of kitchen electronics. "Next time that you're not sure you can make it, do us all a favor and skip the RSVP for me."

I mean, at this point, I knew that I was going *and* taking along the damn hot pink Lily Pulitzer bag with the green polka dot handles and trim. There was just no way around it. As I walked past the front hall mirror, I tried to ignore my reflection, but still managed a glimpse and enjoyed a reflexive shudder. *SHE* did this to me.

I was a Wall Street trader. A cool guy. An alpha. As an athlete in high school, I had hit the game winning single off future Cubs pitcher Derek Wallace to beat a heavily favored Chatsworth team in the Valley Regional finals. Was Lisa even aware that my unwillingness to try cocaine had kept me from once hooking up with Naomi Campbell while partying with Leo DiCaprio and the NY Yankees after they'd hosted *Saturday Night Live*? I was a real fuckin' person who knew real fuckin' people and did real-guy shit!

But none of this, it seemed, erased the fact that I was now wearing light brown Tod's, sporting a pink diaper bag and a cloth belt with some kind of fucking freshwater fish on it. Did it really even matter how I looked?

Ultimately, I decided to relax and just roll with it. What difference did it make if I was carrying a bright pink bag? Hell, I was going to Greenwich. I would probably seem more out of place there with the plain bag. And as long as I was carrying the pink one, "I might as well throw on my Kobe's," I shouted at Lisa, who was unable to hear me over the din of her Cuisinart.

A few minutes earlier, I had come downstairs with a blue polo shirt half tucked into my shorts, wearing a pair of black and yellow Kobe Airs. I figured my footwear choice would be controversial, but at least up for debate. As I walked into the kitchen, Lisa took a break from delivering avocadoes to guacamole heaven and offered a simple, "Uh, uh. No way. Go upstairs and put on your Tod's. We're going to Greenwich, not Studio City."

But now circumstances had changed, and I was flying solo. Back upstairs, Kobe's back on! Still king of my castle! Lisa glanced over at my feet when I walked past the kitchen, and decided to let it go.

I nodded and smiled. Oh yes I was.

With the diaper bag on one arm, and Cam in the other, I played the parents' pre-trip version of treasure hunt which included finding diapers and wipes, putting snacks in Ziplocs, filling spill-proof drink cups, and packing up hats, sunscreen, and any other items that I could bring along to help maintain my sanity.

"Remember, Michael, you have to take your car; I need mine for work," Lisa shouted.

I got the kids in the car and then remembered my car meant no GPS, a semi-devastating turn of events. Sure, I had once backpacked through the Oregon Desert alone for a week, armed only with a compass and a map, driven cross country on multiple occasions with my friend Rand McNally, and navigated the streets of LA selling popcorn machines with only a Thomas Guide and a tin of mint Skoal—but that had all been many years ago. Ages. I'd seen the tech light since then. In today's world, a road trip to Greenwich with just an address and two pissed off kids? This was downright barbaric, bordering on an outtake from an episode of *The Amazing Race*.

After finding the address and Mapquesting directions for the first time in years, we were finally ready to go. I wrestled the second car seat to a draw before successfully popping it in. I strapped the kids in, maxed out the AC to cool the sweat off my face, and headed for I-95. I took a giant breath and checked the rearview mirror. Cam looked content. He was old enough now that his car seat could face forward, and he was drinking in the world speeding by. Syl, on the other hand, looked like she was on the verge of tears, and we hadn't even left our neighborhood.

"You okay, sweetie?" I asked her.

"Why can't Mommy come? She said she was going to come with us."

"Mommy has to work, sweetheart," I said. "She wanted to come but she couldn't. We'll have a great time."

Divert and deflect.

"Do you want a snack for the ride?" I asked her. "Or a drink?"

"Okay," she said with a big sigh. I handed her the bag of Wheat Thins and a bottle of cut apple juice. She was quiet for the rest of the ride.

I surprised myself by using the Mapquest successfully. We arrived at the party, and I soon found myself enveloped by other parents and kids.

"I'm so sorry Lisa couldn't make it," Patrick's mom sing-songed as we walked inside the house She leaned in for a cheek air kiss. She was the picture of Greenwich style, white cropped pants, and an obviously expensive embroidered shirt with matching ballet flats. She looked as if she hadn't consumed non-blended food in the six months since I'd last seen her.

"She was *really* looking forward to seeing everyone."

I did my best to sell it.

Lisa's friend Amanda put her hand on my shoulder and asked, "How is the new guy treating you?"

I looked into her sincere brown eyes, and wonderfully pouty mouth, and told her.

"Better than the girls," I said, referring to both my famously difficult wife, and my hardheaded daughter.

Sylvie's angelic phase had lasted approximately thirty months. Somewhere around the time that we'd moved from the city, she'd started ripping the hair band out of her pigtails, refusing to wear dresses, and was basically never was the same kid again. The "terrible twos" would have been a monstrous upgrade. This was something else entirely. She was independent, immune to discipline, and at times nearly impossible. Although I was a college graduate, a CFA, and a lawyer—who had presumably, you know, thought about a lot of things—I was utterly out of ideas for how to handle her by the time she turned three. I read parenting book after parenting book. Nothing. If there were solutions out there, I had yet to find them.

It was a beautiful day in Greenwich. The sun was shining. After a miserable winter, it was finally starting to warm up. The party was a heavy drinking Greenwich-Rye crowd. For the first year after Syl had been born, Lisa had bonded with these women as they all shared the travails of a first child. The social roles were clear here: women watched the kids and orchestrated the parties. The men did what they did best at these events: drink beer, and talk hobbies and shop. At some point, the birthday kid's dad gets yelled at by his wife because he is off drinking, or doing something other than filming pivotal events.

Right away, I saw a couple of familiar faces—Patrick and Jeff.

"Mike, how's it going?" Patrick was an investment banker for SocGen's Real Estate group, and Jeff was in mortgage origination at Bear Stearns. After a bit of small talk, they demanded that I go get myself a beer.

"You know what, let me get Syl and this little guy set up, and then I'll definitely join you for a cold one," I said with a smile.

I still had Cam in my arm, an oversized pink diaper bag over my shoulder, and Syl was clutching my hand like the was terrified to let go. Exactly which appendage did they envision me drinking a beer with?

Privately, I found drinking at these kids' birthday parties overrated. You still had to drive home, and afternoon drinking made me tired. Not to mention that there was nothing worse in my humble opinion than *one or two* beers. Once I had one, I ached for another. And if I had another, I generally consumed six more. This was not exactly the way I wanted to spend my Saturday with my kids, so the obvious solution was to have none at all.

The central focus of this party was a real old-time fire engine with an open top that had been hired out for the kids. It was going to take them on a little tour of the neighborhood, and seated about ten kids at once. If I could get Syl to get on the fire engine and ride around with the other kids, I'd be home free for a while.

I took her over to the engine, watched her climb up the ladder in back and wait for a seat. She was biting her lip, a nervous habit, and putting on her brave face. I gave her a thumbs up and a smile, and then Cam and I both waved to her. The fire truck pulled away and I allowed myself a ray of hope.

According to Donnie the Firefighter (who, let's say, must have normally been stationed in a Chelsea or Castro District firehouse), the ride would last approximately twelve minutes. There was a quarantined section of the house set up with lots of foam and toys designated for "babies," and I happily dropped Cam into the middle of a foam pit filled with blue and red geometric shapes, toys, and other little kids. I said hello to a nearby mom that was watching her child, and asked her if she'd mind keeping an eye on Cam while I grabbed something to drink.

The answer—like it always was at these things—was "Of course!" I ventured off and found a Diet Coke, which I poured into a red plastic cup to confuse the beer swillers.

On the way back to baby pit, I ran into three more guys I knew from these things—Liam, Tom, and John. They worked for BAC Capital Markets, an SAC Capital spinoff, and Morgan Stanley Prime Brokerage, respectively.

There was a round of obligatory "I'd rather be playing golf" (after a careful glance around the room to make sure that the birthday boy's dad wasn't among us). Although watching the birthday boy's father madly dashing around the yard, furiously snapping away with the camera, and refilling the ice chest with beers, I imagined that he probably felt the same way.

"Where's your wife, Mike?" Liam asked me.

I looked down at the floor.

"Actually, we separated a few months ago. She found an email on my Blackberry from our Bloomberg rep that had nothing to do with the markets."

I gave it my best deadpan, but they still saw through me. Part of Bloomberg's business model seemed to involve sending hundreds of very young, attractive girls to testosterone-infused trading floors throughout the city under the guise of "tech help."

I got a few smiles, followed by big gulps of their beers.

"Not really," I assured them. "She's just working. But a guy can dream, can't he?"

They chuckled. The "other woman" humor played well in this kind of inebriated crowd, but also hit a bit close to home with many in our social set. "But for the kids" was a common refrain heard in bars, trains, and confessionals throughout the neighborhoods of people who worked in finance.

Despite doing everything we could to avoid the subject, the talk eventually turned to the carnage in the financial markets, and a series of horror stories began to flow. Most of these guys were only secondarily involved in markets, meaning they were investment bankers or some other arm of the Street. Their livelihoods didn't depend on outsmarting the markets day in and day out. Many of them had multi-year guarantees, and didn't feel the constant stress of those of us matching wits with the markets each morning. (Those of us who had less job security, less hair, and more circles under our eyes tended to drink a little more heavily than the rest of the crowd.)

"Well, I have to go check on the little guy," I offered, looking for an excuse to break from the conversation.

"Why? Where's he gonna go?" Jeff asked. "Can he walk yet? He'll be fine."

I was sure he was correct, but I didn't like the idea of leaving my two-year-old alone in a strange house for very long. I also wanted to make sure we were waiting outside when the fire truck came back from its tour. The guys caught me looking over at Cam.

"That is a cute fucking kid," Liam said. "Are you sure he's not Irish?"

Cam had red hair, light freckles and green eyes.

"There's only one way to be certain . . . and then what do I do if I find out she's not the mother?" I joked to more laughter and demands that I return for another beer with them. The truth was, I knew who the mother was, having been in the delivery room from start to finish, and even performing the absurd fantasy surgeon ritual of cutting the umbilical cord. (I thought they might give us a discount on the hospital bill. No dice.)

Back at the foam pit, I found that Cam was fine. My impromptu babysitter was gushing over his eyes and hair. I hoisted Cam onto my hip, grabbed a few pretzel chips for the both of us, and snuck back out front just in time to hear the fire engine's ancient duck horn in the distance.

"Come on, no tears," I chanted, the way contestants of yesteryear implored the gods of chance for "no whammies" on *The Joker's Wild*. A few similarly minded moms heard me and gave knowing smiles. The fire engine soon pulled into view. I found Syl's face. No smile but no tears, either! I'd take that trade any day. I waved wildly, making sure she saw me, and went to help her off the fire engine. I stroked her head and asked her if it had been fun.

"Umm. It was OK. A little windy."

"Did you guys fight any fires?"

"Nooo." That got a small smile. Even at four, she knew her daddy could be a merry prankster.

I suppressed a giant smile of my own, and tried to disguise the pride spilling out of my heart. For a girl whose anxiety typically sent her to the nurse's office twice a week with a stomach ache, this was a giant victory. Swallowing her nerves and climbing aboard an antique truck with a bunch of boys and girls she didn't really know was a big step.

I could imagine how she must be feeling. This was a win for her, and I let her know it.

It was announced that there would be another ride. Parents and children could ride together, so I told Sylvie we would go again. That got another smile, and we climbed aboard. As the truck took us slowly around the neighborhood, I held my children's hands and pointed out the white sailboats on the horizon, rocking their way across the Long Island Sound. The duck horn sounded and I jumped. This produced a hysterical laugh from Cam. The full chortle emanating from such a little redheaded body made me smile, and I joined him. The laughing was infectious, and soon Sylvie was laughing along with some of the other children aboard.

Xanax, Vitamin K, a bottle of Opus—these are the tried and true synthetic somas, but I'll tell you something. Their palliative effects don't compare to the powers of your own child's laughter. It can't be replicated or replaced. And no matter what pit of hell you are in, it has the power to find you there.

A couple of hours before, I'd been on the verge of staying home on the sofa for the rest of the day. It was the easy way out, but a way out nonetheless. Now, instead, I had a memory of a lifetime to cherish, and I fucking knew it. In a perfect world, I'd go round Ocean Avenue forever on top of this fire engine, with my two kids laughing and the Long Island Sound shimmering in the distance. Circling and laughing forever.

"Time for cake!" a thin, blonde Greenwich woman announced gleefully as we pulled back in the driveway.

"Oh boy," I said. "Cake!"

I didn't want to be overconfident, but I was beginning to feel there was a chance I might actually pull this trip off—disaster free.

I encouraged Syl to go find a seat at the table while there were still a few open places. After an off-key "Happy Birthday" (and the annoying modern-Greenwich additional verses "Are you one? Are you two?"), Patrick made the first cut, and cake was passed out to all. Noticing that there were extra slices, I furtively handed Cam a slice. I walked into the living room where the men were gathered, and positioned myself with a clear line of sight to my two cake-faces.

Since the "heavy lifting" of the party was winding down, beers were flowing more freely now, and a decidedly more festive atmosphere was building among the gents. On the outskirts of the cake tables, the women were now cracking into the beer chest themselves, and exchanging their own war stories. (I noticed how the women had the sense to linger just on the outskirts of the cake tables; close enough to intercept trouble, but distant enough not to be summoned for trivial help.)

After Liam shared the news that his wife was pregnant with their third, an informal straw poll broke out regarding who would be joining him at three. Surprisingly, almost every hand was raised, including my own. Several men offered five as their magic number. I was blown away. Half the guys here wanted a basketball team.

Back in Los Angeles, two had been the norm. The rare family that had three kids was considered "prolific," and the subject of some good natured ribbing regarding "mistakes" and "insatiability." Here, three was the new two.

Banter was light despite the gathering storm on the Street. I glanced into the dining room to make sure my children were still on board the happy cake train. Syl was eating quietly not speaking to anyone, and I suppressed a wave of sadness by recalling her bravery earlier in the day.

Cam had chocolate all over his face and was grinning wildly. His smile was only surpassed by my own. I was about to go over and wipe him down when I thought, "Who cares, let him enjoy it for a bit." Also, I was curious to see if anyone else would take pity and wipe him down. Sure enough, a sweet gaggle of moms came over and fussed over him, wiping his face clean and then some. He didn't even protest this unsolicited handling by strange females.

Then my phone started buzzing. I suddenly noticed that the conversations around me had died down, and that the rest of the men in the room had their phones out too. Blackberries were chiming all over. Every one of us had been sent a hot-off-the-presses release from the Treasury. The chatter ceased as we tried to digest it. Furrowed brows and poker faces quickly replaced toothy grins as we stared at our screens.

JPM to Buy Bear Stearns for $2 per Share:
Federal Reserve to Provide Financing

JPMorgan Chase said Sunday it will acquire rival Bear Stearns for a bargain-basement $236.2 million—or $2 a share—a stunning collapse for one of the world's largest and most storied investment banks. The last-minute buyout was aimed at averting a Bear Stearns bankruptcy and a spreading crisis of confidence in the global financial system. The Federal Reserve and the U.S. government swiftly approved the all-stock deal showing the urgency of completing the deal before world markets opened.

"Does that say $2?" John asked the room.

"That has to be a typo, doesn't it?" a nervous, high-pitched voice followed. "There has to be a zero missing, right?"

"But even $20 is ridiculous," John said. "This can't be right."

"It's not $20," Jeff said, a little louder and more definitively than everyone else, trying his best to erase the stunned look on his face. "It's $2."

That was the end of it. Jeff would know.

He worked for Bear Stearns.

From a birthday party to a funeral in the time it took to check a Blackberry. I don't know how much stock Jeff owned in his employer, but whatever he thought he was "worth" had probably just been cut by more than half.

Star Trek IV flashed through my mind: *The Undiscovered Country*. There was nothing else to compare this to. No precedent to call upon. This was a financial 9/11. Capitalism, efficient market theory, our entire regulatory structure—all said that what had just happened to Bear Stearns was impossible. A 100-year-old investment bank doesn't go from being worth $50 billion one week to a couple hundred mil a few days later.

But it just did. They just had. All of us had seen it.

We were no longer simply in a recession. Something far more serious was unfolding before our eyes. This was an entirely different animal, and it was simply not possible to know what the fallout would be, or how or where it would take place. We were living in strange, dangerous times. Only one thing was certain: Very few of us—if any—would get out of this one without a good deal of pain.

I thought about the coming week at work, and that was all I saw. Pain, and a lot of it. Stocks, commodities, P&Ls—all flashing red, all draining money out of the pockets of traders and investors worldwide. The collapse of Bear was either going to be the dramatic "thud" that creates a bottom—as Zvi and many others were arguing—or the beginning of the end for life as we knew it. Nobody had a grasp anymore on what was happening, or on what it all meant. This was uncharted territory: the place on the map "where dragons lie."

The Undiscovered Country.

I kept asking myself the same questions. Who bought the Bear Stearns puts? Who made hundreds of millions of dollars while Bear collapsed? Was it Goldman? If not them . . . who?

Whenever there's a rumor or conspiracy suggesting skulduggery, fingers always seem to get pointed at Goldman first. As the most powerful and ethically challenged of all the ethically challenged banks, Goldie was permanently parked in a gray zone and the ideal bogeyman. But that didn't necessarily mean they were always the culpable party.

Whoever was shorting Bear off the initial bump from the headline and press release knew a lot more than the public. The press release didn't tell you that Hank Paulson had given JPM the weekend to come up with a deal, but was quite prepared to write Bear's obituary otherwise. *Someone* knew, though. And from the prints left on the corpse, it was more than one person or firm.

The only thing better than having friends in high places, is having friends in the *highest* places.

It was beginning to look like a whole lot of people did.

CHAPTER THIRTEEN

OF BANKS AND ROYALTY

———

WITH THE FALL OF BEAR, IT became more and more clear that we had been living on borrowed time. Nu, Zvi, and all the rest of us felt like we needed to get our shit together, and fast. No more pursuing rappers. No more following every lead. Certainly no more fucking up investor meetings at the last minute.

It was time to get back to basics.

Our playbook was sound. The phone calls from talented traders looking for a place to work were pouring in now that the world was falling apart, and the only thing keeping us from getting things rolling was the absence of a real-deal capital partner. The twin gutshots of Bear Stearns and CCU* prompted me to revisit an option I had already once turned down. The Monday after Bear went down in flames, I had called back Dave Abramson of RBC and told him we should talk.

"You and Deigs coming back in?" he asked, referring to John Deignan.

"Not Deigs. Just me. I opened up a firm with Nu Goffer."

"Zvi's little brother?"

"Ha! I've never heard Nu referred to as 'little,' but yes, Zvi's younger brother."

"Yeah, I heard you guys were doing something. Nu had a monster year last year, and Zvi is crushing it at Galleon."

"All true. We're in the right spot, Dave, and we're putting together a firm that's going after the First New Yorks and other big league prop firms. This is

———

* We had piled into a "long CCU" risk arb trade on Zvi's advice, only to see the stock collapse from \$33 to \$27 when there was talk of the banks refusing to fund CCU's acquisition.

going to be big. At the moment, we're deciding whether to partner up or raise private capital. From what I hear, you're in business with the right people too, and they have deep pockets."

"Some of the deepest. And you can ask Zvi; I love that kid. We were together at Carlin. I've wanted to be in the Zvi Goffer business for years—and you know I think extremely highly of you too. Been trying to get you to work for me for two whole years now."

"Well, let's sit. Office or bar?"

"C'mon. Is that a real question? Let's do Capital Grille. We can always walk back to the office if we need to."

"Tomorrow? 4:30?"

"See you then."

We were drinking at Redemption after the close that evening when I told Zvi the plan.

"I'm coming with," he insisted, beaming from ear to ear. "Dave *loves* me. Let's go in and ask for the world. They've got pikers there now. Dave Plate is the only guy at RBC worth a damn."

"Dave Plate? The guy who sat next to you at Schottenfeld is there?"

"Yep."

"You told me he was going to put $500K into Incremental and come trade with us."

"Yeah, well it didn't work out. Rick fired him after he blew up."

No doubt on your AMD tip, I thought, recalling a conversation outside of Schottenfeld on 48th and 3rd between me and Shankar and Plate. I'd been walking to Grand Central down Third Avenue, and Shankar and Plate were on the corner of 45th and 3rd, in the midst of a seemingly serious discussion. After a quick hello, they asked in a solemn tone if I was in AMD. "Not anymore," I admitted, after losing $100K-plus on a Zvi "sure thing."

Horrible company, horrible call.

Plate admitted he had lost almost $800K plus in AMD alone last month, Shankar about half that. So I guess it shouldn't have been a surprise that Plate had now "decided" to go elsewhere after being led blindfolded off the cliff.

But I still had to wonder why Zvi had never bothered to update me about Plate's status. After all, we were talking a $500K investment, which, along with Plate's trading tickets, I had incorporated into our models when pitching Incremental's projections.

Given what Abramson had said to me about Zvi, it was only natural that I bring him along to the Capital Grille. We shot the shit over a few drinks, then got down to business and tried to lay it all out for Dave. You could see his barely contained excitement when we spoke. He was leaning in and tapping his right foot like a jackhammer. The pitch was simple. With my trading and operational skills, Nu's capital and experience, and Zvi's Galleon research, calls, and very able traders who just missed the Raj/Stevie cut, Incremental was poised to be an inevitable powerhouse.

Abramson asked what we needed. Seeing that he was already hooked, we went straight for the dream list:

A minimum of a $100 million to play with, going up to $250 million in twelve months. Tickets at a penny or less (since we charged ten cents, we made at least a nickel on every share after all fees). And a two-tier payment structure—tickets paid . . . profit and loss (P&L) paid . . . and *no netting*, which meant if we made money on tickets and lost money on P&L, he couldn't offset one with the other.

Abramson didn't flinch. He said it didn't sound unreasonable, but that he would still have to run it past RBC's legal department. That was more than fair—so we shook on it and ordered another round of drinks.

One week later, Zvi and I walked out of RBC's offices at 666 Third Avenue with a term sheet giving us that deal . . . with just a few constraints. For starters, RBC would have a hand in approving new traders. In addition, per the P&L, RBC got a 10 percent slice, while we took 40 percent, with the remaining 50 percent going to the trader. There was no capital risk, a guaranteed $500K-plus in pure tickets profit per month into our pockets (something which would only increase as Incremental grew), and a brand name bank umbrella we could recruit under, coupled with the promise of all the capital we needed. We wondered with one another if it was really too good to be true—except it was actually both, too good and definitely true. Still, I had questions gnawing at the back of my mind. Would RBC stick with us once they realized they were taking all the risk for only a paltry slice of the upside? Sure, as long as we never lost money, it was a great deal for everyone; but what happened when we lost, say, $1 million in P&L, while also making $1 million in commissions, and then demanded RBC pay us our million (yeah, that's what "no netting" means)? For now, none of that mattered, it was a future worry. We had our deal, and, in a pure "The world is mine" *Scarface* moment, we were off to Sutton Place to swim in fountains full of vodka and champagne.

Flash forward to a long hot August spent getting used to each other, not unlike new lovers early on in a relationship. Both parties were putting their best feet forward and on their best behavior. A good solid August naturally emboldened us, and we started to turn up the gas, as Incremental was up more than 3 percent in September. But almost immediately, we were met with resistance from Dave: intraday limits, holding times, you name it. We were already getting the feeling that RBC's reins on Incremental were just too damn tight. We had gone on the customary three dates, and it was time for some action. Deep down, I know that Dave understood this was the right move, but he wasn't ready to stick his neck out for us. Then again, he was politically cautious, a survivor who understood these were dangerous waters, and it was unlikely he'd ever risk his neck for anyone.

So this inevitably led us up the chain to Dave's boss, Jeremy Frommer, who was in charge of RBC Cap Markets. The prop desk fell under his jurisdiction. He said we'd been getting a lot of buzz around RBC. We told him we were now asking them for some more rope and leeway. So Frommer decided it was time for us to meet, and suggested drinks or dinner. I thought it was a great opportunity to explain our strategy to someone other than Abramson.

Zvi and I were waiting for him at Capital Grille. Frommer arrived late, with an aura of brusque arrogance, as if he were doing us a huge favor just by being there. After some inevitable small talk, I launched into our pitch—it was the same one RBC had already signed up for, but this time I offered a lot more details and specifics. Frommer kept playing with his cocktail, mixing and stirring it, then ripping off pieces of bread and slapping on lots of butter. Maybe he was just hungry, but it felt an awful lot like he wasn't even listening to me. I started to get annoyed, and was three seconds away from asking him if he needed a fucking Ritalin to focus, when Frommer swiveled on his bar stool toward us. He raised his hand, as though he intended to say something original and important, and then proceeded to echo Abramson's overly cautious approach. He spoke about how he'd come to the conclusion that taking very small bites at the apple—the no-risk model—was the best way to go. He didn't use the words "piker model," but that's what he was talking about—a model that took very little risk, and made very little money.

It was definitely *not* the model we were having so much early success with at Incremental. You sure as hell can't ask someone who ran $75 million at SAC to have a $5000 intraday loss limit *and* put a deposit down. You'd be laughed at right in your face. But Frommer clearly felt that he'd made his point convincingly and asked—with seeming earnestness—"So, do you guys understand what I'm sayin'?"

For a few seconds neither Zvi nor I so much as blinked.

And then, Zvi loudly proclaimed, "With all due respect, you couldn't be more fucking wrong!"

The place went quiet. People in nearby booths stopped eating, drinking, and gabbing, and instead leaned over to listen in an E. F. Hutton moment.

"Jeremy, that model is dead!" Zvi boomed. "All the places that still operate like that are folding or making no money. These aren't the glory days of day trading. To succeed, you need more leeway, more capital, and more talent to extract money from the market. Right now, you have a once in a generation opportunity to land real talent. A huge restructuring is underway on Wall Street. Guys who returned double digits for ten years and made millions, tens of millions, are suddenly free agents on the market. They need jobs. It's like Derek Jeter is suddenly available to play for our expansion team, and we can sign him with no upfront, just on a per-hit basis. I'm telling you, you won't get another opportunity like this. Incremental can build a world-class desk that rivals any of the funds out there, for almost nothing. This dislocation will last less than ten months. We can build something in that time that would normally be impossible. Just think about it, Jeremy. You can either keep clinging to that last dead model until RBC takes you off life support, or you can"—Zvi paused here for effect—"grab your balls and become a presence in the space. Either way, you know I'm right."

Zvi stopped and took a long sip from his drink.

He had done it—completely reversed the tenor of the meeting, and knocked Jeremy back on his heels. By the end of the meal, Frommer was ready to play ball. There are moments, few and far between, when I understood exactly how

Zvi got his admirers. This was one of them. Frommer went back to the office and greenlit us, and all that October we knocked it right out of the park.

November went well too. We were up slightly, but most firms were in a tailspin. During December we were flat or down small, yet we still got a large check for our commissions. This left Abramson fuming. Then, as we had known it would, it dawned on the RBC brain trust that they had been shouldering all the risk even as they were forced to eat the losses. Abramson started making noise. Over on the risk management end, he was also doing a lot of head-butting with Zvi and myself over trader risk.

Ultimately, RBC also wanted veto power over who we hired as traders. A great example of this was Franz "I'm Best Buddies with Fitty" Tudor. Dave Abramson wanted no part of Franz, but Zvi was ready to go to the mat for him. Loved the guy, and wanted us to hire him. Abramson grudgingly agreed to allow Franz to plead his case at RBC's office . . . to a young trader on Abramson's team named Martin Shkreli.

Shkreli was a freakishly skinny, on-the-spectrum biotech trader who had worked under both Jim Cramer at Cramer, Berkowitz & Co. and Wayne Holman at SAC Capital. While the general public knows Cramer from CNBC, Holman is a legitimate hedge fund legend and, after Stevie Cohen, the second biggest SAC Capital earner of all time. Holman made a fortune taking huge positions in early stage biotech companies like OSI Pharmaceuticals (OSIP), and profiting enormously when OSIP's acquisition by Astellas was announced. Word on the Street was that Holman had an unholy "edge" with OSIP, speculation which remains unproven to this day.

Shkreli strolled in wearing dark, poor fitting jeans, a sweater a size too small, and an off-white Hanes T-shirt that had seen better days. He was five foot nine and junkie-thin at 130 pounds. His uncombed, wild hair fell over a disturbed child's face. The visual presentation had me mentally running through the DSM-IV table of contents before we'd even said hello.

Deep down, at heart, nearly every person harbors the inner fear that he may not be as good as everyone thinks he is. That he's one market move or event away from being exposed to the world as a total fraud. This biotech showdown was like Tyson-Spinks. Everyone thought Spinks was one of the best boxers on earth, maybe in history. The undisputed light heavyweight champion and a master of the sweet science. He would assuredly be able to stick and move and keep Tyson off him. But Tyson exposed him as an overrated, historically insignificant heavyweight champ and brutally ripped away the whole façade with one uppercut to the gut a few seconds into the first round. Spinks crumpled.

That's what Shkreli did to Franz, peppering him with rapid fire questions about stock values, Net Present Value (NPV) methodology, and ongoing Phase II results. Franz couldn't hold a candle to Shkreli's psychopathic level of statistical recall and brainpower . . . but trading is only about half brainpower. Equally important are discipline, psychology, and perspicacity; figuring out what everybody else knows (and doesn't know), where everybody else is on a trade, where the market is, what's priced in, and where the pressure points are. You have to know at what level do the longs give up, do the shorts get squeezed, and does the risk manager come tap-tapping. Shkreli was an NPV absolutist, finance's equivalent of the data geeks that think fashion, religion, art, or any other matter can be broken down into a precise quantifiable algorithm. The NPV absolutists think investment is a neat little science, and that they can precisely model what future earnings and revenues will be, then discount that back to the present to get the exact number a stock should currently be trading at based on all available information. If a stock is trading for less than NPV, buy it. If it's trading for more, sell it (while giving yourself some cushion on both sides, of course, because nobody's perfect all the time). But like most modelers, and certainly all of the guys in the risk departments leading up to the crisis, they all suffer from the same fatal flaw: a model is only as good as its inputs. If the inputs are off (which they almost always are when you're trying to handicap the likelihood of future events), then the model is much more of a directional compass than a set of exact GPS coordinates. It's the correct starting point for stock valuation, sure, but it's only one part of the equation.

That should have been Franz's short rebuttal. But instead, he was drowning, drinking from a firehose as Shkreli fired off question after question, cutting off his answers, or dismissing them as ridiculous or wrong.

I wasn't sure if Franz was holding back because they thought this was a friendly discussion, or if he wanted to appear civil because a possible capital backer was in the room. Either he didn't have the tools to fight back or didn't realize there was an actual fight going on. Whatever the case, the ref was about to step in and call it based on the three knockdown rule. I realized it was time to let Franz know this was a "gloves off" encounter. If the interview/interrogation ended like this, there was zero chance he would get an offer from Dave, and Incremental would look foolish for having offered this stumblebum lamb up for slaughter.

Franz's performance might have been pathetic, but I still had a soft spot for him and wanted to give him an opportunity to work for us. And this Shkreli guy was insufferable. I enjoyed his act for about six minutes . . . then it started to piss me off. He was a bully, and an obnoxious one at that.

"You can't accurately model most early or mid-stage biotech," I interrupted. "Everyone knows that. Look at the moves in that sector. Volatility is massive. Biotechs get cut in half all the time. And it's always because someone modeled the likelihood of approval or clinical results wrong. You can't model FDA approval from Phase I with *any* real degree of confidence"

Shkreli looked at me and hesitated. He had orders to go after Franz. What was Dave's partner doing stepping into the fray?

Shkreli glanced over at Dave, as if asking permission to engage. With a subtle nod back at Shkreli, Dave took the leash off his pet.

"Of course you can," Shkreli sneered back at me, gloves off. "But the very fact that some modeled it wrong means someone *could have modeled it right.* They just didn't do their homework!"

"Except 90 percent of that 'homework' involves talking to people who shouldn't be talking," I countered. "The biotech mafia is awfully good at modeling a double blind placebo. How does researching that work? How do you read data if there's no data to read?"

"It's not as difficult as you make it sound," Shkreli countered. "We *can* model likelihood of success to a statistically significant point and the resulting share value. We do it all the time."

"Oh, oooookay," I said sarcastically—my gloves coming off as well. "So *you're* the one on the other side of all those trades that go wrong. Now I understand. That explains why you're running a $5 million prop account for RBC instead of running three billion for Stevie or Oracle. I gotcha."

All the stereotypes I harbored about quants and geeks came bubbling to the surface. Those guys could debate and massage data, peer review and tinker with models until the sun rose—sure—but *ad hominem* personal attacks, sarcasm, and humor—things that were a big part of big boy life on the Street—completely threw off their game and scrambled their antenna.

"It *is* a science, and that's why Wayne and the rest of the true stars in biotech know me on a first name basis!" Shkreli shrieked loudly. "The fact that you don't even know that makes me question why Dave would be in business with you in the first place!"

I had to give Shkreli that much. For a quant, he was holding his own.

"Dave, you can call off your attack dog," I said with a smile. "He's made his case."

"Attack dog? I've merely proven this trader is incompetent!" Shkreli said, motioning to Franz. "But I can show you an attack dog if you'd like."

He gave me his best "tough guy" stare. It was like watching a starved poodle with rickets trying to impersonate a Great Dane.

"You've proven nothing other than an overreliance on mechanical valuation formula that only works with *suspiciously* perfect info," I told him. "And even then it doesn't account for shifting outcomes, like Phase II results, or changing reimbursement guidelines."

There was something more I wanted to say. I knew something I shouldn't. But then I did. Shkreli had a way of making you set aside your better judgment.

"And if you speak to me like that again, I'll walk around this table and choke you out right here in this conference room," I added quietly.

The physical threat snapped him out of his catbird seat. He stuttered for a few seconds and began to turn red. Then Dave stepped in.

"Thank you, Martin. That's all we needed you for. Please let me finish with Mike and Franz alone. I'll talk to you in a few minutes."

Shkreli got up and walked out, turning back to glare at me once more from the doorway. I gave him a nice big smile in return.

"Okay, that was . . . interesting," Dave said. "Mike, I'll give you a call later today and we can discuss. Thank you guys for coming down. I apologize for Martin, he's really smart—just a little rough around the edges and immature. Either way, we'll talk soon."

"High IQ or not, I'd be careful of anyone who has absolute faith in anything," I told Dave. "We both know how much of this comes from real experience."

"Well, I've got 'absolute faith' my wife is going to kill me if I don't head home and give her a break from the kids. So let's chat tonight or tomorrow, yeah?"

We left.

Dave Abramson won that day's battle, rattling poor Franz. Even so, Dave ultimately came to regret his relationship with Shkreli. Shortly after the Franz ambush, Abramson was forced to fire Shkreli after some highly questionable trades that cost RBC a huge chunk of change. Yet Shkreli then landed on his feet, becoming a successful biotech hedge fund manager, specializing in short-selling early stage biotech companies. Years later, of course, Shkreli famously raised the price of Daraprim, a life-saving pill, from $13 to $750, creating a tidal wave of outrage at greedy pharma companies during an election year. The powers that be—pharma, insurance companies, politicians—collectively turned their eye on Shkreli and suddenly "found" multiple securities laws violations he had committed. He was arrested and is scheduled for trial in June of 2017. I expect he will serve a dime if convicted.

In the meantime, the verbal arguments between us and RBC on the trader and risk front continued to escalate, culminating with Abramson cutting off and then firing Bryan Roth within a few ticks of a temporary market bottom. Roth was down maybe $50 thousand on the day, $250 thousand total, which is far from a huge amount in this business, and easily erased with one solid trade. But RBC was adamant: Roth had to go. From Zvi's little cubicle, the entire trading floor could hear Zvi and Ralph, RBC's risk manager, going at each other over the phone. It quickly devolved into a "Fuck me? Fuck you!" back and forth. That triggered a call from Abramson and his sidekick, Marc Schwarz, asking for a summit at RBC to try to work things out after everyone had cooled down. We scheduled it, but when we got there, Abramson had not cooled down at all. In fact, he was more livid than ever.

He started off the meeting by banging the table. Then he screamed at Zvi.

"You're trying to fuck me right in the fucking ass, and if you think that's gonna happen you're out of your fucking mind!"

This was, of course, a big mistake. It showed he had totally misjudged Zvi the Hulk.

Zvi said: "First of all, you scream and start making threats, I'll come over this table and slam your head through the fucking wall."

Silence all around.

"When have I ever disrespected *you* like that?" Zvi asked.

Abramson did not answer.

I tried to steer the meeting back in a productive direction. I told them that we recognized their concerns—which drew a harsh glare from Zvi—but that we saw things in a different light. At the end of the day, all I could get them to agree on was a six-month extension of the status quo. After that, RBC wanted a new deal. We barely shook hands when we stood up from the table. In the elevator, still livid, Zvi said, "Fuck those guys! We'll get a new, better deal elsewhere. What a bunch of fucking no-talent bureaucrats. They don't even understand our business. We've got *whales* that want in. Did I even tell you Slaine is back, and wants to give us $10 mil?"

"Seriously?" I said.

"Yup. And according Craig Drimal, Todd Deutsch wants in too. And don't forget Raj. And we'll close a deal with Stevie by then. Stevie knows the game. He makes these punks look like toddlers."

"Okay then . . . let's pursue Stevie, I guess," I said earnestly.

We did.

Stevie was the only one who really mattered. The legendary Stevie Cohen ran and ruled SAC. One of the ex-SAC traders who worked for us had put us in touch with Stevie's funds guys—Sohail Khalid and Jason Karp. Jason, a well-known portfolio manager, was head of research for Sigma, Stevie's more old-school, research-driven fund. The operations side was run by Sohail. They both knew about Incremental and were impressed with our plan.

After a few meetings and some time spent drilling down into hard numbers and strategies, we started drafting documents for a $10 million capital infusion to start, allowing us to nestle under Stevie's Midas wing.

As Karp told us at one of these early meetings: "Stevie doesn't get involved in something unless he thinks he can make it a $500 million dollar firm. He definitely sees that potential here with Incremental."

We were golden, right? Well, as it turned out, not exactly. It was hard to get things signed and sealed. With the RBC clock ticking, the discussions with Stevie's boys dragged on for months. We were scheduled to meet twice with Stevie—or "The Big Guy," as they referred to him—but it always fell through. One time was on a Sunday, we were actually already on our way out to Stevie's house in hedge fund guru heaven—Greenwich, Connecticut—but Stevie had to reschedule. We hadn't even been told that he was stuck in Europe because the day before Karp (allegedly) had blown Stevie up for about half a billion on the Volkswagen squeeze.*

The second time was at the Palace—the upscale Palace Hotel on Madison Avenue, not the greasy spoon Palace Diner, as Nu initially thought (providing some much needed, and unintended, comic relief). That second cancellation was due to some family emergency. Even so, Sohail and Karp showed up. They spent their time making the novel case that Stevie deserved 50 percent of Incremental, and not the 10–25 percent we had previously discussed.

"You guys have built something impressive, in the worst market any of us have ever seen," Karp said to butter us up. "Now imagine if you also had the ability to say you were backed by the Big Guy, and that his capital and resources were lined up behind you . . ."

The thought alone was making me salivate. I could see Zvi start clenching and unclenching his fists under the table while he rocked back and forth in his chair. But 50 percent was certainly new, and a big jump from the 10 or 25 percent we had been looking at.

Privately, I would've given 80 percent to Stevie if he had wanted it, and if it had been my call alone. Let him bring in his people to run it as well and make me a consultant. I was getting sick of this nonsense. I was tired of trying to manage Zvi, while simultaneously trying to raise money and navigate the most treacherous markets in a generation. I'd walk away tomorrow for a decent check and go do charity work somewhere warm. That was the truth. We weren't curing cancer or changing the world, and I knew it. We were in it for one thing.

The problem was that Incremental had become Zvi's baby now. I had sworn I wouldn't let that happen, and then found myself powerless to do anything but watch as it did. Zvi did not just want to make money. It was about more

---

* Karp had recommended shorting Volkswagen, and when it was announced that Porsche might take a stake in the automaker, the shorts got decimated and the squeeze drove the stock into the stratosphere. That was effectively the end of Karp's career at SAC. He took a job at Colson Capital in Dallas shortly thereafter.

than that for him. Some part of him needed to avenge/revenge himself on every risk manager who ever reined him in, every trader who had ever scoffed at his calls, and even the great Raj, who had fired him for losing more money in a shorter period of time than most people had thought humanly possible. This was Zvi in charge. When Rick Schottenfeld told him he would be the next Stevie, Zvi intended to prove him right—to show Raj and everyone else out there who ever doubted him that they had been wrong. That meant keeping control. That meant keeping his name on the door.

"Jason, I hear you," Zvi said. "We definitely want you and Stevie involved—and as our partners—but if you think you guys can just come in and minimize what we've built here and grab a majority of the firm for next to nothing, you're not on the same plane of existence we are. People have refused him before. First New York told Stevie 'No thanks,' and we'll do the same. You know how hard it is to build something. You've been at it for years and do you have anything remotely like FNY or Incremental to show for it? If it was easy, you guys would have already done it. Especially with the name and resources behind you."

Taken aback by Zvi's words, Karp said: "We've taken a different approach and you know that. We have different projects. We have staked dozens of—"

Zvi just cut him off.

"Whatever the case, 50 percent is more than we're going to consider. Why don't you guys talk it over and let's get together again next week when you're ready to do this for real."

Zvi stood up, apparently prepared to leave a $17 Grey Goose on the rocks half-finished to punctuate his point.

Zvi had made a possibly powerful, possibly ridiculous statement by comparing us to First New York, a firm likely netting $100 million a year.

I wanted to check him, but I adhered to the cardinal "Sonny Corleone" rule of business: *Don't air your internal disagreements in front of others.* I couldn't think of anything to say, or any way to redirect this exchange that wouldn't come off that way. But if this was a Mafia movie, then it was only Stevie who carried the aura of the Godfather. (Incidentally, Karp had nearly given Zvi an on-the-spot orgasm early on, when he'd told him straight-out: "You know, you kind of remind me of the Big Guy.")

Whenever I asked Zvi why we shouldn't take the deal, he would stress that we did all the work. I would counter by arguing that the pie would be so much bigger with Stevie on board that it wouldn't matter. We could give away half but get a $500 million dollar firm, or stick to our guns and own all of a $50 million dollar firm. "Just do the damn math, Zvi!" I'd shout at that point. Yet Zvi remained unflinching. It was the principle of the thing. Zvi also liked to say: "I can get Raj to give us $10 million at the drop of a hat, and he'll want no more than a 20 percent stake . . . so fuck Stevie."

Looking back, there were several occasions when Raj indeed seemed to be just around the corner with $10 million in hand. Sometimes. I was even in the room for a few of these encouraging Raj/Zvi phone conversations about how close Raj was to investing.

But here's where I have to remind you that I was a dealing with an insane man and didn't yet know it.

Things I was about to learn later convinced me that, on *all* of those occasions, there was nobody on the other end of the phone.

Our talks were still getting bogged down, on all fronts, so we had to keep shopping furiously. This was made painfully clear one day in March of 2009 with RBC's ninety-day termination notice came in the mail, with an official certified stamp on the envelope that might as well have read, "FUCK YOU!" across the front. Once you have a firm deadline for something like that, things take on a terrifying clarity. We had a mere ninety days to replace $150 million in buying power. That meant three months to raise at least $10 million, if not $20, and find a platform that could house us.

We were immensely fortunate that Dave Plotkin had come over as a trader. Dave had left Schottenfeld when his six-year-old son Max was diagnosed with leukemia. He devoted almost all his time to coordinating health care, doctors, and treatment. Later, he launched the Max Cure Foundation with his father Richard. As a parent, I couldn't fathom the suffering he was going through, and yet the guy was still engaged, and still good for Incremental's morale. Dave genuinely loved our firm. He even invested $250K for a small stake. More remarkably, given the sword of Damocles hanging over us all, he wanted to arrange meetings with Todd Deutsch and his friend Adam Gittlin, two folks with a wealth of experience and Marianas Trench-deep pockets. Plotkin felt that both men would be eager to invest in Incremental.

With the days ticking down, one slow trading afternoon Plotkin and I stepped off the desk to eat lunch in the conference room and talk shop. After walking me through some personal trivia on Gittlin ("His wife is a producer for *Good Morning America*, and he's a published author . . .") and Deutsch ("He's memorized over 1500 stock symbols and charts, and is supposed to have a memory like an elephant . . ."), Plotkin asked me what else we had planned on the capital raise front. I mentioned that David Slaine was back in again, thinking he'd be impressed.

"Whaddya mean 'again'?" Plotkin asked.

His face looked like he had just received an "I think I'm late" text.

I told him about how Slaine had nearly become an anchor investor and trader at Incremental in early 2008. He'd been hesitant because we were still in the concept phase at that point, but now we'd proven our trading chops. Slaine was finally ready to write a check for $10 million and wanted in as a partner.

"Listen, man," Plotkin said, in a tone of absolute sobriety (putting down his Italian sub to impress upon me that this was super important). "I gotta tell you something. You don't want anything to do with Slaine. That is one *bad* guy."

"Really?" I said in genuine surprise.

Everything I'd heard about Slaine centered on his wonderful trading feel, his nine-figure bank account, and his massive share volume (which is important when you're upcharging traders' commissions and negotiating with clearing firms for a good rate).

"I can speak from personal experience," Plotkin said. "One of the *worst* human beings I've ever met."

"One of the worst?" I said doubtfully. "Rank him against Ronnie Weiss."

I was urging a comparison of Slaine to Schottenfeld's universally hated risk manager, a man I knew Plotkin despised. While Dave had been working at Schottenfeld, Ron never asked how his son Max was doing, knowing the poor kid was battling for his life. But if Dave went three cents over his buying limit or daily loss limits, Ron was there to hawk him. Weiss seemed heartless, totally devoid of any sympathy whatsoever.

Plotkin's answer was telling: "Ron Weiss is just a bad guy. A jerk. But Slaine is one of the *worst*. Ron is triple A, but this guy is Hall of Fame first ballot. Remember, I was David Slaine's assistant-*cum*-partner at Chelsea."

"You were Slaine's partner? He was at Chelsea?" I asked, wondering how I wasn't aware of either of those facts. "Chelsea was a bad shop from what I heard, right? There were a lot of rumors flying around about that place. Like, I heard the owner flipped on Frank Quattrone to keep himself out of prison."

Plotkin raised his eyebrows and nodded slowly.

"What you heard was right," he said. "Chelsea was a mess. But Slaine is even worse. I had a deal with him to be his trader, and anything I made him I'd get to keep 25 percent. At the end of the year, he was up almost $3 million off my ideas and trades. Instead of giving me the $750,000, he gave me $50,000. He told me he had a 'tougher year than expected' and if I didn't like it I could walk. I was struggling to put a roof over my family's head, and this guy was not only one of my closest friends but somebody already worth $50 million plus! *That's* the type of guy Dave Slaine is."

To give you a sense of how correct Plotkin was, it's worth taking a moment to review precisely what Slaine was up to at that time . . . namely dialing for scalps. Slaine had secretly agreed to cooperate with the FBI to ensnare his friends and colleagues. With a wire attached to his rumored-to-be-"enhanced" body, Slaine recorded dozens of conversations with his supposed best buddy, Craig Drimal (known as "Ruby"), to keep his sorry ass out of prison. He also wore a wire or taped calls with dozens of others, including me. The FBI had knocked on the door of his West 57th Street home in 2007, telling him he could either snitch or stand trial for numerous charges of rulebreaking and financial impropriety. Saving his ass would prove a pretty easy endeavor, for one simple and sad reason—namely, Drimal trusted Slaine, trusted him like a brother. Too bad that brother took his cue from Cain. Drimal was well situated inside Galleon and had a solid working relationship there with Raj. Slaine also knew Raj personally, having briefly worked for him at Galleon after leaving Morgan Stanley's OTC trading desk under a cloud of suspicion for market manipulation in the late '90s. It was while he was at Morgan Stanley that Slaine met Drimal, then a bouncer at the Vertical Club in Manhattan. The two quickly formed a friendship based on a shared passion for weight-lifting and their mutual ability to bench-press 400 pounds. Shortly after arriving at Galleon, it was Slaine who persuaded Galleon's top brass to give a job to Drimal. So it was no wonder poor Drimal would remain grateful and trusting of his old pal.

In the end, this shows just how oblivious we were at that time. The government was already rounding traders up. People were already wearing wires. It was all starting.

And I was so out of the loop I was talking about having informant #1 invest.

CHAPTER FOURTEEN

MERCS AND THE GALLEON DUO

IN ADDITION TO BRINGING IN SOMEONE who was secretly recording conversations with everyone he touched, we were also talking to MERC, a group of commodity traders from Long Island that had done well and which was now looking to expand into equities. My good friend, Pete Bogart introduced the two groups to each other. At the time, Pete, a former lawyer himself who had triumphantly billed the least amount of hours in Skadden history over a four-year period, was trading for a hedge fund in the upscale Westchester County suburb of Rye—a fund which was, like most funds in those days, acting out a Lily Tomlin spinoff entitled *The Incredible Shrinking Asset Base*. Pete's friend Nick Aaron was working there and he thought Incremental and MERC would make a perfect fit. They sounded interested and had already pledged $10 million, but were nervous about Equities Demi-God Stevie Cohen taking a stake too.

Now that Plotkin knew that Slaine wanted back in, Plotkin suggested we talk to Todd Deutsch and his good friend, Adam Gittlin. We met with Deutsch at Opia, a bar/restaurant partially owned by Raj. The downstairs was closed for construction and loud as hell, with a crew of undocumenteds hammering away in the dining room, so they escorted us upstairs to a private room and had a bartender take our order. Being a partner with Raj had its benefits, both in finance and in the broader culinary world. With their mutual love of basketball (stoked by Zvi's fictional embellishments), Todd and Zvi hit it off like long lost cousins. After twenty-five minutes of small talk and five minutes of strategy, Todd proclaimed he was in . . . he just needed to figure out the mechanics for making the investment. Todd suggested we reconvene at Incremental's office that Friday, early, and get down to business. I could barely contain myself.

We went drinking Thursday evening, but agreed to cut our customary twelve to fifteen drinks to a sobering six to eight. Around 7:30 p.m., Zvi took a call from Craig Drimal, and when he came back told us we'd be having an extra guest the next day at Incremental. I asked who.

"The one and only Gary Rosenbach," Zvi said with a devilish grin, referring to Raj's partner and billionaire cofounder of Galleon.

Sure enough, at eight the next morning, ninety minutes before the market opened, Todd and Gary arrived. Todd was decked out in hedge fund master casual—charcoal-gray slacks and an expensive blue cotton mini-check oxford with the sleeves rolled up. Gary was a bit more casual, wearing cotton khakis and Timberland slip-ons, a light gray wool V-neck sweater, and a white T-shirt that was frayed around the collar.

The meeting began well. Our pitch seemed to work its magic, just as it always did.

Perhaps it was because he had recently left Galleon—or because he was in the process of retiring—but Gary came off as less fearsome than his "Sicilian Jew" reputation.

At first.

Towards the end, Gary suddenly grew restless—just as Zvi would often do—tapping his hands and rolling his eyes in their sockets.

"So, let me just cut to the chase," he said as our pitch concluded. "What makes you guys different? Why should I give you my money? How do I know you're not just going to blow it up like every other asshole out there?"

Zvi could sense a kindred spirit in Gary, and opened his mouth to say something bellicose and braggy. I cut him off before he could even get started.

"Because we're fanatical about risk management," I said. "So fanatical, in fact, that we sat down with RBC and reprogrammed *their* software to meet *our* needs. Strict position limits, concentration limits, in real time. We keep reserves to protect against netting risk and, again, what Galleon and the others missed. You guys paid tens, maybe hundreds of millions in commissions. Now it may have been a net plus because you got the first call from analysts and got hooked up in the IPO and secondaries, but we're *still* going to get some of those on the strength of Mike Curtis's* relations and, even better, we cut a very aggressive deal with Goldman where we keep those commissions in-house. We'll pay them .03 a share, charge our traders .10, and keep the million or more in monthly commissions in the till. If we're trading with an unlevered $25 million capital base, with the turnover you're talking anywhere from $10 mil and up in commissions. That's a 40 percent return . . . if we *break even* trading. Let that sink in. Even if we if we lose money, we've got a $10 million cushion, giving us the ability to withstand some serious drawdowns and not lose a penny! That's the model you guys want to be involved with. And this is a golden age for fallen angels—guys like George Rubis, Tim Pierotti**, and a bunch of SAC folks who have returned double digits for years, and just suffered a once-in-a-lifetime setback. We're picking these guys up for pennies on the dollar."

Gary bought it all. You could see it in his face. He saw the chance to do something on his own, without Raj. Moreover, it was something that wouldn't require major oversight on his part. He could check in from Colorado while he was rustling steers on the high plains, and/or make Todd his eyes and ears.

"I might not do the whole $25 million," he allowed cautiously.

$25 million?!

Then I understood.

Without telling me, Zvi must have told Drimal—or even Gary himself!—that we wanted $25 million . . . not the $10 million we were actually looking for.

"But I'll do *at least* $10 million," Gary finished.

Jesus. That was the best "bad news letdown" I'd ever heard in my life. It took everything for me not to smile and ask Gary if he needed the wiring info, then and there.

---

* Curtis was formerly head of syndicate trading at Galleon, meaning he was responsible for getting the firm allocations of stock in an IPO or secondary offering based on the huge amounts of commissions Galleon paid to those same firms and the strength of his contacts in the industry.

** Both skillful former Galleon portfolio managers.

Zvi and I walked Todd and Gary to the elevator and shook hands, making plans to speak again soon. When we turned back around, with ear-to-ear grins, there was Tim Pierotti, a former Galleon trader who was now working for us. He looked as though he'd seen a ghost.

"Was that Todd Deutsch and Gary?" he asked, incredulous.

"Yup," I said. "We've been talking to Todd about investing, and now it looks like Gary might be along for the ride."

"Wow, I was thinking about talking to Leon Shaulov about coming in, but I'm glad I didn't if you guys already have Todd."

"Why not both?" I wondered aloud.

Tim's jaw dropped.

"Are you kidding me? Those guys want to kill each other . . . and practically did on more than one occasion on the trading floor."

"Todd and Leon almost fought?" I asked. "Seriously? I never heard that."

Tim nodded.

"When Todd was getting mauled in 2007 at Galleon, Leon was printing money and being very loud about it on the desk. Todd snapped one day and screamed at Leon to shut the fuck up. Leon came right back at him with, 'Oh, I get it, Todd. The reason you're losing money is because I'm too loud. Okay. I got it, big guy.' Todd had been merciless on the desk for the previous three years, calling anyone that couldn't keep up with him 'a member of the JV' or 'an amateur.' Anyway, Todd rushed him and the rest of the floor broke it up. I really think they might've killed each other if it had been allowed to go on."

"Good to know," I said. "We'll put them on separate floors if Galleon goes under."

At the bar that night, Zvi and I were genuinely psyched. It had been an ungodly grind, but it looked like we could be close to finished. Maybe we had really done it. Maybe this was it!

I kept my emotions in check, however, since I'd seen more than one deal fall through in the "paper up" stage. With Todd already on board, and now Gary wanting to play the bank, we seemed in good shape, though. I was still a little disappointed that we hadn't been able to finalize the deal with Stevie yet, but this was still a big development. Enormous, in fact. And there was a chance that we might still be able to *also* work Stevie into a minority investor deal with us, as they were with MERC.

"What does this mean for MERC?" I asked Zvi.

"What does it mean for *MERC*?" Zvi almost spat the last word. "It means they can sit on my dick and spin. Fuck MERC. Those guys are fucking scumbags anyway. I would never go into business with them except as a last resort."

I didn't agree with the scumbag part, but certainly wasn't jazzed up to have them as a partner.

"Okay, but let's not say anything to them until Gary and Todd have money deposited, papers signed and we're rolling," I cautioned.

"Gotcha," Zvi replied.

Would he actually have the sense to hold his tongue? I could only pray.

The next thing that happened was I got a call from Craig Drimal. You'll recall that at this point, Drimal was a limited investor in Incremental, but still worked for Galleon.

"It's Gary Rosenbach," Drimal said, naming his investor friend. "He just called me and . . . well . . . I think something very bad is happening."

"What?" I said. "Spit it out."

"It happened at a party at Steve Starker's house," Drimal began.

Starker's house was near Old Oaks, the elite old-guard Jewish country club in Purchase where Starker, Gary Rosenbach, Eric Mindich, and dozens of other Westchester power players were members. Drimal explained that all these folks had been at the party, along with Mike Brown, MERC's co-CEO. Brown mentioned he was putting money into this hot new prop fund called Incremental. Gary, somewhat surprised, said he was also looking at us and possibly considering investing. Then Brown mentioned that an ex-Galleon guy was running it.

Gary had been blindsided by this detail and belligerently asked who the hell it was.

"Why, Zvi Goffer," Brown had said, confused that Gary could be considering making an investment of his own without knowing this most-basic basic fact.

Incredibly, Gary, a managing partner of Galleon, had never known that Zvi had been employed at Galleon! Apparently Raj had kept Zvi a secret from Gary. Such a thing seemed almost impossible! Even if Zvi didn't sit on the main trading floor, he attended the morning meetings. And Drimal had never bothered to tell Gary about Zvi's background either—he just assumed Gary knew.

"He was pissed, Mike," Drimal told me. "Very pissed."

And he was.

No one could have predicted Gary's response. Gary felt deceived and lied to, and soon cut off all contact with us.

The deal was off.

If that seems extreme to you, then you need to understand Gary.

He was very controlling—with a legendary, vindictive temper that had more than earned him his "Sicilian Jew" nickname, in both his personal and professional life. Galleon was his baby and he wanted to be in control and have a say/stake in every part of it. But Raj was the real power behind Galleon. Gary knew this, and their partnership had been fraying for years. For Gary not to know that Zvi had been a portfolio manager *at his own shop* was beyond humiliating. More than that, it raised red flags for Gary that Drimal might be working with Raj to do things behind his back. Gary thought of Drimal as one of his acolytes. Gary expected Drimal to stay loyal, and to keep him abreast of everything. That, obviously, had not happened.

So less than a week after our savior had appeared, he was gone, felled by an offhand comment at a suburban BBQ. This chance conversation also probably erased any prospect we had that Starker was going to invest. On top of that, MERC knew we were still shopping. Zvi, Drimal, and Raj's complicity had essentially knocked down nearly all of our investment prospect pins with a single bowling ball.

The loss was devastating.

Just as it all began to feel totally hopeless, Todd Deutsch called to say he was still interested. Yeah, MERC was pissed, he said, but their deal was still on the table; they were also getting more aggressive on the terms . . . and all the while the doomsday clock was ticking steadily down.

Todd, at thirty-eight years old, did have one major oddity: his dad ran all his money, estimated at around $150 million.

"Go out to Long Island and talk to him," Todd told me. "If you can get my dad on board, then I'm in."

Matt Subilia, our CFO, accompanied me on a hurried journey out to the Deutsch estate, which was in fact a fairly average house in Oyster Bay, with a big backyard and a swimming pool. We were given the grand tour personally by Todd's dad. This tour included mementos of Todd's basketball accomplishments at Oyster Bay High School, with mandatory viewings of video of some of his high school playoff games. Having attended a Los Angeles public school with several alums who'd gone on to play for UNLV, I politely feigned interest in Todd schooling a group of short Jewish kids for a few minutes before suggesting we catch one of the last Indian summer days out on his elevated deck. Deutsch Senior told us to get comfortable, that his wife would rustle up some food, and brought out an eighteen-pack of Coors Light from the fridge. The sight made me grimace. After a particularly rough Tuesday night—so rough, I didn't realize until I found my receipt in my pocket the next day that I'd caught a cab from 46th and 3rd to Grand Central, a mere three blocks away— I'd decided it was detox time, and had committed myself to not drinking for three days, just to dry out a little. But that had been yesterday, and today there was a bunch of Coors Light in front of me and a guy with an expression that seemed to say: "Time to chug, son, and I'll write you a $75K check for every beer you get down." Since Matt was the designated driver, I ended up knocking back about half of them on an empty stomach. To his credit, Mr. Deutsch knocked back quite a few himself.

And all the time I had to listen to Mr. Deutsch reminisce about famous people he knew.

"Marty Schotteheimer kicked my ass in college."

"Doug Kass and I are friends, but I don't want to give him money."

It went on and on.

His wife made some unidentifiable hors d'oeuvres, which I whispered to Matt that he'd better eat if he wanted to keep his job. (I watched him point out things in the greenery behind Mr. Deutsch while tossing most of it over his shoulder in the bushes). But at the end of the day, it was a done deal and we stumbled out.

Todd would put in $250K on October 1, with another $500K to follow January 1. The amount was irrelevant; the important part was we had another hedge fund all-star with an impeccable reputation in our corner. From a recruiting and training perspective, there weren't many names that could compare (sans the Big Guy, of course).

At the same time, in a move I couldn't have been happier about, Gittlin accepted our offer to come over as Incremental's new CFO, and said he wanted to put some of his family's money to work, in the area of $2 million to start with the promise of much more to follow.

Bruce Gittlin, Adam's father, was a big-time NYC landlord, with a net worth of "it doesn't matter anymore." The RBC cover was now less than thirty days away from vanishing. And as the squares on the calendar ticked off, the stress of trying to find capital to keep the firm afloat while simultaneously trading (and risk managing) one of the toughest markets in history was becoming increasingly brutal. We drank too much and I seemed to always have a hangover. I was simultaneously losing hair and gaining weight. *Tick-tock, tick-tock,* went everything in my life. Meanwhile, MERC was starting to make things difficult—first by telling us that they didn't want Stevie Cohen involved *at all* and then by making unreasonable requests (aka demands). For example, they wanted to keep all the money in their own accounts, wanted to have a say on risk, and then on who we could hire. Soon, it was like RBC all over again. Instead of being a passive capital partner, what they really wanted was to co-manage Incremental, and with absolutely zero equities experience on their end.

Is this how it happens? I wondered. Is this how it always is? How it must be? As good as it fucking gets? Is there no other way?

It all felt so, so, hopeless.

Then the king died.

CHAPTER FIFTEEN

THE KING IS DEAD

—————

WITH THE DOOMSDAY CLOCK TICKING AWAY, my day-to-day the stress was borderline debilitating. Life at home suffered as well. I had started taking Ambien every night—alcohol alone, even in copious quantities, couldn't quiet my wired mind anymore. I'd come home and listen to Lisa bemoan her catering disasters—the wrong extra virgin olive oil, or a stale crab puff causing a fury with some sexually frustrated Greenwich housewife. Yet when I mentioned my own concerns—the market tailspin, the back and forths with Incremental, the way every ally slowly became another RBC—all I heard, when I had a good trading day, was about our getting a second home, a new car, or a refinished kitchen.

At Incremental we were beyond desperate now, and had decided to turn to a guy named Uri Cohen, whom Nu had once worked for at Spectrum Securities. Uri was a brilliant Orthodox Jew, strictly kosher, a tall, skinny thirty-year-old who wore thick eyeglasses and made a point of keeping out of the limelight. He was, more importantly, a trader at heart who made a fortune on the "rebalancing" once a quarter or year.*

————

* Major stock indices like the S&P, Russell 2000 or Nasdaq 100 are typically "rebalanced" once a year. According to companies' "market weight," the indices decide the appropriate weight that each company makes up in the index, thus causing all of the index mutual funds (Vanguard, Fidelity, etc.) to buy or sell certain stocks as they are added to and taken out of various indices. Computers took this over too, but for a while, back in the day, smart, connected traders could get a feel for the flow and dislocation caused by S&P 500 having to buy five million shares of a stock and sell five million of another when they rebalance.

At our first meeting with Uri, he got us instantly. He loved the model, and was willing to give us exactly what we needed. I didn't love it, but only because, frankly, Uri was a no-name brand—and yes, names mattered in the trading world. Besides, from a purely business perspective, we still had Gittlin's money. But Nu and Zvi genuinely adored Uri. Nu had been trading his account at Uri's firm only last year, but had allegedly made upwards of $7 million there. And Uri was the only one left who understood the risk, had the capital, and wasn't making us dance through hoops. Deutsch's dad had agreed to wire us the money on October 1 but then Todd had called us to say there had been a glitch of sorts, travel-related, I believe*, and after apologizing profusely promised the wire would be authorized on the first of November. One month away felt like a goddamn eternity.

And hey, Uri was onboard and ready to go all in with just a few minor details regarding structure and percentages left to work out. We scheduled a final meeting with him for October 16, 2009, to ink the deal. So it was a day like any other, right? Well, not quite. A mere few hours before we were scheduled to meet, Wall Street was rattled and the hedge fund world was rocked to its core by a 9.2 Richter scale event.

With CNBC and Bloomberg streaming from multiple flat-panel televisions on most trading floors all day, it takes a lot to actually grab traders' attention through the daily mash of noise. But the "BREAKING NEWS" scrolls and pictures of Raj being escorted handcuffed by FBI agents in flak jackets with the sub-headline "Galleon Co-Founder Raj Rajaratnam Arrested" did it in a big way.

"Turn this up!" came screams from the trading floor as we all stopped what we were doing and looked on in stunned silence. With half a dozen ex-Galleon guys on our floor, and Zvi's close ties with Rajaratnam still very much intact, the news blaring from the TV speakers was very, *very* relevant to all of us. As we sat there quietly and digested the CNBC loop, Franz Tudor slowly walked over to Zvi's desk and motioned him over. I could hear them speaking.

"This is crazy, right?" Franz said. "Do we have anything to be concerned about?"

---

* In retrospect, I believe something far more sinister had taken place.

"It's fucking nuts. I don't know. I mean this is . . . this is really fucked up."
Zvi did not sound confident—a true rarity.

Franz did a walk-by on several other traders—Nu, Joe Mancuso, some of
the Galleon guys, and myself—just to get a read on how we were feeling.

"Mike, are you worried?" Franz whispered.

"About what? Raj? What do you think they got him on?"

As I said at the start, when I first heard about Raj, I was only thinking
about sex. Raj was supposed to be an over-the-top hedonist. To me, the like-
liest scenario was that someone had snuck into one of his famed parties who
wasn't quite eighteen.

For the moment, we had to pretend all was fine and dandy and focus on
raising this much-needed capital from Uri at our meeting later that morning.
When we entered Uri's simple, understated office on an upper floor at 120
Broadway, just before lunchtime on October 16, he had on the TV in the conference room: it was CNBC, and all the talk was Raj, Galleon, and the arrest.
Uri was watching Raj, in his cashmere cardigan sweater and Prada loafers,
doing the perp walk on a loop. It was now clear that they had arrested Raj for
insider trading. This was a move by Uri. He knew that Zvi's ties to Galleon
and Raj ran deep.

Zvi tried not to linger on it, but dove headfirst into his final pitch.

On our side, I could see Adam Gittlin quietly scratching his head; he had
already made the connection that Zvi had worked directly for Raj during the
period of Raj's criminal complaint. Still, Uri had yet to experience fully the
salesmanship, the gamesmanship, the staggering exaggerations and outright
lies that comprised Zvi's alter-ego when he pitched. Even I was still unaware
how deep these rivers of deception ran. (Gittlin had gone farther than any of
us. In a moment of infatuated drunkenness during his first meeting with Zvi,
he had signed a "friendship contract" with Zvi—insisting that he wanted to be
more than just a business partner with Zvi, but a friend. Zvi liked the idea so
much that he even drew up a three-sentence "cocktail napkin contract" they
both inked, committing to the bond, and Zvi posted it above his desk.)

I was more or less incapacitated during this meeting with Uri—busy running doomsday scenarios inside my head. Adam and Zvi did most of the negotiating, somehow managing to turn an ELE (extinction level event)—Raj's
arrest—into the greatest thing to ever happen to Incremental. Instead of Zvi

going to jail for conspiring with Raj—and Incremental getting shut down—
we were now going to have the pick of the litter at Galleon. We could get not
only Galleon's B team, but the A Team superstars as well. Studs like Leon
Shaulov, who made money hand over fist. It was all on the table. You could see
Uri go from predator to prey as Zvi wove his fairy magic.

Next, I began to worry about Deutsch. Surely this news—that Galleon had
been sunk at sea, and "Baby Galleon" still wanted his funds—would mean the
end of his investment. Not only was Deutsch one of the managing partners
of Galleon, but his Captain's Fund was specifically mentioned in the criminal
complaint. The same would happen, I was certain, with Stevie Cohen and
SAC. As Zvi pitched to Uri, I sat at the table getting more and more paranoid.
Then I thought about the man himself. What was Deutsch's actual situation?
He must be on the SEC's radar, given where he was with Raj and what he
traded. Had Deutsch been tipped off or leaned on by the Feds? Was he a target
in his own right? Or possibly a cooperator? Was that why he and his dad were
making excuses regarding the wiring of money? And based on Raj's complaint,
was that the only "wire" I should really be worrying about?

This was all the more extraordinary because I ended up being almost right.
My suspicions were correct—sort of. I was fishing with the right bait, but in
the wrong waters.

As we'd soon find out, our friend Franz had been sitting next to me on the
trading desk wearing a wire for over a year.

Anyhow, Uri was all in after the meeting and it was just a matter of finaliz-
ing a detail or two. Zvi had successfully flipped what should have been a "game
over" or at least "proceed with caution" type event into a once in a lifetime
opportunity to grab talent from one of the best known hedge funds on the
Street. Within ten days or so we had everything signed and the accounts set
up, Gittlin's money came in, and we were ready to roll.

And a week after that? The FBI paid me an unexpected pre-dawn visit, and
Incremental vanished forever.

Chapter Sixteen

A TALE OF TWO TRIALS

RAJ RAJARATNAM WAS LIKE A BLACK hole. That's not a ding on the man's legendary physical girth. Rather, I use those words because, as the head of one of the most impressive hedge funds on the planet—one that managed to stay afloat and even prosper right up until his arrest on October 16, 2009—Raj sucked all of us into his orbit. Pulled us in whether we wanted to be there or not. My destiny became inextricably tied to Raj's, even though he and I had never exchanged more than a few innocuous pleasantries.

Raj's company had become the Enron of hedge funds. Remember that before Enron's collapse, the big investment banks had wanted in and all the savvy financial journalists touted its impressive success. That was Raj. That was Galleon.

Just as Enron's undoing had surprised so many, Raj's arrest also came as a total surprise, even to some of his own staff. (An unnamed colleague of Raj's at Galleon famously came into work, noticed the changed environment, and asked if Raj had been arrested for terrorism.*)

Roughly a year and a half would pass until Raj stood trial, professing his innocence till the very end, even while the folks tied most closely to him—most notably Danielle Chiesi and Anil Kumar—pled guilty or cooperated with the prosecution. Raj's trial was the big one. The one the Feds all dreamed about and looked forward to. Feds looked forward to trials like this the way Wall Streeters like us looked forward to deals big enough to put us out of the game. We all knew that grandstanding was going to be a massive part of the

---

* Raghavan, *The Billionaire's Apprentice*, page 317.

proceedings. The lead prosecutor Preet Bharara saw this—perhaps correctly—as his career-defining case. The importance of its outcome, on the eve of my own trial, cannot be overestimated.

So I wasn't going to miss it for the world.

In the real world, even the most scintillating trials—featuring marquee defendants and famous lawyers—would be shockingly disappointing to a generation raised on the likes of *Law & Order* and *Ally McBeal*. On those shows, evidence is all sexy smoking guns, and whichever side delivers the most spectacular bombshell finale is the winner. In the real world, both sides must telegraph their evidence, witnesses, and lines of questioning well in advance. Instead of showing fireworks and passion, counsel spends huge chunks of time mindlessly setting the foundation, just to get some minor piece of evidence admitted. Even a desperate insomniac would flip past a Court TV broadcast at 2 a.m. for a random *Law & Order* rerun. Any sane insomniac, anyway.

When the highly anticipated "Raj trial" began, it was a sensation on Wall Street. Not since the days of *Giuliani v. Boesky* had the public and the press been treated to the spectacle of such a good white-collar criminal case at 500 Pearl Street, the Manhattan Federal Court—home field of the Southern District of NY (SDNY), and also known as "The Office." The SDNY prosecutors consider themselves (and generally speaking probably are) the best the country has to offer. Their track record is 98 percent conviction rate, courtesy of an extremely uneven playing field, with the laws and procedures heavily tilted in the government's favor, not to mention their near unlimited resources. And pitted against them are many defendants who can't even afford to pay for a competent attorney. A big part of the drama in Raj's case was that the boys at the SDNY would be facing a well-heeled defendant with enough resources to pay for—not just a *good* attorney—but for practically any attorney he desired.

Raj eventually settled on a team from powerhouse DC law firm Akin Gump Strauss Hauer & Feld, captained by John Dowd, a grumpy old Marine famous for defending Senator John McCain during the Keating Five debacle, and repping Major League Baseball in its case against Pete Rose. Dowd had been practicing law longer than I'd been alive.

Of course, we all went to watch.

Before the first morning court session, I was in the eighth-floor Federal Cafeteria, trying to order an egg sandwich from a surly cook, his government tenure empowering him to provide neither service nor a smile while working. Nu and Zvi came up behind me and tried to strike up a conversation.

"How long before Dowd puts that runt Brodsky in a headlock?" Zvi asked, a big smile on his face, referring to Reed Brodsky, one of the AUSAs prosecuting the case.

I offered a quick hello after looking around to make sure the cafeteria was empty of possible enemies.

"No fireworks today," I opined in low tones, "but by the end of the first week I expect the prosecutors to be pleading for an intercession from Judge Holwell over hurt feelings stemming from some Dowd comment. He's going to hurt their feelings a lot."

I was confident when it came to Raj's lawyer. I thought he had hired the ultimate badass. Zvi thought so too.

"They'll be crying like little bitches when Dowd gets through with them," Zvi agreed. "Anil Kumar is going to be called 'Anal FUBAR' by the time Dowd's done with him."

It was a bit inelegant, but I liked it.

For Zvi, this was all sound and fury—prologue to a dance that could end in only one conceivable way. Raj would be acquitted, and then so would he. Zvi was sure of it. At that point a woman and a man walked through the door in classic government haircuts, short and combed to the side, deliberately unstylish. I turned my back so they couldn't see my face and, after they passed, rotated back to the Brothers Goffer.

I said: "Listen, I'm not trying to be an asshole, but I can't be seen talking to you guys here."

Nu scrunched his face like he wasn't sure what I was talking about. But Zvi got it instantly. The government's case against me operated on the assertion that the three of us were thick as thieves. The government needed me to be part of the mega-conspiracy.

I didn't know if Zvi knew it, but my only real avenue to salvation at this point was to convince Zvi to plead guilty, to own up. The AUSAs on my case had not only offered me a generous probation-only deal to plead guilty to one count, but in further discussions, they had also indicated that if Zvi and Nu were to take a plea, they would drop my case and offer me a "deferred prosecution"—the home run outcome. So it was friends close, but enemies closer until

I could pry open Zvi's stubborn eyes and wake him to the fact he was DOA, facing a "dime" if he saw this through to the end.

"You got me?" I continued. "This is just the way it's gotta be for now. I'll meet you later at Sutton Place if you want to compare notes, but not here."

Zvi nodded. He understood.

The government's opening statement was delivered by Jonathan Streeter. Prior to Raj's arrest, Streeter had actually been in the process of interviewing for a job with my lawyer, Michael Sommer. With Raj's arrest, he'd decided to stay where he was to captain the high profile prosecution. It's easy to understand why. Such cases come but once in a lifetime. The opening statement was just about laying out the government's case in broad strokes. There were a few dramatic details to hook the jury, but mostly it was just the overview of what the government would "prove" throughout the course of the trial.

By then, most everyone knew that the case against Raj was strong. The government wasted no time painting Raj and Galleon as a cesspool of dirty money, and as corrupt insiders bending good men to their will and making obscene, unlawful profits. Making more in a day than decent folks like "you and me, who play by the rules" will make in a lifetime.

When Raj's champion John Dowd took the podium, the entire gallery waited in eager anticipation . . . and kept waiting. He reminded me of a former heavyweight champ climbing back into the ring after an extended absence, a dusted Ali in his fight against Larry Holmes—thirty pounds overweight, no bounce in his step, no sting in his jab. Dowd droned through a long, scripted opening that did little to dampen the government's theory. It was the last proof I needed that Dowd was finished, a warrior past his prime living off a once-vaunted reputation.

I'd gotten a sinking feeling this might be the case during the pretrial hearing when Dowd had inexplicably allowed Agent Kang to wiggle off the stand during the *Franks* wiretap hearing (a hearing to determine whether a search warrant was legally obtained). Pretrial, Judge Holwell had granted Raj's motion for a *Franks* hearing to determine whether the government had filed a misleading wiretap application. The mere fact that a *Franks* hearing was held at all was a huge victory. It meant that Raj's team had demonstrated to Holwell that they had met the preliminary burden of proof showing that (1) the government had *knowingly and intentionally*, or with reckless disregard for the truth, included a *false statement* in the wiretap affidavit and (2) that "the allegedly false statement was necessary to a finding of probable cause." In other words, the government had lied their way through the wiretap affidavit.

But then, Dowd had not pursued it. He had not delivered the knockout blow. This was more than a little disconcerting.

The Goffer brothers attended Raj's trial with Kucharsky, their "paralegal," a balding, chain-smoking friend from SUNY Binghamton, who struck me as more of an inept hatchet man than any sort of actual paralegal. When Zvi introduced me to him, I asked what firm he worked for (none) and what kind of legal experience he had. ("He's good at that stuff," Zvi said, which also meant none.) But a lack of education or legal experience didn't stop Kucharsky, or Zvi for that matter, from opining with absolute certainty on every aspect of Raj's case.

Even though the deadline for a deal had passed, I knew the government would accept a plea from Zvi up to a month before trial. The Raj case was my last real chance to convince Zvi that his decision to go to trial was pure suicide.

I wanted to say: "If Raj has a 10 percent chance, you have a 1 percent chance. Take the deal."

But Zvi's focus was, unbelievably, elsewhere.

"Did you see that smoking blogger for *Biz Insider*?" he asked me one day. "Tall brunette with an accent? She's all over my dick. Kept asking who I was, who my brother was. I finally told her with a wink on the way out of the courtroom, 'You'll find out soon enough.' Teased her perfectly. I bet she was soaking."

It was infantile. It was insane. Ten years of Zvi's life were on the line, and he was talking like Donald Trump in an *Access Hollywood* trailer.

Sure enough, the next morning *Business Insider*'s Katya Wachtel posted a blog entry about the three mysterious men, sweating in their Jos. A. Bank "Buy 1, Get 2 Free" ill-fitting suits and mismatched dress shirts, looking like contract killers from Belarus.

On Day Three of the trial, I called my good buddy, Peter Bogart.

"You've got to see this, man," I told him. "Trust me. Come into the city."

Pete and I linked up around 8:45 a.m. for the 9:00 a.m. start. A healthy crowd was already buzzing. Press from the *Wall Street Journal*, *New York Times*, and other top media outlets and cable channels were camped in the front, along with the Brothers Goffer, their "paralegal," and a colorful mix of Raj team members right behind them. A few news anchors stood in front of cameras, announcing highlights of the trial. When they ran out of specifics, a woman with the *NY Post* pondered what it must be like for Reed Brodsky's wife to have given birth to her first child while he was spending eighteen hours a day on a case. Others offered bland congratulatory words, while mentioning the incredible sleep deprivation and pressure Brodsky must be feeling, working to balance such a high profile case and the birth of his new baby girl.

Zvi took in snippets of all this. It made him grind his teeth. Brodsky's recent fatherhood was news to Zvi. He had a slightly different take on the event, which he shared with Nu in a voice loud enough to be overheard.

"So he had a baby girl, huh?" Zvi said. "Fuck. I was praying the baby would come out stillborn."

It was insane. Unbelievable. (*Fucking Zvi!*) Nu tried to shush him, but Zvi was only spurred on by the wide eyes and dropped jaws rotating in his direction.

"What?" Zvi said, gesturing to no one and everyone. "He wants to take my children away from me, and for what? For hearing a few secondhand ideas and not making a penny? Fuck him. I want to see how that scumbag likes losing a child."

Even Nu was smart enough to know that praying out loud for the death of a prosecutor's newborn in front of the press wasn't wise. Nu stepped in front of him and physically shut him up. Zvi had gotten what he wanted, though. He had successfully shocked the press corps. For me, it was the final proof I needed that my fate was tied to a madman, to a sociopath that cared for and about no one other than himself.

Pete leaned and asked: "Did Zvi just say what I thought he said?"

I nodded.

There had always been a part of me that had feared Zvi on some primal, animal level. Now I feared him even more—and on new levels. Zvi could hurt me from a legal perspective, he could hurt my reputation, he could hurt my chances of going free, and he could still hurt me physically. There were probably other ways he could hurt me too, that I hadn't even thought of yet.

Desperate people make desperate moves.

I was finding that out the hard way.

Hundreds of trials take place every day around the country. No more than one quarter of those courtrooms are anywhere approaching full. In fact, a completely full courtroom is a rarity. Yet that was precisely what we had for the trial of Raj. The stiff marshals were reveling in their newfound attention and power, directing traffic like it was opening night at a Broadway show.

"*No drinks! No papers! No magazines!* Agents and press first. Please sit in the first row."

After fifteen minutes of waiting, the crowd busy scoping and gossiping, one of the marshals barked the only part of a trial that would be familiar to *Law & Order* fans: "All rise."

In strolled Judge Holwell, a deliberate, soft-spoken Sam Elliot lookalike, and we were seated.

He offered a courteous "Good morning" and asked if there were any issues that needed to be discussed without the jury present. When both sides demurred, he instructed the marshal to bring the jury in. After a minute, there was a loud knock at the jury room door and in sauntered Raj's jury, sixteen of the most motley-looking individuals you'd ever seen. These were not the folks you wanted juggling with your fate. In Hollywood, "wardrobe" dresses *Law & Order* jurors in generic, dull, business casual clothing that doesn't stand out. In real life—as anyone who has been in a courtroom can attest—jurors often don't hesitate to dress like they want to be the center of attention. This jury was no different. They wore everything from neon lime-green Hawaiian shirts to long, disheveled dreads that made them look like the monster from *Predator.*

"Can you imagine having your life in the hands of that crew?" Pete whispered, looking them over, having the same thoughts.

"Can I?" I asked incredulously.

"Oh yeah. Shit. I forgot."

Pete hung his head.

At the break, Pete and I stood in the hallway, where I pointed some of the players out to him. "That's Nathanson. He's one of Galleon's attorneys from Shearman and Sterling. And that's Susan Pulliam. She's a reporter at the *Journal.*"

"Who's the sailor from Nantucket?" Pete asked, referring to a bespoke-dressed man in his forties. He had a double-breasted navy blue sport coat with a white silk pocket square, and looked like an extra in a yacht club's "Boating Safety" video.

"Oh, that's McCarthy," I said. "Raj's PR guy."

Just then, the door to the stairs was yanked open and FBI Agent B. J. Kang and another agent I didn't recognize—a burly dude with his brown hair shorn to the scalp—shouted, "*MAKE A HOLE!*"

Each had a hand on one of Anil Kumar's arms, and speed-marched him into the courtroom. Anil's head stayed lowered. The FBI agents were barking and swiveling their heads, scanning the room for potential threats. The crowd of reporters and spectators parted like the Red Sea, and Anil was pushed into the relative safety of the courtroom. It seemed laughably silly to treat Kumar like a stool pigeon at a mob trial, but I guessed the feds weren't taking any chances.

When they were through the courtroom doors, Pete turned to me, an inquisitive smile on his face.

"Make a hole? Who talks like that? How about 'Excuse me, please'?"

"I'm going to use that from now on. When I'm boarding the subway during rush hour, I'm just going to scream at the people in front of me, *MAKE A HOLE!*"

We laughed and went back inside.

Kumar, a longtime friend of Raj, testified competently and did the two things the government needed him to do. One, he made clear that he had been getting illegal information from his employer, Intel, and two, that he had been passing that information along to Raj—who also knew it was illegal. On cross, Dowd made a few minor dents, but did nothing to really damage Kumar's core testimony.

From a psychological perspective, the most interesting part wasn't the trial itself—which provided few surprises and even fewer moments of drama—rather, it was the reaction that Zvi's presence was beginning to produce in others. His miscarriage tirade had made him a marked man. Everybody looked his way now. You could feel a palpable hatred emanating from the FBI agents in the courtroom, many of whom may have assisted on our case. They all knew the cocky, handsome fool parading around the courtroom with a permanent smirk on his face, awaiting his turn.

It was almost unheard of for a high profile defendant like Zvi to attend the related trial of another defendant. So much so, that *Bloomberg* wrote an article on the spectacle Zvi was creating, again referring to him as Octopussy, and including a big photo of him, unshaven and in one of his many loud track suits. Prosecutors and FBI agents alike gave Zvi a wide berth, but their sneers made clear that they considered him nothing more than a common street hoodlum. They were salivating at the prospect of sending him to rot in jail.

I could hardly blame the Feds for their reaction. I knew Zvi had crossed a line. At the same time, there was still something about the parading of Zvi and Raj around like two financial super criminals that reeked of disinformation and propaganda. And maybe even something else. Here they were, two foreign-looking swarthy gangsters, up against the white-bread boys of Washington. (Preet Bharara was the lone brown face on the government's side.) The big banks had collectively just lifted somewhere in the order of $1 trillion from America, but nobody there was ever shackled. A few people got slapped on the wrist. That was it. Yet these "ethnic" boys with their strange names had been targeted for financial misdealings that weren't all that different from what the big banks had done.

However you looked at it, Raj had not "stolen" millions from anyone, and Zvi had not made a dime from his trades. Their crimes were technical violations. No one lost their life savings (which is more than could be said for the pre-recession machinations of Goldman Sachs, Merrill Lynch, Bank of America and the rest), and no one, ever, was physically hurt. These weren't con men stealing Social Security pensions from hapless widows *a la* Madoff. What Raj and Zvi—along with dozens of others in the money management industry—had done was the financial equivalent of jaywalking. They had broken a technical rule that those in the know had been breaking since the turn of the eighteenth century when traders would gather underneath a large Buttonwood tree at the foot of Wall Street to trade securities. Type up any chart of any stock before a takeover or major event, and you can see the movement *before* the announcement—*someone always knows*. But it was easier to present Israel Brooklyn and the Dark Man as the bad guys to a hurting American populace hungry for justice, than it would ever be to go after the big banks, or the bought and paid politicians who had changed the rules to make it easier for crony capitalism and power consolidation to take place. It was a PR blitz, designed to show the American public that while the feds had missed Madoff, Stanford, and others stealing billions over the last twenty years, and that mortgage fraud in the trillions had been going on right under their noses for years—the Good Guys were fighting back . . . and winning!

To a way of thinking, this trial was Oligarchs 1, Outsiders 0.

Zvi was an asshole and a bully. Raj was an information junkie and a glutton. These were not "good" men. But neither did they play any role in the financial collapse our country was suffering through, nor were they even remotely the most egregious or high-level insider traders out there. And that being the case, it did lead one to ask why they had really been put on trial.

I never for a moment forgot that I was caught up in a *staged* drama.

The week of our arrest, AUSA Brodsky had told Cynthia, the first of Zvi's many attorneys, that he had no interest in negotiating separate pleas. "Come in for a global plea and everyone will be in much better shape. Otherwise he'll spend the next fifteen years in prison. The case against Zvi is airtight."

When Zvi relayed the story to me later, he added his own color: "If that's his definition of airtight, it's a good thing he's not a submarine commander— he'd kill his entire crew."

The real value in Zvi lay in his ability to string up Raj and Gary Rosenbach. The government knew Zvi could be a devastating cooperator if he'd only turn informant. The standard *modus operandi* of prosecutors is to extort and coerce a defendant until he's under unbearable duress. Keep adding new charges and more dollars until the defendant faces the unbearable prospect of bankruptcy and decades in prison, and then flip him and work up the chain.

According to Brodsky, the deal for Zvi could get pretty sweet. All he had to do was offer up info on Raj, Gary, and, get this . . . *me*. Billionaire I, Billionaire II, and a mortgage-saddled nobody. It was strange, but indicative of the phantom nature of their case that they were pressuring Zvi to flip on me downstream, along with those two whales upstream. The mantra typically went, "*Work up the ladder, not down.*"

I was way, way down.

After watching the first week of Raj's trial, I was having serious doubts that he would be able to win. It looked like they were going to prove that Raj had done what they said he'd done. But Raj still had a strike force of the best lawyers money could buy, and they'd been working on his case 24/7 for the past eighteen months. The entire back row of the courtroom was filled with Raj's lawyers, and there still weren't enough seats. His team also occupied the first row of the spectator gallery—paralegals, PR people, and other miscellaneous assistants. Raj was using a large chunk of his billion-dollar fortune for his own version of the Powell Doctrine—if you choose to go to war, go all in with overwhelming force. Think Iraq as opposed to Vietnam. Raj could afford to pursue every investigative avenue and every litigation tactic out there. I, on the other hand, couldn't afford *any* investigative work. Neither could I afford jury selection consultants or trial strategy focus groups. I couldn't even mount the proper and necessary pre-trial motions because of my financial limitations. But even with this "one hand behind my back" reality, I knew I had to fight. I was innocent.

Sommer still believed there was a chance that the government would blink and offer me something. Unfortunately, this was based largely on his analysis of Zvi and Nu as rational actors who would realize they had no other good choice than to cop a plea. I had long ago given up on this possibility, and knew that we were either going to trial with Zvi, with Zvi and his brother together, or with the entire group of derelicts including Drimal, Jenkins, and Cutillo. I knew it was going to be uphill. Forget 3Com; that was a sideshow. But "conspiracy," as my lawyers constantly told me, while it sounded like a fictionalized nightmare charge from *1984* or *The Hunger Games*, was, in the end, brutally real.

Zvi and I nearly came to blows over "conspiracy" on more than one occasion at Sutton Place. I tried to convey the high-caliber spiderweb that "conspiracy" could become in the hands of a motivated prosecutor, but Zvi poo-pooed my concerns.

"You don't understand," Zvi scoffed.

"You're not worried about this?" I said sarcastically. "Then why don't you explain it to me?"

"I've done my own work," Zvi began.

In trading, when Zvi talked about doing his "own work," it usually amounted to little more than piggybacking someone else's idea, or spending a few hours on Google spinning his wheels and selecting articles that confirmed his preexisting bias, while disregarding any evidence that might have made him think again. Not exactly an exhaustive, top-notch approach. The phrase was disturbing to hear because I now realized Zvi had likely used it while passing off extra-legal information as his own regarding trades.

"And I've come to the conclusion that no one . . . *no one!* . . . has ever been convicted of conspiracy unless they were *also* convicted of an underlying substantive trade."

"No one?" I said doubtfully.

"Nobody. And Cynthia couldn't show me a case either."

Zvi's lawyer at the time, Cynthia, had probably tried to tell him that his idea was absurd, and Zvi had likely responded by being Zvi. By saying something like: "Then, prove it. If it's silly, show me a case; that shouldn't be too tough."

"I can show you a dozen cases in an hour of legal research of people just convicted of conspiracy," I growled at Zvi. "I've been told more than half the people in jail are there on a conspiracy charge alone."

"I'm only talking about insider trading. Find me an insider trading case where the guy gets convicted of conspiracy, but acquitted on the other charges."

Zvi's filter of insanity and narcissism had just cut about 99.99 percent of the cases out there. Very few people in our industry actually go to trial, and those that do tend to be convicted of all counts, both substantive and conspiracy. Zvi's idea was that he would not be convicted on the underlying substantive of 3Com or Axcan, and thus his dozens of hours of conspiratorial phone calls and informant testimony were irrelevant. It was novel—I'll give it that—but ultimately meaningless. He was going to get convicted on both substantive charges, every conspiracy charge, and anything else the government wanted to throw into the indictment. He was glomming onto minor inconsistencies, while in the big picture, he was already a dead man.

"Remember I didn't trade Axcan," Zvi wheedled.

"I know, but the guy you gave it to did, and he made a few million," I pointed out.

"I told him I heard an idea," Zvi said. "I didn't even believe it myself, and that's why I didn't trade it. How could I be held responsible for what some other guy does?"

"Because the lawyer that stole the idea is going to get up on the stand and say he passed it to your buddy. And then one of the traders downstream is going to say he got the idea from Drimal who told him he got it from you and . . . and that he *knew* it was inside info at the time. And then if that isn't enough, the government is going to play an hour of recorded calls of you telling Drimal that shit. So just because you didn't trade it doesn't mean they're not going to hang you."

"You're fucking insane, you know that?" Zvi replied aggressively. "Try telling a guy on the jury, one of those $35K a year bums, that if you had a lotto ticket worth a million dollars, you wouldn't cash it? That's essentially what you're telling them. I had an idea worth over a million bucks and did *nothing* with it. And I should go to jail for that?"

It was true that Zvi could describe a situation in which he had heard big inside information and chosen not to act on it himself for financial gain. And yet he *had* received something for it. As the recordings would show, he had received the gig at Galleon.

"Raj isn't going to win," I reminded Zvi quietly. I didn't want to fight the real battle now, and my tone told Zvi that I was just voicing an opinion, not looking for a challenge.

Moe had been right virtually every time, whether it was the wiretaps, *Contorinis**, or any of the motions we had filed. From Day One, Moe had said "Raj has no shot," and I agreed with him. I knew Raj was done. I think by this time everybody in the Northern Hemisphere knew that, with the exception of Zvi (and of course Nu, who was only following his brother).

What I didn't say aloud was that I suspected Zvi had an even worse shot at winning than Raj.

"You don't understand," Zvi fired back, incapable of letting it go. "Anil Kumar is done. They made him look like a fool. His whole testimony was suspect."

"Why? Because he forged a doctor's note?" I asked incredulously.

"Goes to credibility," Zvi said, suddenly turning nebulous and general.

---

* While we were on pre-trial, Joseph Contorinis, a former Jeffries money manager, was convicted of insider trading that prosecutors say netted $7 million in profit. He was tipped off by UBS AG investment banker Nicos Stephanou about upcoming acquisitions and mergers. There were no tapes and only testimony by Steohanou (that was inconsistent). Contorinis also testified in his defense and was slapped with a perjury charge by Judge Sullivan for doing so. Contorinis was sentenced to six years in prison

"No, goes to *sleep* . . . as in *the jury was going to sleep*. You don't get it. Raj is like a murderer with the victim's blood all over him, fingerprints on the weapon, and three eyewitnesses—but wait, one of them says he thinks the shirt Raj was wearing when he butchered that woman was sky blue, yet it turns out the shirt was actually robin's egg blue. And you think *that's* going to save him? It won't make a fucking difference. Every witness has the same story on the important parts, and most of it is on tape!"

Tapes that aren't a tenth as bad as your tapes, I'm sure, you fucking scumbag, I thought.

By now, Nu had sidled over to listen. Accustomed—addicted?—to drinking every night with me, or Zvi, or the other friend or two he still had, Nu heard the same propaganda from Zvi day in and day out. At this point, I wouldn't have been surprised if Nu genuinely thought there was no chance of Zvi being convicted.

"What about the tapes and Santarlas?" I asked again, since Zvi was mugging for the crowd around us with a "Ya believe this guy?" shake of his head

But before Zvi could respond, someone pulled the string out of Nu's back and he began squawking.

"You know, the government thought they had a much bigger case. This was so trumped up . . . six stocks . . . the Octopus, whatever . . . And now it's just one stock."

Nu drank every night until he couldn't remember. Not to black out, *per se*, but just enough to wipe the slate clean. *Tabula rasa*. On multiple occasions he would repeat the exact same stories on Wednesday night that he had regaled us with on Tuesday. His absentmindedness had become increasingly worse as Raj's trial dragged on. Now, hanging out with Nu was like having my own personal Groundhog Day.

"Nu, that doesn't fucking matter," I barked at him. "None of that matters. Just shut the fuck up."

I wanted to hear Zvi's answer, not his. I had already told him fourteen times in the last fifteen months that the government could charge 200 stocks, 200 different counts, and you could be innocent on 199 counts, but if there's one—just one—that you're not clean on, jail still awaited.

"Remember that terrorism case that was going on during the *Contorinis* trial?" I cried. "The guy that was acquitted of literally 199 out of 200 counts?

Literally 199 out of 200! But guess what? The one count he was convicted on still carried a life sentence.* Big win for the defense lawyer and defendant, huh? Is that what you're saying?"

"I don't know," Nu said as though I were quibbling over something minor "The government blew this whole thing up out of proportion. They kept saying this was a massive conspiracy, $20 million run by the Octopus. But where's the money? Where's the . . ."

"The Octopus?" I interrupted. "Are you fucking serious, man? It's Octopussy! Not Octopus."

"Well, Octopussy. Whatever. You got what I'm saying."

"Yeah, we do," I said, shaking my head, and turned back to Zvi, who was, by now, red from both alcohol and glowering.

"So the government drops the entire case except 3Com?" I said to Zvi. "Now what?"

"We throw that in their face and make them look stupid," Zvi said. "Agent Makol perjured himself all over the arrest warrant and wiretap applications. Shankar perjured himself at his own allocution. Plate's whole story is a fabrication he made up to cut a deal."

Here it was again, the same litany. A broken record when the entire world had moved onto MP3s. It might have carried some weight back in 2005, when everyone was rich and getting richer, unemployment was below 5 percent, and nobody gave a fuck about what Wall Streeters did. Now, people were ravenous for justice, and the government had to toss Main Street some banker-trader red meat.

"All we need is *one*," Zvi said, repeating a familiar refrain.

He meant one juror, one angry man, one lone wolf nutcase.

Nu and Zvi tossed this revelation back and forth like a baseball. Then Zvi commanded Nu to fire up another round along with some shots while he went to the bathroom. I turned to take in the scenery and try to remember why I was here again—what was the damn point of coming to this place? The utility had passed, and now it just seemed like punishment, penance,

---

* On November 17, 2010, Ahmed Ghailani was acquitted of all but one of the charges against him. He "was found guilty conspiring to destroy property and buildings of the United States." (from an FBI press release) http://www.internationalcrimesdatabase.org/Case/954/Ghailani/.

Sisyphus on Wall Street. The drinks were large, top shelf, and free. Would I have been there without that perk? I didn't know the answer, and didn't want to think too hard about it because a "no way" meant I had a serious problem elsewhere.

Zvi seemed to be turning even more aggressive, if that were possible. We hadn't yet had a serious altercation; I knew an actual fistfight or serious argument would mean the end of my opportunity to persuade, the end of my information conduit. But still, now I could barely contain my disgust when looking at Zvi. The way he acted, what he had become.

Yet the sad fact remained that we were likely to be linked, now. Barring a miracle, the window had all but certainly closed, and we were going to trial. I saw little to be gained in making open enemies of Zvi and Nu at this point.

So instead, I mostly watched Zvi prattle on. I tried to feign interest in his lies about the different attorneys falling over themselves to represent him.* Or the fantasy of Raj winning.

A week later, Zvi's new attorney was David Markus—the second attorney he hired that he claimed had "never lost in Federal Court."

"What happened to Glover?"

"Grover. It's not Danny Glover. It's Grover. Douglas Grover."

"Okay. What happened to Grover?" I asked. The image of the Muppet Grover still popped into my constantly aching head.

"Nothing happened. He still wants the case, bad, but I think I may have found someone better."

"Better how?"

"Undefeated better, that's how."

---

* This week it was legendary defense lawyer Gerald Shargel. Zvi told me how Shargel had brought him into his lush, paneled office and clicked a hidden button under the desk that brought down a soundproof reflective black glass cover over the windows to prevent the feds, and other intrusive parties, from eavesdropping or reading lips—apparently a common practice against Shargel's clients. Zvi claimed Shargel offered him a $500K "all-in" deal to represent him in this case. Shargel's fees normally run minimum seven figures for a trial. Furthermore, another defendant had already met with Shargel and debriefed him, so it's likely that he was conflicted out. But I would only learn those facts later. For now, as always, they weren't about to get in the way of a good story from Zvi.

I looked up the resume and saw David Markus had few "name" cases. There was no place to find actual stats on lawyers—there was no Bill James Handbook or ESPN.com equivalent for an athlete, to confirm career home runs or touchdowns. However, a Google search quickly revealed that this was the guy representing Buju Banton, the big-time reggae superstar indicted for conspiracy to distribute cocaine.

"He's fighting them. You watch this case," Zvi exhorted.

I had heard of the case. At this point, I didn't care. Anyone would be superior to Cynthia. Zvi needed someone that would smack him in the face, make him stand up straight, then look him in the eyes and tell him to play ball because he had no fucking shot. Zvi had no legal ground to stand on. If he was intent on fighting, his lawyer's only real shot would be to put the government on trial—put on a show and do anything he could to divert the jury from the fact that his client sounded like the offspring of a Bonanno family street goon and Bernie Madoff. Yet even that, I knew, would probably not work in the end.

It didn't matter. Nothing mattered. Zvi was still thrilled with the new development.

According to Zvi, the best part of "hiring" Markus had been that the deal included getting his partner, William "Bill" Barzee, for free.

"Barzee thought the case was so outrageous that he agreed to help Markus with the defense—no charge!" Zvi gleefully announced.

A former federal public defender, Barzee had tried hundreds of cases and had what Zvi claimed was "invaluable" courtroom experience. At this point, of course, I knew I couldn't believe a word coming out of Zvi's mouth regarding anything. At least the falsehoods he was telling now showed that he had taken my criticism of his former attorney's lack of actual defense experience to heart. There's a world of difference between prosecution and defense. The biggest difference is probably that it's challenging to get evidence admitted when you're on the defense side. It's an art, and you have to learn it. The prosecution, on the other hand, is allowed to present virtually anything, no problem.

Then, within a week of Zvi's hiring him, Markus lost his first case ever when Buju Banton was convicted of conspiracy to distribute cocaine. The next time I saw Nu, I made sure to tell him that Buju's case was 100 percent more triable than Zvi's, and that Zvi's "undefeated superstar" had just gotten his ass kicked by a prosecutor who wouldn't get a call back after a first round interview in the Southern District. After a few drinks, Nu admitted for the umpteenth time that his brother's case *might* have some "problems." Not his brother, mind you, just the case.

"I guess it's not going to be easy to explain some of those tapes to a jury . . ." he allowed.

Yet Nu stayed committed to following his brother.

Once Zvi started running with the ball, it was going to take an immovable object to stop him. Abstractly, I sort of admired this—or at least stopped to realize I was seeing something rare and remarkable. Almost no one has that type of faith and persistence when faced with long odds. He was just wired differently. But would that save him? Could that kind of insane focus and denial of reality save anybody?

I realized I was going to find out very soon.

"Holy shit, turn on the TV. Did you see the news?" I shouted into my cell phone. President Obama was standing at a podium in front of the White House telling the American people that an elite special forces unit called Seal Team Six had just killed the world's most wanted terrorist, Osama bin Laden. The man responsible for September 11th, the man who had caused greatest heartache of the young century, was apparently now in a pine box after being killed in a raid deep inside of Pakistan.

"It's about fucking time!" I continued.

"Yeah, no, it's great news," Moe replied into my ear. "Great for everyone . . . except you . . . and bin Laden, I suppose."

I assumed he was joking and laughed. But the tone in his voice and lack of follow up told me he was serious.

"Wait, what are you talking about?"

"You're a smart guy, Mike. Do the math."

After a brief pause, it registered. And I wanted to puke.

"Fuck that. No way."

But even as I offered these protestations, some part of me already knew the answer.

Bin Laden's capture was sure to cause a spike in American pride and patriotism. The greatest country on earth had offed its greatest nemesis, and the outpouring of love and nationalism would surely engender chants of "USA . . .

USA . . . USA" as it was now literally doing in corner bars and town squares all across the country. It was great for everyone. Except bin Laden and me. Except for Case No. S1: 10 Cr. 56-06 *The United States v. Michael Kimelman*. The prosecutors I was facing wore American flag pins and called themselves Team USA in public. In light of the current mood, I was going to come off like one of Osama's henchmen going up against Ronald Reagan with a bald eagle on his shoulder.

"*The United States v. Michael Kimelman*," Moe announced in case I hadn't made the link yet. "You'll be lucky if the judge doesn't ask for a moment of silence and the jurors to recite the Pledge of Allegiance before deliberation. When they get done with you, Zarqawi will be more sympathetic."

I knew that Moe was right. It was only a question of "To what degree?"

After two weeks of deliberate, persuasive testimony from informants and lots of circumstantial evidence on trade timing, the government rested its case against Raj. During cross-examination, Raj's all-star legal team had managed to isolate some small discrepancies in the cooperator's testimony and actions, but nowhere near enough to challenge the fundamental idea that they had been engaged in a criminal conspiracy headed by Raj to secure inside information. I had to hand it to them. The feds had presented a compelling case, and unless one of the jurors was looking to pull an OJ and vote for Raj just because they were a melanin match, Raj was cooked.

Not surprisingly, the Brothers Goffer still maintained a different view of things.

"Now that the defense gets to put on their case, you're gonna see what Akin Gump is all about," Zvi boasted to me at Sutton Place while fist bumping Joe Mancuso and Nu.

"What Akin Gump is all about?" I scoffed. "They're all about collecting $50 million in legal fees and saying we did the best we could with an unwinnable case. You're still fucking kidding yourself, Zvi. This isn't a poker tournament, where Dowd's been hiding an ace up his sleeve. This game is *over*."

Zvi bristled.

"That's exactly what Dowd has. You're naive if you don't think so, Michael. You don't spend $50 million on lawyers and not get something special. These guys are the A-team. You'll see."

"Dude, this isn't a TV show," I replied. "Dowd is not going to call Agent Kang to the stand and make him break down and say he made the whole thing up. Defense cases are made *during the government's case*, by blowing up the government's witnesses and destroying their credibility. What could Dowd possibly come up with at this point? Give me an example, Zvi. What's going to rebut the things that Raj said on tape, or that Adam Smith and Anil Kumar said on the stand? All these people have made it clear that Raj received inside information, and knew precisely what it was. And how about his good buddy Rajat Gupta calling him the second after the Goldman board meeting ended and teeing up the Buffet investment for him? C'mon. Give me an example of something that rebuts that?"

"I don't know what it is," Zvi said confidently. "But I know it's going to be spectacular."

Nu nodded along.

I wasn't buying it.

"The only thing that even raises the possibility of something interesting happening is if Raj gets on the stand," I told Zvi. "That's all they can do. There's no Galleon analyst out there that's going to get up there and say, 'Yeah, I gave Raj the same exact picks based on my research and that's what he traded. He did nothing wrong.' So, unless Raj gets on the stand, there *is* no defense case."

This was winding me up tightly, so I paused to take a large gulp of vodka. As per usual when we got to talking after watching the proceedings, I felt like punching Zvi in the fucking mouth. I had been warned by Moe that if we actually had a fistfight one night, it was likely both of us would be remanded to Brooklyn MCC until trial. ("Good luck preparing for trial in that hellhole. No sunlight, no outdoors, TVs blaring 24/7 and predators roaming everywhere.") Moe's words kept my hands in my pockets. For the moment.

"And even if Raj takes the stand," I continued, "there's nothing he can say that will be credible. What's he going to do? Convince the jury it had all been a misunderstanding? And good luck handling the prosecutors on cross exam. They'll tear him a new asshole."

"I don't see why he couldn't handle himself," Zvi said. "He fooled the SEC when he was in front of them for a full day's deposition."

"He didn't fool anyone, Zvi. They *knew* he was lying, they just didn't have the proof yet. That's why they referred the case to the FBI. You guys are insane.

I told you before, there's a one percent chance Raj gets acquitted. Now I think I'm down to zero percent. This one's done. But for the fact that it's the job of most of the spectators to be there, that courtroom would look like Dodger Stadium in the seventh inning—empty."

Zvi shook his head dismissively.

"Okay," he said sarcastically. "*You* know more than Dowd and Terrence . . . and Raj. That's why they're worth tens of millions or billions and you're walking around with a Poland Spring bottle filled with vodka."

"That's your brother, not me."

"Yeah, you're worse," Zvi snapped, oozing scorn. "At least he bought that vodka. You're begging for free drinks from bartenders I have a relationship with."

It was the first time he had said something like that. I was sick of his idiocy, and he was tired of my "negativity." Only I was right, and he was a fool. Our relationship, long in limbo, was starting to seriously disintegrate. I couldn't humor his blind confidence anymore. He just wanted to remain a super-optimist until the moment the cell door clanged shut.

For the rest of the night I drank silently, and kept my fists curled in my pockets.

The next morning was Day One for the defense. Everyone was on tenterhooks to see what they would do. As their first witness, Raj's team called Rick Schute, a smart and tough analyst and portfolio manager. The defense team had him lead the jury through the basics of Galleon, the industry, and the regular flow of information for traders. I wasn't sure if it would connect with the jury, but he was putting some real yardage on the board—making sense and being engaging.

At the lunch break, Team Raj spilled out of the courtroom in high spirits, apparently thrilled with Schute's performance. They weren't the only ones. Zvi, Nu, and Kucharsky came out with big grins, practically high-fiving each other. This was all part of the master plan. A Raj acquittal followed by a Zvi acquittal. The only thing missing was the four of us riding off into the sunset together while the credits rolled. The plan had been diagrammed for me in at least a half dozen late night boozefests at Sutton over the last year. It had always felt like a guy planning in detail how he'd spend his future Powerball winnings. (At least with Powerball, if you lose, your life is technically no different than it was before the drawing. Here, if you lose, you're cut off from your family and locked in a cage for an indefinite period of time.)

But after Schute's testimony, Zvi felt like The Plan was within reach. If we'd been on the Sutton Place deck, he would have had a big cigar in his mouth, saying: "I love it when a plan comes together." For the moment, Zvi spoke to his brother in a voice purposely loud enough for a nearby fed to hear, "That just erased all the government's gains from last week in one morning!"

A team of federal agents, looking like they had been sucking on Lemonheads for the past hour, marched right past him to the break room. The prosecutors were not far behind. It was then, with Zvi standing near the elevator, still cackling and smiling, that I saw Raj walk out of the courtroom, surrounded by his cadre of Akin Gump sycophants and cheerleaders. After a brief exchange, he patted one of them on the shoulder, excused himself, and headed straight towards Zvi. My codefendant turned away from Nu and locked eyes with his former boss, the man he idolized. Zvi's arrogant smile was now in check, his lids all aflutter. Raj had been arrested eighteen months ago, Zvi seventeen. They had not spoken since. Zvi had claimed that Raj had acknowledged him in the courtroom, with the occasional nod, but I hadn't seen it, and I had been watching carefully. Yet here was Raj, in the middle of his trial, at the center of a feeding frenzy of press, lawyers, and other random observers, heading straight for Zvi. My mind flooded with images of Hinckley, Jack Ruby, or Squeaky Fromme. Was this what it was like for witnesses at those kind of events? Did you freeze while everything moved in slow motion? Because that's what was happening for me. Raj opened his arms for Zvi while they were still several feet apart, and Zvi walked right up to Raj and returned a giant hug.

"I know," was all that Raj said to him, making some powerful eye contact, then breaking it off and returning to his cadre of lawyers.

It was probably the single most important moment of Zvi's life. He turned to Nu, perhaps to see his response, but probably to hide his face from the crowd. Zvi was tearing up. The crowd moved past and slowly dissipated. Soon it was just us.

"I'm the only one . . . the only one," Zvi said to his brother. "He knows, Nu. I'm the only one. Everyone else stabbed him in the fucking gut. His lifelong friends? They couldn't wait to walk up to him and twist the knife. But I'm the standup one. Raj'll never forget that. You can't put a price on that type of loyalty. *He knows.* He might put $50 million down with Incremental Day One. Our future is wide open. This is gonna be real."

Zvi eyes were misting over as he stared out the eighteenth-floor window at the East River. In a year that had been painfully short of hope and good news, I let him enjoy his moment. I didn't have the heart to tell him a $50 million investment was about as likely as an acquittal.

The feeling of exhilaration we got from Schute's spirited bunker defense lasted less than twenty-four hours. I took a pass on Sutton Place that night, knowing that it was going to be an unabashed Raj lovefest. My last best hope was still to have Zvi cop a plea. And now I was farther away from it than I'd ever been before.

The next morning, it was Assistant United States Attorney Reed Brodsky's turn to tackle Schute on cross examination. Little did we know he had a golden gun in his pocket. After a couple of opening feints, Brodsky let it fire.

"So, Mr. Schute, Raj Rajaratnam gave you $25 million for your fund, isn't that correct?" Brodsky asked, already knowing the answer.

"Yes. Mr. Rajaratnam is an investor in my fund," Schute had answered.

Little did we know, but that was already checkmate.

Schute spent the rest of the morning trying to explain that the $25 million was still Raj's money, and he could take it back whenever he wanted. That it wasn't really *his* money, and that Raj had not really *given* it to him. But Schute's protestations did little to help. The jury, mouths agape, simply heard that Raj had given him $25 million. No wonder this guy was up here testifying about how aboveboard Raj was.

Two-bit corner drug dealers might leave $15K cash in a manila envelope under the door when they wanted to see a witness change their tune, *but here's how we do it in the hedge fund world, folks!* The jury saw it as an enormous bribe.

"For $25 million, he *better* be a good witness," I joked to the agent sitting in front of me, just to see if I would get a response. He gave me a big smile and a knowing snicker.

As the prosecution continued, the gist of the cross became clear. It was a very simple idea, and would be easy for the jury to understand. *This guy has been . . . PAID. You can't believe anything he's saying. For $25M, I'd tell you Raj was better looking than George Clooney and hung like John Holmes.*

Once again, it felt like game over.

The next day's witness was Geoffrey Canada, founder of the Harlem Boys Club. His was a tremendously inspirational story, and Raj was a critical and consistent backer of Mr. Canada and his vision. At the same time, at this stage of the game, a character witness wasn't going to cut it. I could almost hear the jury thinking: *You're a billionaire. Giving to community improvement organizations is what rich people are supposed to do. So what?*

The mood in 2011 was so angry and rife with socioeconomic envy, a billionaire wasn't about to get extra credit for giving a little of his hard-earned (stolen?) millions to charity. And the racial connections between the communities Mr. Canada served and some of the jurors left a bad taste in many people's mouths. Raj had given his money to this organization years before any investigation—and it was obviously a heartfelt gift of incredible generosity to a worthy cause—but why bring it up now, like this? In the hallways during the bathroom breaks, everyone whispered about "black jurors and little black kids."

Soon, the only question remaining was whether Raj was going to take the stand and testify himself. The first three defense witnesses, Schute, Canada, Gregg Jarrell (an expert paid a small fortune to present charts and stats showing Raj *could have* received his info from publicly available sources), had proven ineffective at best. After Jarrell concluded, it wasn't clear that Raj had any other witnesses left to call.

So either the big man himself was going to take the stand, or Akin Gump was going to fold and hope a "king high" hand was good enough to win. When pondering whether or not a defendant should testify, the standard defense playbook instructs the defense to *always make it seem as if the defendant will testify.* This makes the prosecution lose precious time preparing to cross examine the defendant. It's time that could be better spent on other witnesses. Raj's team went with the textbook bluff.

Each time Judge Holwell asked Raj's lawyers—usually at the prosecution's behest—whether their client would testify, Dowd gave the standard response: "We plan on making a game time decision, but believe the defendant will in fact testify."

Dowd uttered it in such a deliberate and believable fashion that by the end of the trial, every article predicted Raj would take the stand. The defense bluff may have been standard operating procedure, but it worked. *I* also felt it was likely Raj would indeed testify—if only because if he chose not to, at this point, to any educated observer, he was clearly finished. Done. Why not play that final card? You never know.

Unless Raj had a juror in his pocket, this trial was over, and the King of Hedge Fund Kings was going to jail for a very long time. Raj taking the stand was the sole remaining chance for the defense to present a compelling alternative to the prosecution's narrative and correct the "misleading" portrait of the defendant that had been presented by the government. Raj and his lawyers *had to know* that.

Then it came.

Dowd stood up and mucked the defense's final hand.

"The defense rests, your Honor."

It prompted surprise murmuring from the gallery, and quiet exhalation from Streeter and Brodsky. Closing statements were to begin the following day.

"The defense *rested*!" were my first words to Moe and Sommer as I walked through their conference room door.

"Doesn't matter," Moe quipped. "That one was over before it began."

"So how long do they deliberate for? Want to do a pool?"

"Sure," said Sommer. "Seventy-two hours."

"We're doing days, forget hours. So you're at three days?" I said. "Moe?"

"Two days."

"I guess I'm at four," I decided. "I like three, though. I think that's the real number."

What we left unsaid was the expected verdict.

"So what are we doing today?" I asked my team.

"I want to review some of the 302s," Sommer began.

I agreed that this was a good idea. I had been looking through the 302s myself.

302s were written FBI records of statements proffered by cooperators. You'd think, in the twenty-first century, that such things would be kept as digital audio files. According to Sommer, there was a reason the FBI wanted to hang on to the paper transcript format. Namely, because they could selectively omit (unintentionally, of course) any part of a statement given by a cooperator that did not help their cases.

"I don't see how Shankar and Tudor don't come off as completely insane, in these," Sommer said. "So where should we start?"

"I've been compiling sort of a 'greatest hits' sheet on the 302s," I said. "Why don't we start with Shankar, since he's about half the case with Hilton?"

Hilton was one of the trades I was charged with having made improperly.

"Shankar it is," Sommer said. "What are your thoughts so far?"

"Well, as you know, before we were arrested, Shankar was the only part of the case that I knew about," I told him. "Like, I didn't know at the time I traded it, but eventually I found out that the Hilton call originated with Shankar. On the afternoon of July second, Zvi called me when I was trading at Quad and told me he was 'hearing that Hilton might be in play.' That was what he said and how he said it. Nothing illegal. No inside info. I bought a small position and sold most of it the next day, when it was up pre-market. Not long after, the Jeffries analyst came out with a note saying Hilton was in late stage talks with private equity. I added to my position and the stock started ramping from there. That evening, Blackstone announced it was buying Hilton for $47 in cash. The stock had been trading in the $34–$37 range beforehand."

Sommer said, "Okay, I'm with you so far. How much stock did you own?"

"About 15,000 shares."

"So you made around $150K?"

"A little more. I traded it that day too, and made some more money."

"Go on."

"So it seemed like a good call, but not too suspicious. The Jeffries note was right on, and the trading action before the note seemed to indicate there was some speculation. There were multiple instant messages coming out of Schottenfeld and other firms that the Hotel Group was under accumulation and the rumor was that a top-tier analyst was going to upgrade the group. At the time, I didn't give the call a second thought. Zvi didn't know where Gautham got the call from, or if he did, he wasn't telling, and based on the Jeffries note, clearly there were some leaks and management was talking to someone. A second-tier bank like Jeffries doesn't publish a note like that unless the news is outrageous. So it didn't bother me until Raj got arrested and the criminal complaint specifically mentioned Hilton. That made me think maybe Shankar got Hilton from Raj or maybe they both got it from the same person. It turned out to be a little more complicated."

Moe stepped in.

"Deep Shah, who worked at Moody's, gave it to Roomy Khan. Roomy passed it on to Raj directly, but she also passed it on to Tom Hardin, who worked at the Lanexa Fund, a hedge fund affiliated with Tiger Management. Then Hardin to Shankar to Zvi, and from Zvi to Mike and about fifteen other people."

"That's correct," I said. "Tiger and SAC are the two big dogs in the equity hedge fund game. They're responsible for seeding and spinning off more managers than nearly every other fund combined. As to Gautham, I only met him twice—actually three times; once was when he interviewed for a job at Incremental. He seemed odd—annoying and egotistical, and a bit shady. After Raj's arrest, Zvi 'confessed' to me that he thought Shankar was the rat mentioned in the Raj complaint. Zvi also believed Shankar had worn a wire. I asked Zvi if he had anything to be concerned about and he basically said no. However, he did reveal that he paid Shankar cash on multiple occasions. Zvi paid Shankar cash for his calls as a 'thank you,' he said, and also because Shankar kept asking to borrow money. Zvi said Shankar needed cash to pay his dying grandfather's medical bills in India, and because he was having trouble paying his mortgage. Zvi made it sound like he paid him not because it was a part of a tit-for-tat arrangement, but because he wanted to help a guy out when he was struggling."

"Shankar talks in the 302s about Zvi Goffer paying him $10,000," Sommer said.

"Well that's the thing," I told him. "I was kind of willing to give Zvi the benefit of the doubt with the cash payments . . . that is, until one day when I asked him how much he had given Shankar. Zvi told me that, all in, it came to over $100,000."

"Holy shit," Sommer exclaimed.

"That was literally my response."

Moe said: "Just the sheer amount, $100,000, makes it all feel . . . less clean."

"Again, that was my reaction," I said. "And when I kind of freaked out a little, Zvi started downplaying the significance. Shankar was talking about having to permanently move back to India, he said. Zvi just wanted him to be financially secure."

"So he's backpedaling a little," Sommer said. "It's like he's just trying to keep you from panicking."

"Yes and no. On the tapes, you hear Shankar—this is before he starts cooperating—you hear him telling Zvi he needs money for his mortgage and for his sick relative. So that part's true. But I don't think he's asking for $100,000. Maybe that's the cumulative total Zvi gave him over the course of a year. $10K here, $20K there. Who knows?"

"The best part about Shankar's 302 is when he says he feels totally guilty about the $10K payoff so instead of keeping the money, he gave it away to an Eastern European homeless woman in Grand Central," said Sommer.

"That's basically the craziest thing I've ever heard," Moe said, livid as hell. "It's clearly bullshit. He just doesn't want to have to give it back, or he knows something is up and is trying to make himself more 'likable' for the FBI and the judge who will ultimately sentence him."

"A jury will laugh him out of the room," I added. "It totally destroys his credibility when he says he felt so guilty about the cash. And then his next move is to go out and extort Dave Plate for another $5K!"

"Plate also said he didn't think Shankar was paying anyone off," Moe noted. "He thought Shankar was just keeping the money."

"I am confident Shankar got a lot more than $10K from Zvi, and that he kept most of it," I said. "I think there's got to be a way we can nail him on that."

Sommer said: "Unless you testify, or Zvi testifies, I'm not sure we can."

"Anyway, it's interesting that I wasn't worried about 3Com or any of the R&G stocks at this point. I thought the case was pretty much Hilton. I knew Zvi had some issues though, Shankar or not. His time at Galleon overlaps with the time the government cares about in Raj's criminal complaint."

"Anything else for Shankar we should note?" Sommer asked.

"You mean besides the fact that during his allocution, he pled guilty to insider trading in Avaya? A stock that even the R&G guys had never heard of. It was just another Zvi vapor tip, but Shankar pled guilty to it. Also, in his allocution, he claimed that he now understands that 3Com was insider info, but didn't at the time. He has to *know* it was insider info in order to be guilty."

"That's good; we can hit him hard on that during cross," Sommer said with a smile. "Let's step back now and review. The highlights for Shankar are as follows:

1. He pled 'guilty' to a stock trade no one alleges there was inside info on, which shows the FBI and USAO were completely fooled by circumstantial evidence, the same circumstantial evidence they're trying to convict *you* on. This is important. It shows they did not even understand what was happening.

2. He testified Hilton 'could be in play' when he pled guilty. That's a rumor, as opposed to real inside info.

3. He lies about the size of the cash payments he got from Zvi and then compounds that lie by claiming he gave the money to an Eastern European woman in Grand Central."

"Maybe we should hire OJ to find her?" I chimed in. "Because she's so definitely real."

"Or, we could do a five-person lineup and see if he can pick her out?" Moe added.

"And four," Sommer continued, not missing a beat. "On the tapes, there is a tip Shankar gives to Zvi which Zvi doesn't relay to you. There's also a series of phone calls where Zvi clearly excludes you from the insider info he has and tells Raj and Drimal."

"This is all solid stuff," Moe noted.

"Now, ahem, Michael," Sommer said as if broaching a delicate topic. But what on earth, I wondered, could be more delicate than these facts which would decide my fate?

"There's one more thing I wanted to bring up," Sommer said, doing his best Columbo. "I don't think we've had this discussion before, but we are not going to get any surprises at trial *about your background*, are we? What I'm asking is, have you ever been in trouble with the law before or is this your first time?"

Technically this wasn't my first experience with the FBI. Technically.

There had been a little incident in which my father-in-law had called the FBI after I'd failed to come home one night, felled by an all-night drinking contest against Jason Giambi. I awoke the next day around noon on Yankee reliever Tanyon Sturtze's couch. (What do you want me to say? I was a Wall Street guy who sometimes did Wall Street guy things. Hanging out with MLB players was sometimes part of it.) I'd awoken to a series of worried messages from my wife, my father-in-law, and the FBI, but it had eventually amounted to nothing. I had apologized profusely to each, and promised to do a better job of letting my family know where and when I was about to black out in the future.

"Nothing more than a speeding ticket twenty-five years ago," I responded, deciding to leave that tale untold.

"Good," Sommer replied. "Our position is going to be that you're a family man who is active in the community and in philanthropy. We're going to say that you're a guy who has never had even a hint of trouble with the law before. I want to make sure that story is intact."

"It's the truth, it's not a 'story,'" I said defensively.

"There is no 'truth,' only what we can prove to a jury," Sommer responded with a hint of disgust at my naivete. "Now, let's get back to work. Where were we?"

CHAPTER SEVENTEEN

PISSING OUT OF THE TENT

———

AFTER YET ANOTHER GRUELING PRE-TRIAL SESSION, I made my way east on 53rd Street, crossing a handful of avenues along my well-worn path to Sutton Place. I paused to look north, toward the corner of Park Avenue and 55th Street—the offices of Incremental—which now seemed like an ancient dream from another life. To the south was 270 Park, the building I'd worked in for Chemical Bank right after college, now a Bear Stearns mausoleum. Morbid bookends of my adult existence. I'm not sure I would recognize either today.

The more we delved into the information about my case at these pre-trial sessions, the sillier and sillier it seemed that my life could be destroyed over it. The fact that it was so silly, and yet so serious, made me feel angry. The anger was a pilot light, a steady blue flame that was always on and could never be entirely shut off. It produced fury directed toward the federal government at one end, and toward Zvi Goffer at the other. Yet there was also, underneath it all, frustration with myself. I had not been smart enough to dodge the bullet. I had taken the risk of riding passenger with a drunk sociopath.

And perhaps I was still doing it. I was still in that car.

There was no reason on earth why I should have ventured to Sutton Place that night—or any other. Zvi's opinions were objectively worthless, and had been for some time. My lone remaining hope of convincing him to plead out had all but evaporated. If I'm being honest, the offer of free drinks among the similarly situated was a siren song I couldn't resist. Amid the fear and stress was a yearning for empathy and belonging. I justified these visits to the bar by focusing on our tribal identities: we were federal defendants traversing the same dangerous paths. It made sense for us to stick together and learn from one another.

In truth, I had a problem.

Starting at noon, I would literally count down the hours until I could have a drink. I had trouble remembering the last day I'd gone without one. Stopping or slowing down was never a consideration. In the city, I could pretend it was about fellowship or ritual. Drinking alone at home, or in front of Lisa and the kids, meant hiding refills and being subtle about it.

This afternoon I was amped up, and kept reminding myself on the walk over to have two drinks before I opened my mouth about the conclusion of the Raj case. Two would temper me—would temper us—I thought. At first it went okay. Tired and dispirited, we engaged in strained small talk about weather and the Yanks. But then Nu went for the jugular.

"So, what do you think?" Nu finally popped the $64,000 question after just one drink.

"What do I think?" I feigned ignorance.

"About Raj. Not taking the stand and all."

"Three days," I answered, and took a long sip of my cocktail, trying to act casual—as though the subject of our discussion did not chill me to the bone.

"What d'you mean three days?" Nu said.

"In three days, Raj will be remanded to Brooklyn MDC to await sentencing," I said, taking another large sip to numb myself. "He's probably looking at fifteen years, which at his age and with his health is a life sentence. So he has three days of freedom left before he steps inside of a prison for the remainder of his life."

Zvi started laughing, a harsh, forced laugh. Nu smiled along. The rest of Zvi's drinking-buddy drones laughed too, although I doubt they were sure what they were laughing about.

"Keep dreaming," Zvi scoffed. "This thing is far from over."

I hesitated, knowing tensions were only bound to escalate. But I also knew that ignoring Zvi was the only thing worse than disagreeing with him.

When I didn't instantly respond, Zvi pressed down hard on the accelerator: "What I can't understand is, why are *you* going to trial, Michael? If you think we have such a small chance of winning—as you always say—why bother? You've got a great deal on the table. Why not take it? They didn't offer me anything I could take. Five years. If I lose I get six, so there's no 'choice' to make. It's a no-brainer to go to trial."

I laughed—I couldn't help it. This triggered Zvi. He turned red. It also kick-started his jaw muscles into overdrive, like he had just scarfed a gram of cocaine.

"Were we watching the same trial?" I asked. "Dowd and Co. got their asses kicked all over that courtroom. There wasn't any sleeve ace at the end, either. Just the government scoring point after point. This one's done. At best, Raj has a 5 percent chance of a hung jury and zero of acquittal. And you know what? The sad thing is . . . his odds are better than yours."

This time I was direct, in his face: You're fucking going to prison, Zvi, and you are dragging me and your brother with you.

Zvi turned claret red, lips snarling. He responded before he checked himself:

"I can't listen to this nonsense. They're not going to destroy my life and family without a fight. You may have lost the faith, Mike . . . and your nerve. But I haven't. I *can't wait* to see the inside of that courtroom. They're not going to know what hit them. We're going to blow this bullshit case out of the water and put *them* on trial. When this is over, the jury is going to laugh the government right out of that courtroom."

I let Zvi storm off to the other end of the bar. Nu and the crew crept away from me. Silence followed. Whether it was a bathroom break or a time out, Zvi didn't stroll back for another fifteen minutes.

"You've got to keep the faith," he said, now relatively calm. "You're giving them way too much credit, Michael. Their whole case is based on a guy who was two for twelve, and one of those stocks, we didn't even trade! Remember, they've got one stock. One! And the *Wall Street Journal* ran an article right before we bought it saying, in the clearest terms imaginable, that 3Com was in takeover talks with Bain Capital. If that's not public info I don't know what is. Their witnesses are absurd! Don't forget that I lost a total of $50 million or so trading these calls."

"Raj lost $50. You lost about $7 million."

"Okay, excuse me! I lost $7 million! And the guy I tipped lost $50 million. Those numbers show what a joke this case is. An insider trading case where the defendant lost millions? That's a helluva edge!"

These were sentimental arguments. I did not think they would mean much for a jury.

"That stuff counts," I admitted, "but the law is twisted. And the judges and prosecutors aren't going to emphasize the losses; they're going to point out you made $400K in a single day on 3Com. They're going to play tape after tape of you sounding like you're conspiring. And they're going to lie their asses off to make you and your brother sound like complete criminals. It doesn't even matter anymore. You've made your choice. And you know what? I hope you guys break 'em off something. I really do. But I have to live with your choice too. I'm here because of you. I need to do the best I can to present *my* side, because it's a lot different than yours and you know that. And six years? That's *your* guess, Zvi. I know your lawyers didn't tell you that. Word on the street is that the real number is eight to ten. And if you go strictly by the guidelines? Then it's ten to twelve years. There's a huge difference between five years—home in three—and ten years. Huge for you, your family, and your life. But we've had this conversation already. And you're going forward with the trial, so it doesn't matter."

"You're fuckin' right I'm going forward," Zvi said. "If we put the government on trial and highlight the ridiculous errors in this case, we'll win. There are guys on the government's side who should be in jail for perjury. There are hundreds of missing wiretap calls the government deleted because they helped our case! There are *illegal* wiretap calls. The ACLU is going to have a field day when we make this stuff public."

I shook my head.

"If you were going to get the ACLU involved, the time to do so would have been during the wiretap suppression hearing. You guys didn't do that. You guys didn't even flag that the feds accidentally wiretapped an innocent guy in Boston for two months because they had a wrong number! You didn't do any of that! So it's irrelevant."

I for one didn't have enough money to file my own motion to suppress the taps, and the motion that Zvi's old lawyer Cynthia had filed was mediocre at best. It had omitted several key points.

"If it was so critical, how come *you* didn't weigh in?"

"I've got limited funds, and have to pick my battles," I explained. "The tapes don't really hurt *me*. They're a big problem for *you*."

"Yeah, big problem," Zvi said sarcastically. "Whatever. It will all be fine when I testify."

"You're not going to testify," I scoffed.

"That's where you're wrong. I *am* going to testify. Nobody can explain it better."

"So what will you say about promising Jenkins $500K in a bag?"

"I was just getting him pumped," Zvi said. "That's what I'll say. It was a figure of speech. Besides, where am I going to get $500K in a bag from?"

"I dunno. Where'd you get $100K from for Shankar?"

"It doesn't matter. That's all puffery, see. I was stroking that idiot Jenkins to get him excited and hungry. Five hundred in a bag? Gimme a break."

Things got quiet for a few seconds while we reloaded drinks. Like fighters on the stool between rounds, we looked away and gathered our thoughts.

"Look," Zvi said when we began again, "the important thing to remember is that we're all on the same team. We're all in the same tent, and we have to make sure we're pissing out of the tent together. Otherwise, it's going to be a mess."

This was the speech his lawyers had given him, both Cynthia and now Barzee. Keep Mike on your side, because for him to defend himself, to proclaim his innocence, he has to contrast himself with you and your brother and that's not good for us. Simply put, Zvi understood that my defense could pose a danger to him.

"If you think I'm climbing inside the tent with you and saying we're one and the same, you're out of your fucking mind."

Then, counting off on my fingers, I shouted: "I didn't have a prepaid phone. I didn't make any cash payments. I didn't know Jenkins, Shankar, Cutillo, Santarlas, Drimal, or any of these other fucking lunatic idiots you were speaking to. If you think I'm going to sit quietly and say I did, you need a new lawyer."

That was it. Zvi had always known, but now he really knew. I was approaching green-eyed, gamma reaction angry, and with the full import of my words now fully dawning on Zvi, his rage began to spike.

"That's . . . " He started stuttering, couldn't decide how he wanted to finish, and changed gears. "I was the one that lost the most. I put up most of the money for Incremental. The firm still owes me $500K in trading gains. I'm the one that got the least back and is facing the most time!"

"You lost the most money?" I replied in disbelief. "So what? I lost my life and reputation. Everything I've worked for since the age of eighteen is gone. Every degree, every dollar. My family is falling apart. And it's because of you. Had you been a man and walked in and owned up to what you did, I wouldn't even be here. Your brother might not be here either, and there's an outside chance Incremental would still be in business. So I don't want to hear, 'You lost the most.'"

Zvi took a long breath and then said: "I can't believe you're buying into their lies and BS. You let me down, man. I would have done anything for you."

"Anything but face the music, and tell the truth," I quietly countered, also trying to tone it down.

This was going to end badly if I stayed. Using the excuse that I needed a refill, I took a timeout and lumbered to an opening at the other end of the bar. My hands were shaking as I ordered a vodka and reached for my phone. I thought, *Thank God I convinced him to hire Katten Muchen to oversee the wind-down of Incremental.* Granted, they had done little other than drive up a big bill and get our accounts frozen, but eventually they had been able to get us a portion of our capital back in a somewhat equitable fashion. Without a neutral law firm orchestrating the dissolution, Zvi would have transferred all the unfrozen money in the Incremental account right away to his and Nu's account, leaving me out to twist in the wind.

I got my drink, took a long slug, and walked to the smoker's ledge overlooking Second Avenue to check my messages. I could see Zvi shouting at his brother, his hand running from cheek to chin over his red face.

Watching Zvi, I experienced powerful new feelings of self-hatred and disgust. Four years of my life dedicated to partnering with a madman . . . four years, and counting. We had built a massively profitable firm that was supposed to be both my exit from the rat race and a culmination of a lifetime of hard work. Now all of it was washed away. The nausea I felt at that moment wasn't from drinking on an empty stomach.

I walked the long way around the bar and was soon out the door, unseen, and onto Second Avenue. I headed south to Grand Central. A little bird told me that that was probably the last time Zvi and I would ever speak.

The lunch menus weren't provided on May 11th, a telltale sign that the Raj jury had reached a verdict.

Surprising everyone, they had deliberated for eleven days. The trial had lasted two months, but each day felt like seventy-two hours. Each day without a verdict crushed me, and created a vacuum in which Zvi could grow bolder and cockier. A lightning-fast guilty verdict might have convinced him to rethink taking a plea. When the best law firm that money could buy . . . lost, what chance would a broke Brooklyn knucklehead on his fifth lawyer have?

But Zvi was still eyeing a Raj acquittal.

An acquittal would mean, in his mind—and possibly in the minds of the government's representatives—that these cases truly *weren't* triable. A Raj acquittal would have meant that the government, with all the structural advantages and endless resources, had failed. It certainly would have meant a new round of pleas offered, perhaps three years for Zvi, one for Nu, and a big beautiful DP for me.

But the reality was, unless Raj had bought a juror or two (the way Gotti Senior was rumored to have done), there was no chance that was happening. The delay in getting a verdict meant that our own trial was mere days away, and that I had run out of landing strip.

At 10:15 a.m. the jury foreman notified the court that the jury had come to a unanimous decision. Raj, who had lost nearly one hundred pounds since the start of the trial, arrived and took a seat beside his lawyers. The tension was at heart attack levels—with lives, liberty, and careers all on the line.

Then the judge's deputy, William Donald, announced the counts and rendered the same decision on each.

"Guilty."

Raj remained mostly stone-faced, but blinked precisely once each time the word "guilty" was spoken aloud. I learned this detail later. I was not in court, but walking up Lexington Ave., when the text from Moe arrived. "Guilty." One word, but I knew exactly what it meant: an emboldened, triumphant government; no courtroom-steps sweetheart deals for us; and a trial that started the following Monday.

I had an uncontrollable urge to drink, to hunker down and drown my fears in a Rodney Dangerfield "keep 'em coming until someone passes out, and then bring 'em every fifteen minutes" vodka binge. But I knew that would solve nothing. After that final night on the roof at Sutton, I had resolved to stay sober until after the trial. It was Thursday. On Monday morning I would be in the same building that Raj and his $50 million team of lawyers were now walking out of, heads down, having been handed an ass-whupping of epic proportions. In a mere eighty-five hours, those doors would slam shut and it would be me against the mighty, multi-headed leviathan, me against the Goffer brothers, and me against one Judge Richard Sullivan. It was almost game time. In what moments still remained, I needed to stay sharp and focus on prep. There were still things to do.

Nu had transcribed a series of key body-wires recorded at Incremental the morning of Raj's arrest, which the government had decided to dump on us at the last second. It was yet another dirty trick by the prosecutors, and, in my opinion, it broke the Brady law. (Under that law, they should have included them in the original discovery material shared fifteen months earlier. Brady exists because most cases are resolved by plea, and some defendants would not plea if they knew there was exculpatory evidence out there. Imagine pleading and then finding out after sentencing that there was an eyewitness, tape, or test that cast serious doubt on the prosecution's case?)

I met Nu on the corner of Lexington Avenue and 44th Street, two blocks north of bustling Grand Central Station. I was hopping a 5:35 p.m. Metro North train home, and Nu was off to Sutton Place to end, or more accurately, begin his night. We exchanged discs. I had a moment of intense panic, scanning the parked cars on the street, imagining an FBI photo surveillance team snapping a series of shots through the tinted window of a navy blue Crown Vic. I had read enough John LeCarre novels to know that a still photo of two people exchanging discs on a street corner *always* looks like a conspiracy.

"You coming out for one?" Nu asked expectantly.

I told him no.

"Come on, one beer," Nu implored.

"I don't think so," I answered. Nu asked again.

"How about just one? I know Zvi will want to get your opinion on the verdict, and see what you think."

"I've got too much work to do," I said. "And you know my opinion. You and your brother have known it for months, Nu."

I looked Nu in the eyes, and we stared at each other for a few seconds.

I had spent many nights with Nu over the last year and genuinely felt for him. He was like Lenny from *Of Mice and Men*. He was the loyal but decidedly

slower younger brother—willfully blind to his much brighter brother's machinations. But Nu was also likable. He could be hilarious. A doting father with
a big heart, a decent person who had trusted his kin. Sometimes the double
helix is the toughest dealer of all. Nu didn't choose to have Zvi Goffer as his
older brother. Who knows: had I been in his shoes, I might have done the same
things he had.

"Goodbye, Nu, and good luck," I said, extending my hand.

"You too, bro . . . and come here," he said, brushing past my hand to wrap
me up in a bear hug. "See you on the other side."

After a thirty-minute Metro North express train to Larchmont, I was walking home down Palmer Avenue from the station when I received a text message
from Nu:

"This is crazy here. There's like ten FBI agents toasting and celebrating
Raj's verdict on the Rooftop, including Jan Trigg and a few others from our
case. Hanging out and eyeballing us right in our f'n backyard!"

It was a warm spring night, and yet I shivered head to toe. The FBI's choice
of Sutton Place for the Raj after-party was too much of a coincidence, and after
all the coincidences of the past year, the entire concept of "a coincidence" was
becoming hard for me to credit. The feds had to have known that for the last
fifteen months, Sutton Place had been the Goffers' watering hole, their tree-
house and temple. Either they had been tailing and observing us on a regular
basis, or simply triangulating our phones. We never used a credit card because
the drinks were on the house, and we always tipped in cash. Yet the feds clearly
knew. Oh yeah, they knew. And here was one final Fuck You from them. One
last pre-game psych-out. A giant serving of smack talk right in Zvi's face. The
enemy was dancing on Raj's grave, right in the house that Zvi built.

I said nothing, shook my head, and called Moe.

"I'm glad I didn't go."

"You're *GLAD*? You're fucking lucky as hell, Mike. Had you gone, they
would've snapped a few pictures of you three retards toasting together and
put them up on the whiteboard as the centerpiece of their opening statement."

"That bad, huh?"

"What'd I tell you about surveillance photos? They do them because people
always look guilty in them. We've all seen too many TV shows and movies,
or read too many spy novels. You can be sitting at Starbucks, reading a paper

alone, enjoying a Mocchacino and fantasizing about the hot barista, and in a surveillance photo you look like an double agent awaiting a drop from the KGB. The image of you three clinking beer bottles the day before trial would have been a very bad thing."

I hung up and continued my slow walk home. After catching several stray bullets in the chest over the last two years, was it possible that I'd actually dodged one?

The more I thought about it, the more my opinion changed. I almost had to hand it to the FBI. During the hearings, tapes, and various trials I'd attended, they always came off as humorless drones—modestly competent postal workers packing firearms. But holding their post-verdict party right in Zvi's face, on his hometown turf? It was ballsy. Hell, I might have pulled it myself had I been on the other side.

My one regret—I realized as my house came into view—was that I hadn't be there to see Zvi's reaction. To see how he'd actually handled it. Had he been surprised, or even cowed? Had he stayed defiant and brash? Had he maybe tried to start some shit with the agents after having a few? Anything was possible, I realized.

Because I was dealing with a straight-up madman.

CHAPTER EIGHTEEN

AND JUSTICE FOR ALL

"Courts are the places where the ending is written first and all that precedes is simply vaudeville."

—Charles Bukowski

THE BREAKFAST LINE AT THE SUBSIDIZED Federal Cafe on the eighth floor of 500 Pearl Street is an eclectic mix of defendants, clerks, prosecutors, functionaries, and administrators. It felt exactly how I expected it to feel . . . not completely real. It felt like a dream. Not actually happening to me, Michael Kimelman.

The only one with whom I seemed to be able to share this absurdity was Moe. "Feels crazy, doesn't it?" he remarked at one point.

Oh yeah. You bet your ass it does.

Moe understood the surreal horror such grievous stakes could conjure. Your mind doesn't want to acknowledge that this can really be happening. That your future can really hang in the balance.

Because of the nature of our case, Zvi, Nu, and I were being tried together—before the same judge and jury. We each had our own legal defense team, and each defense team got its own table in the courtroom. During jury selection, each of the three teams would get a few strikes to exclude jurors. (The prosecution and the judge would be able to exclude jurors too.) When the trial properly began, Zvi, as the head defendant, would go first, and it would round-robin from there. Zvi's lawyer would make his opening statement. Then Nu's lawyer. Then mine. It would be the same during any cross-examinations. When the prosecution brought up a witness, Zvi's lawyers would get to do cross first, then Nu's, then my guys. At the end of the trial, the government would get to make an initial closing statement, then it would go Zvi, Nu, me—with each of our lawyers giving closing statements—and then the government coming back to do one final rebuttal.

As we had prepared for the trial to begin in earnest, Lisa had manifested her fear and anxiety in different way—by seeing everyone around her, with the exception of our children, as the enemy. The tension in the house over the last eighteen months was nothing compared to the trial. My parents flew in to stay with us, adding the more pedestrian "in-law tension" to the mix. They wanted to do nothing but help, to be there for us, and yet were only pure kindling, sending the flames of stress higher and higher.

My dad arrived from LA the night before jury selection. After searching unsuccessfully for me in the courtroom, he returned to the Federal Cafe, where he recognized Zvi. And Zvi recognized him.

Zvi introduced himself and said: "I'm really sorry for putting Mike through this."

My dad told me later that Zvi's sentiment seemed genuine, but anger still rose furiously inside of me. I could picture the exact face that Zvi made—that Bill Clinton/Bart Simpson hangdog look where you want to believe that he's truly, truly sorry. Deep down, you know he's lying, but you believe him anyway because you want to, and because it's easier than acknowledging the truth and what that cup holds.

I had to set my dad straight.

"Dad, here's the deal. You don't talk to him, his brother, his lawyers or his family. These people are not our friends. They're not even on our side. That piece of garbage is the reason I'm here. If he was truly 'sorry,' he could have walked into 26 Federal Plaza and told the prosecutors that I was a dupe in his little conspiracy. He didn't. He lied to me over and over again. He isn't sorry. He's just playing a game. There are fourteen people in jail, or waiting to go to jail, solely because of him."

"I understand," my dad said, looking down at his shoes.

I'd come on too strong, and now I felt like an asshole. One of the three people in the world that would have literally done anything for me, and the first thing I'd done was scold him. I tried to explain myself.

"Look, Dad, I didn't mean to come on so strong. You didn't do anything wrong. You didn't know any better. Sommer already lectured me about appearances. We don't know who in the Cafe might be a potential juror, or an FBI agent. If they see Zvi shaking hands and talking with you, they're going to think we're one big happy family—and for the next few weeks, perception is reality. I have to make everyone believe that we were business partners only, that he did all of his dirt before *we* went into business together, and that he lied to me about what he'd done."

"I understand," my father said. "I know you're just trying to protect us, and you're under a lot of stress. This is torture for your mom and me, so it's gotta be murder on you."

"That's still no excuse for snapping at you like that. I'm sorry. You guys are the best, and I love you."

We both started tearing up. I didn't know if it was good or bad to be seen crying with my family, so I excused myself and went to sit with Moe.

"It's too bad I'm not a praying man," I said to Moe. "Now seems like the time to do that."

"I'll get down on my knees with you here if you want to," he responded, a slight smile on his face.

"Naw," I said.

I thought back to the blessedly brief times my kids—or the kids of people I knew—had been in the hospital. Sylvie had once gotten sick, and was so small and dehydrated that the doctors couldn't even find a vein to start an IV. Try holding down your screaming child while someone she doesn't know sticks her over and over with a needle. And then there was Cam's friend Leo, whom he adored, in a bed at Sloan-Kettering battling for his life against leukemia. *Those* are things you pray over.

Just then Sommer arrived. He gave me a small smile but the mood stayed somber.

"I just want to thank you for having the confidence in me," he said as he sat beside me. "We're going to do our best to show the jury and everyone else what we've known all along. But here's the deal. Starting now, we're always 'on.' You don't talk to your codefendants, you don't talk to jurors. No smiling or laughing. If something doesn't go our way, no reaction whatsoever. If you've got a poker face, put it on and keep it on."

"*If* I've got a poker face? You want to play head to head for the last $150K of your bill?"

"I believe that's against the American Bar Association guidelines," Sommer said. "Regardless, it's game time. Be aware of everything, but react to nothing . . . unless I tell you to."

"Okay," I said. "Done."

"Before Sullivan calls in the potential jury pool, he's going to ask if we want to present anything else on the motion we submitted," Sommer continued, referencing our request to show the jury the non-jail probation offer I'd received from the government. "We think it shows not only a 'consciousness of innocence' on your part—because you rejected it—but also the weakness of their case on the insider trading charge. Juries deserve to make their decisions with all the facts at hand. If I was a juror, knowing that the government had offered a defendant probation would probably have an effect on how I viewed the case and the evidence. If it might produce a little more skepticism, we want it in evidence."

"What do we do about the coverage this weekend in all the papers showing pictures of us and Raj together?" I asked. "The headlines called him 'the greediest man on the face of the earth.' How is it possible for me to get a fair trial when the jury pool has been digesting that?"

"I saw those headlines too, and that's going to be our second motion," Sommer assured me. "I'm going to ask for a delay of a week to let it pass. There's a good chance the judge grants that one. But there's also a chance he doesn't, so we have to be prepared to continue if he denies."

"Why would he possibly deny it? Doesn't the obvious risk of a biased jury far outweigh a one-week delay?"

"Yes, *but* I don't make the decision. And all judges *hate* when their schedules get upended. If he feels it'll cause a domino effect with his other cases, he may try to ram through and keep going."

"Great. Expediency over justice. Not quite '*in veritas*' but I can see its appeal."

"Don't worry," Moe said, trying to cheer me up, "I'll wager at least half of the jury pool hasn't read a newspaper their entire lives."

I smiled at him because I knew he wasn't joking.

The morning session opened with Sommer arguing why my no-prison probation offer should heard by the jury and why a small delay of a week was the only fair and logical outcome in light of the deluge of negative press regarding Raj's conviction.

There was a back and forth in which Sullivan, the judge, appeared to be leaning our way. He seemed annoyed that the government hadn't put forward a more forceful argument against the admission of the plea offer or delay.

Then, out of the blue, Sullivan suddenly announced he'd decided against both.

That was when it finally dawned on me how these things actually worked. The judge was going to do what he wanted, no matter what. When he wanted to rule in favor of the government, he was going to. But he expected the government to give him enough of a show that he might be able to *give the appearance* of having been swayed by what they'd said. If they gave him very little or nothing, he would still side with them, but he would be annoyed with them.

During our motion for summary judgment over a year ago, AUSA Reed Brodsky had forcefully stated on the record that "Mr. Kimelman was only being charged with conspiracy, not a substantive crime." Both Sommer and Judge Sullivan had to embarrassingly remind him that I was indeed being charged with a substantive trade of 3Com as well according to the indictment. Sullivan went the additional step of scolding him and appearing to consider dismissing the charge but relented after sternly admonishing Brodsky.

Then, during the wiretap admission hearing several months ago, Judge Sullivan heard from Sommer how the FBI and prosecutors had violated nearly every wiretapping rule in the books by failing to minimize sensitive personal conversations that weren't related to the investigation, and by continuing to tape and listen in on calls that were protected by two of the most serious privileges afforded under the Constitution—those between defense lawyers and their clients (attorney-client privilege) and husbands and wives (marital privilege).

Sullivan appeared to be furious, delivering a vicious tongue-lashing to AUSAs Brodsky and Fish and to the FBI agents involved in the wiretaps. Calling the government's actions "disgraceful," he actually looked for a second like he was going to toss the tapes. He frowned. He shook his head.

And then he ruled in the government's favor. Again.

After the operatic "sound and fury" of the summary judgment motion, the wiretap motion, and now the plea and delay of trial motions, I realized how this game worked. This was purely political theater, dramaturgic farce. Sullivan was never going to actually rule against the government, but he had to make it seem like it was a difficult decision, a "close call" if you will, before handing the government the decision. We were the Washington Generals, and the government was the Harlem Globetrotters. That was how it was going to be.

Those familiar with the Globetrotters know the Generals are their steadfast opponents, always winning early and looking as if this time they just might pull an upset and beat the legendary crowd favorites, the Globetrotters. But lo and behold, the Globetrotters pull something special out of their bag of tricks and ultimately prevail. Apparently, it was no different in federal court. No matter the argument, no matter the issue, Sullivan had to make it appear as if he just might hand this one to us, before giving the US Globetrotters a narrow victory. At least I knew better now than to get my hopes up at trial when it seemed like the judge was actually leaning toward deciding an issue in our favor.

But this was not the most terrifying part.

After Sullivan denied all of our motions, there was a break during which we were allowed to talk to one another. During that break, I overheard multiple members of the jury pool talking. Already, they were scoffing at my lawyer and what he was trying to do. I heard things like "They don't arrest you for nothing" and "Where there's smoke, there's fire."

I could hardly believe it.

Next, after collecting responses to a series of written jury questions, Sullivan proceeded with the oral part of the juror interview process. The responses were likewise horrifying to me.

How many people here have a negative view of Wall Street? You would've thought Sullivan asked how many people were interested in a free iPad. Hands shot up high and fast.

How many people are familiar with the Raj Rajaratnam Galleon case? Maybe a quarter raised their hands. It was still a giant number considering every paper in the area had blanket coverage and pictures of us with the "greediest man alive."

Walking in that morning, I'd thought I had a coin flip shot on the conspiracy charge and a slam dunk on the phantom insider trading 3Com charge. Now I was seriously contemplating faking a heart attack to give me twenty-four hours to reconsider the government's plea offer.* This wasn't a slightly hostile "away" crowd, it was Jesse Owens walking into Berlin '36.

Dinner that night was quiet. My parents tried to be positive, or at least feign normalcy. I was trying my best to, somehow, remain optimistic, with "level" as a fallback, but deep down I knew I was in trouble. And "I" meant Lisa, and our children too. When the best-case scenario is you're still bankrupt, and your name comes up at the top of a Google search for insider trading, it's tough to stay genuinely optimistic.

As we got ready for bed, I turned on the TV to distract our thoughts and strangle the silence. The tightness in my throat and chest seemed to be blocking my ability to breathe or think.

"Do you want to talk?" Lisa asked hesitantly.

"Sure."

Did I really?

"How do you feel it went today?" she asked. Lisa was trying to be understanding, even sweet. She knew my heart felt like bursting from stress, and she probably didn't feel much different herself.

"I think . . . I think we did okay," I said measuredly. "It wasn't an ideal jury, but nothing's ever ideal. I would've liked to have had at least one black juror. Maybe it's a stereotype, but I feel like black people are the most cynical about law enforcement. And there's also no one like . . . *us*, is there? There's not a single person on that jury that I think has a friend or has ever met someone like me, or that we would ever grab a drink with, or engage in a conversation with unless we were trapped in an elevator together. Nobody who feels like our kind of people. That kind of scares me. Maybe the young girl. I could see her getting drunk at a bar in Hoboken."

I had noted a young Snooki type, albeit more attractive and less sloppy, who had made the cut. She was the only one on the jury that any of us were

---

* The best "fake heart attack" in finance was that well-known floor trader who hit the ground when the stock he was making a market in on the floor of the NYSE received a takeover offer and his firm was heavily net short. The "victim" was able to stop the action long enough for the price action to slow down and the person that filled in for him ended up taking the majority of the blame.

likely to have interacted with in the last five years.* The rest were just . . . different.

"You don't like them? You're not happy with the choices?"

I wasn't. But what could I do about it? Moreover, what should I say? If I told Lisa no, she'd just sink lower, and I knew she was trying to stay upbeat. She needed to maintain. We all did.

"I think the jurors are basically all right," I eventually told her. "They'll either get it or they won't. But remember, all we need is one."

I looked away and winced, realizing I'd just parroted some of Zvi's idiocy.

"At this point, we've got to play the hand we've been dealt," I went on. "We've been dealt eleven people whom you and I would likely never meet during any sort of social situation."

"So they won't be sympathetic to you?" she asked.

"We don't need them to be sympathetic, although it would help. We just need them to listen, to apply the law. The government has to meet the burden of proof, to *prove beyond a reasonable doubt* that I committed securities fraud and that I was in a conspiracy. They can't do the first one. It's impossible. So they have to focus on the conspiracy charge."

"I still don't understand conspiracy."

"Neither do I," I said. "Not fully. But here's the thing. As long as they look at me as an individual, and not just as Zvi's partner, I'll be okay."

Lisa seemed sated by this, but I didn't even know if I believed it myself. I popped an Ambien, finished off my third (large) glass of wine, and climbed under the covers with her to watch reruns of *The Sopranos* until the pill kicked in and extinguished another day of pain and anxiety.

The jury walked in silently, several of them making eye contact with me for a split second before averting their eyes. I had a creeping feeling that if Sullivan were to conduct a straw poll right now—guilty or not guilty—before a single word or piece of evidence was submitted, a majority would raise their hand to convict. It was more than a feeling; I knew it.

---

* Hoboken Snooki, our sole potentially sympathetic juror, ended up being removed from the jury pre-verdict due to a family illness.

"Burden of proof and presumed innocent," Moe whispered to me, as if he knew what I was thinking. "We got this. Stay confident."

Suddenly conscious of my posture and demeanor, I brought my shoulders back, elevated my chin slightly, and tried to affect the countenance of someone innocent and wrongfully accused.

"You may be seated," Judge Sullivan said to the room with a friendly, serious smile. "Thank you, ladies and gentlemen, for being on time and I hope you had a good night. Now that you have been sworn in, it will be your duty as jurors to find from the evidence what the facts are. You and you alone are the judges of the facts. You decide what happened based on the evidence presented at trial."

Through a targeted combination of humor, flattery, and time-tested material vetted on hundreds of previous juries, judges massage jurors and make them feel special and unique, their "service" on par with those in uniform fighting over in foreign lands to defend truth, justice, and the American Way. The flattery from a booming, authoritative figure assures the jury that they are equipped for and worthy of this challenge, and humor dissipates the suffocating tension, mostly originating from the skulls of the defendants. Like wayward children seeking the approval of an intimidating yet beneficent father figure, the jurors want nothing more than to please their Judge Father.

I futilely attempted to perform some stealth deep breathing exercises to slow my heart, which was pounding against my breastbone like a fundraiser at my front door during dinner. The insanity and stress I felt was, once again, off the charts.

Being on trial is not dissimilar from being in a presidential debate that lasts six weeks. Your every move is scrutinized and watched, even when you're not the focus of attention. For eight hours each day, a pure and permanent poker face is required. You can't react to anything; even scribbling furiously on a legal pad can be misconstrued negatively. For someone used to smiling a good part of the day, freezing one's face in a mask of neutral consternation can be physically painful. To be on full alert all the time takes a mind-breaking toll. But you still have to do it. One bad cross exam, one stumped question, or one missed angle and it can be game over. To observe and record for eight hours a day and betray no emotion or reaction is beyond tough; it's torture. And after the court session ends for that day, it's not like you get to wind down and relax. There is no break. After court, it's right back to your lawyer's offices to prepare for court the next day. That goes until 10 p.m. or later. Home by eleven if you're lucky. Kids, if you have them, will already be asleep. Your parents will have questions you can't or don't want to answer. Your partner will be drained, scared, and concerned for you—but won't really know how to engage with you because what's happening to you is so unique. Then you'll wake up the next morning and be out the door by seven to do it all over again. It's like hopping on a horrible treadmill that you can't get off for weeks. The speed varies up and down, but it never actually stops. And maybe at the end of it, you go to jail.

The treadmill of horror gets worse as you get closer to the end of the trial. The tension and torture climb as the trial progresses. During jury selection, the stress and tension are extremely high, but *that's* like a theater dress rehearsal compared to opening statements. Each step gets worse, and your mind feels like you couldn't possibly handle any more. But then you always do. You find a way, and you do. If you think opening statements are bad, wait until closing statements. At least with opening statements, you still have *time*. Things can still happen. Closing statements means it's over, and you have to hope it went well. Soon you will know the outcome that will determine the coming months and years, or possibly the rest of your life. Closing statements, which have the ability to produce dancing spots of whiteout in your vision, nonetheless pale beside the horror of deliberations. During deliberations, the jury knocks on the door to alert the marshal when they have a note for the judge. The note could say, "We have a decision," but it could also simply be a request for more information, for a replay of some evidence, or some other clarifying question.

It's an arrhythmic, insta-migraine moment every time a fist pounds that jury door.

For me, every single knock brought on a flashback to the FBI pounding on my front door the day I was arrested. It's horrible, and yet it can't compare to, or prepare you for, *VERDICT.*

Verdict is the *last* note in the song. Then there is a sickening delay of two hours which the judge uses to give members of the press and family members and friends of the defendants time to arrive at the courtroom.

What do you do when you feel like your head is going to shatter, like your temples are pulsing so violently that people can see it, and like your heart is skipping beats? What do you do? Do you pray? Do you scream?

You won't know until you face it yourself.

Between us, I sincerely hope you never do.

CHAPTER NINETEEN

GUILTY

"THIS EMAIL ADDRESS IS CURRENTLY AT a re-education camp for the indeterminate future and will not be checked. Please try back once its lesson has been learned. Mike."

If you had sent me an email on or around December 11, 2011, that's the automated answer you would have received.

In the *New York Times*, journalist Peter Lattman, who was reaching out to me, referred to my response as "wry." Wry, indeed. Let's try a tongue-in-cheek attempt to divert all the other emotions I was feeling, such as "devastated," "destroyed," "distraught," "despondent," "bitter," "outraged," "terrified," and even, in my darkest moments, when the world seemed such a dark and horrible place, "borderline suicidal." I admit that there were a few moments during the trial when, with an unsettling clarity, I could understand why poor Ephraim Karpel* had hanged himself with a leather belt in that small subleased office on lower Fifth Avenue, hounded by Federal agents, ruined professionally, and driven to despair.

If I had been a fatherless lush, living in a child-free vacuum, then who knows—although deep down I *do* know. Why? Simple. For all the suffering

---

* During my trial, the government played a wiretap featuring Karpel and Zvi and didn't even bother to notify Karpel that he was going to be publicly outed as an informant beforehand. Karpel, a married father of three like me, read the news in the paper like everyone else, and then hung himself in his office. The next morning in court when Sommer asked AUSA's Fish and Tarlowe whether they were aware of Karpel's suicide, Fish shrugged his shoulders dismissively and snickered, "Not my witness", before resuming small talk with Tarlowe.

my poor parents had been through since my arrest two years earlier, to cap it off with their son washing up against a jetty on Long Island Sound, bloated, with a belly full of aspirin and vodka, or swinging, blue-faced, from a chandelier, would have been the ultimate act of thoughtless selfishness. But there *were* my children to think of. Three little kids, who had already lived through this gut-wrenching ordeal.

They were what kept me going—my parents and my children—through this terrifying and confusing time. I could not let them down. Any more than I already had.

If you know anything about me, you already know that I was found guilty. Here's how it shook out.

Throughout my trial, my defense team called only one witness on our behalf, but it was the FBI's lead case agent, Jan Trigg. Please consider for a moment how unprecedented this was. The lead FBI case agent is supposed to be the linchpin of the government's case. She was the one who captained the investigation and built the Fed's case from scratch. We blew up the government's case on cross exam, either shredding their witnesses or mostly getting them to admit they had *no idea who I was* or that they didn't believe I was a part of the conspiracy. And then, the *coup d'etat* was calling Agent Trigg again as a witness for *our side,* and getting her to reiterate under oath on the stand what she had admitted under cross-exam when she'd testified on the government's behalf.

"Do you need some time to review the transcripts and evidence?" Sommer had asked her.

Sommer had Agent Trigg in an armlock, and she was doing everything she could to squirm out.

"Perhaps, your Honor, this would be a good time for the morning break to allow Agent Trigg to *refresh* her memory," Sommer suggested with a tinge of sarcasm.

"I think that's a good idea if no one objects—let's break for fifteen," Sullivan noted, dismissing the jury and calling my lawyer's bluff.

Upon return, Sommer repeated the question before Agent Trigg, to make sure the jury really grasped the implication of what she was being asked:

"Can you show me one wiretap, one body wire, one phone call, one email or instant message where Zvi Goffer, *or anyone*, passes my client Mr. Kimelman inside information and he trades on it?"

After a few seconds of silence, Trigg reluctantly admitted, "No, I can't."

I know it wasn't the movies, but amid the murmuring in the gallery that followed her answer, I couldn't understand why Sommer didn't just leap up and shout: "Your honor, I make an immediate motion for dismissal of all charges against my client!"

I imagined Sullivan pounding his gavel and asking for "Order in the court" before asking the prosecutors if they had any other evidence against me.* It was a pleasant fantasy. Fleeting, but pleasant.

If there was any bright spot for me during my trial, that was it.

I'm not going to drag the rest out.

Despite the above—despite the government not even calling Franz Tudor, who wore a wire and sat next to me on the trading desk *for over a year,* doing his best to incriminate me; despite a year-plus of phone taps, and wire taps, and several informants coming up with nothing; and despite Zvi having done everything he was accused of *before* he became a partner with Incremental, the jury didn't look past the dollar signs. They were blinded by the money. That, and the fact that Zvi and I had become partners and friends at Incremental. Then they offered the damning conclusion: "Guilty."

We were "Wall Street," in a country still feeling the sting of the recession. We were looked on like French nobles after the storming of the Bastille. I could write about the legal minutiae that happened before the verdict, how there were several legal firsts in this trial, but in the end it'd be fascinating to about fifty people. You're likely not one of them.

Sommer wasn't even there for my verdict. He had a kidney stone and was in the hospital, so we put it on speaker for him. Probably the only way to make it worse to hear that your client has just been convicted is to hear it in a hospital with a catheter in your penis. It was just Moe and me at the table.

---

* At trial, the only witness the government had that was able to link me in any way to the 3Com trade was Dave Plate, who testified that he thought I might have been in a crowded bar during happy hour and heard Zvi discussing the trade. On cross exam, Plate admitted he wasn't sure I was even present.

Just as we were tried in triplicate, so did we hear that we were guilty. The jury said that Zvi was guilty, that Nu was guilty, and that I was guilty. One two three. We were three of what would eventually be twenty-four persons who were either convicted by juries or who pled guilty in the Galleon and Incremental cases.

I don't have precise memories of how Zvi or Nu reacted, or even how I did. I was disappointed and numb and not thinking clearly enough to be very observant.

The horror was now complete.

Or so I thought.

I was not immediately taken into custody, and would have several months more of freedom until Judge Sullivan finally rendered his sentence.

That meant months to let whatever traces of hope and optimism I still had fizzle and spark and sputter. And life still went on. The week after my verdict there were games for the Little League team I was coaching. It was also Father's Day. I had to put on my coach/daddy hat and smile, while inside it felt like the world had ended and I could barely breathe.

Two days after the trial ended, Lisa came bounding onto our outside deck where I was seated, staring at nothing and trying to calculate for the thousandth time how my life had reached this point. She was smiling, which totally unnerved me as I hadn't seen Lisa with even a hint of a smile in weeks.

"I've got an early Father's Day present for you," she said mysteriously, which now really had me alarmed. "So I'm in Stop & Shop with Phin getting some groceries when I see someone who looks familiar. We pass in one aisle, and then in the next aisle. When we pass a third time, I realize who it is. Juror number nine!"

"You're kidding me, right?"

"Nope. It's definitely him and I think he recognizes me too. This time when we walk by each other I say hello and tell him I think we know each other. I introduce myself as Lisa Kimelman. I say 'I believe you were one of the jurors on the case that was just decided.' Then I ask him if I could just ask him one question. He's clearly a little uncomfortable. But I just jump right in and ask it: 'Can you tell me how you came to the verdict of guilty against Michael?'"

Lisa pauses.

I'm blown away at this point. I didn't think she still cared about the case. Frankly, I'm amazed she had the nerve to confront one of the jurors. I wondered if I would have had her courage in the same situation.

"Are you serious?" I asked with a rapt grin. "What did he say?"

"After giving about a half dozen 'umms' and 'uhhhs' he said, 'There were just a lot of really bad tapes against that guy Zvi Goffer.'"

My face fell, and I nodded. The answer was crushing, but not unexpected. Guilt by association is always your biggest fear in a situation like mine. Turns out I was right to be afraid.

"So that was it, huh?" I finally said.

"Please," Lisa said, with an expression that screamed, *Give me* some *credit, willya?* "I'm not going to let him wiggle off that easily. I said, 'I know there were some bad things in those tapes when it came to Zvi Goffer. But I'm talking about my husband, Michael Kimelman. Would you mind just telling me what was compelling in the evidence against *him*? We'd really like to know what swayed the jury.'"

"And?" I asked.

"More 'umms' and 'uhhhs' and then finally he kinda goes, 'Just the tapes against Zvi and him being in business with that guy. The fact he was in business with that guy. I guess that was it.'"

Lisa still wasn't done.

"So then I asked him if he knew that the government was going to ask for a sentence of five years. He looked genuinely surprised. He said they'd spoken in the jury room about how white collar guys always get a slap on the wrist. That it's always a year or two, tops. Then he walked off."

I shook my head. Everything I had feared, everything Moe and Sommer had warned me about, had come to pass. The evidence, in the end, hadn't mattered. Guilt by association had. My decision to go into business with a firm even slightly associated with Zvi Goffer had. My decision to trust Zvi had.

I was long past the point of feeling any anger. Lisa's remarkable tale just left me numb.

This juror had been one of only two jurors that my legal team had deemed even potentially "decent" and capable of making a rational, objective decision. And yet he had made *this* sort of decision. Used this sort of thinking. We had never had a chance.

But the encounter with the juror did not end there.

No good deed goes unpunished. While I was still awaiting sentencing, the juror went to the FBI and Judge Sullivan and filed a formal complaint saying he had been harassed and intimidated by my wife. (After proxy-interviewing Lisa and the juror, Sullivan decided that a five foot four, 100-pound woman holding an eleven-month-old infant in her arms had not been a significant threat to a six foot two, 220-pound man in a public grocery store. Not filing criminal charges against Lisa—for innocently asking what anyone else in her position would've wanted to know—was maybe the one time the system showed itself to be reasonable, objective, and decent.)

With my verdict decided in June, I had to suffer through an entire summer to wait and see what Judge Sullivan had in store for me before I was finally sentenced in October. Sullivan had the power, under some established guidelines, to put me away for as little as a few months, or for as much as several years. The government had asked him to give me fifty-seven months. There was some genuine wiggle room here, but given the way Sullivan had behaved during the trial, my hopes were not up. I wasn't sleeping well, and was inhaling liters of wine and vodka.

I would have to read a statement at the sentencing. Sommer wrote something for me, but it seemed a little too careful and perfect. Besides, I wanted to write something myself. Conflicted about what exactly to say, I decided to compose two versions. I wanted to write something that essentially refused to admit guilt for something I wasn't guilty of, while acknowledging that I respected the judge and the jury's decision. It was a very fine line. The standard playbook says that in these sort of situations, you'll get the best result if you throw yourself down in front of the bench, beg for mercy and, prostrate, acknowledge your guilt. Show remorse and the judge will be more lenient.

As you might imagine, Zvi had already taken this angle, giving it his own sleazy spin. Zvi had written a letter to the judge, claiming that he had seen the light, would forego any appeal in his case, and that now his former, greedy self was no more.

To me, it seemed an obvious and pathetic attempt to manipulate the judge. Sullivan didn't buy it, and sentenced Zvi to ten years. This was more than double the plea he had been offered initially. For a short time, it was the longest insider trading sentence in American history. Two weeks later and four floors down, in Courtroom 17B, Judge Holwell would slap Raj with eleven years.

Raj had made over $63 million talking directly to people on Boards of Directors and other "classic" insiders. Zvi, on the other hand, made $380K by getting secondhand information of questionable value from a slip-and-fall lawyer in Brooklyn who was fed that information from his friend working at a law firm, and by eavesdropping at lunches. And yet, amazingly, the end result was almost identical. Laws are supposed to be uniformly applied. Clearly, from a defendant's perspective, it was better to have Judge Holwell than Judge Sullivan presiding over your case. Zvi would go on to file an appeal several weeks later, all revealing that his transformation and contrition were about as honest and sincere as everything else he'd ever said in his life.

Nu took the opposite tack. At his sentencing, when the judge asked Nu if he would like to address the court, he barely stood up to offer a simple "No," and sat right back down again. I learned later that Nu was so outraged by Zvi's sentence that he had to be talked into standing at all.

Fortunately for Nu, his approach worked significantly better than Zvi's insincere change of heart. Nu was facing five to seven years under the guidelines. Sullivan sentenced him to three. Nu was the only one who fared about the same going to trial as he would have done had he pled to the charge.

As for me, my sentencing followed a strange and unexpected event.

I suppose *Elle* magazine is a respected name in the fashion world—if you respect the world of fashion, that is. I, for one, don't. I've never been tempted by Savile Row suits or hand-stitched shirts from Naples. Even Brooks Brothers seems a dandified stretch. Clothes don't make the man, in my opinion.

Anyhow, imagine my surprise—and jaw-dropping, heart-sinking shock—when I learned that Lisa had decided to pen a piece for *Elle* magazine just before my sentencing. She had not told me, or anyone, that she was going to do this. The absurdly long title of the article—*Elle* seems to play a bit fast and loose with these things—was: *The Verdict: When Lisa Kimelman had to face the trial of her life (and look good for it), she found armor, and an ally, on the fifth floor of Barneys.**

---

* http://www.elle.com/culture/career-politics/a11784/the-verdict-608992/

The piece was about how shopping at Barney's had allowed her to prepare herself for my trial. Needless to say, this was not the kind of publicity likely to garner me favor with a judge who seemed to have it out for me (or with a public fed up with rich, spoiled Wall Streeters). Reading the piece, I could tell that Lisa, in her way, had tried to be self-deprecating and down-to-earth. She opened by admitting that she'd only been shopping at Barney's once before, several years earlier, with a few friends and after a couple of cocktails. She even mentioned how hard a time the sales assistant had when helping her on with a pair of jeans, growling, "You gotta tuck your fat in, girl! You tuck that fat in!"

But she also dropped the fact that her father was something of a political and financial heavyweight. And near the end of the piece she told the story of how her mother had once been seated next to Henry Kissinger, back when her husband was in the Nixon White House, and how Henry had complimented her hair.

"Oh, you can wear it too," Connie had told America's Metternich, taking off her wig and dangling it over the White House china.

To Lisa's way of thinking, these were innocent facts and cute anecdotes. And to those in her social circle, they may have been. But to outsiders, they undeniably gave the impression of our trying to "clout" our way out of this. Of signaling that, ahem, we were not the sort of people to whom this was supposed to happen.

To this day, there is no way to know what sort of damage the article did, or to know whether Judge Sullivan read it (I'm inclined to think that he does *not* have a subscription to *Elle*, but I believe people who work for him might have brought it to his attention). What I can tell you with great certainty is that my legal team was very upset, and thought it would bode poorly.

I was upset too, but I also felt for my wife. Here she was, on the brink of being entirely on her own. The magazine article was a smart move as far as publicity for her catering business—which would be all she would have to sustain our family while I was away.

Yeah, it pissed me off—and yeah, I thought it was a pretty self-serving move—but no, I didn't for one second blame her.

So there I was. After two years in purgatory, finally overlooking the abyss. I was the last of the three defendants to be sentenced. The courtroom was packed on the day of my sentencing, the energy and anticipation palpable. I had a sense of fatal resignation, a grin-and-bear-it mentality. I had made the decision to go to trial and now had to accept the outcome and face my punishment. I couldn't risk being defiant in my statement—at least not in terms of tone or attitude. I'd seen enough of Sullivan's "hang 'em high" tactics to know I couldn't risk enraging him. In an attempt to brighten the mood, I slid Moe a copy of the angry version of the statement I'd written—the one I wanted to give but knew I could not give—with the actual orange Monopoly *Get out of Jail Free* card on top of it.

"Do I hand this to the bailiff before or after I make my statement?" I asked him.

Here is what, deep down, I wanted to say. It was sloppy and angry and full of my soul. Here is what that statement said:

> My attorneys have advised me, because of the posture of the case, not to say anything. I would like to go ahead anyway and make a brief statement.
>
> At this point in my life, I am filled with regrets.
>
> I regret not testifying. Not having the opportunity to give my side of the story.
>
> The consensus was you don't testify unless you are losing the case—and at no point during the trial did I or my attorneys feel that was happening. Besides, the AUSAs in this case should have already been nominated for a best actor award in a fiction drama for their performance during the close and rebuttal—and I didn't want to give them additional fodder to feign outrage and confusion over.
>
> It's easy to ask someone on the stand about a date four years ago and get an 'I don't know." The lead case agent offered up some version of "I can't recall" or "I don't know" over fifty-eight times that I counted during one relatively brief cross exam. I can barely remember what happened last week, much less four years ago. Those non-answers would have been pounced upon during the close and rebuttal as evasions or lies.
>
> "How could the defendant 'forget' making $50K or $100K in a single day? I guarantee you I would remember if I made that kind of money."

Never mind the fact that when one manages millions of dollars, swings of this magnitude happen quite often, or that making more in a day than most jurors will make in a year, is, wrongfully, on its own, inculpatory.

While I am not guilty of insider trading, I do know that I am certainly guilty of bad judgment. I regret and am sorry for lowering my standards so far that I chose to go into and stay in business with someone whom I knew had a habit of shading the truth and of serial exaggeration. For lack of a better term, and please excuse my language—a "BS" artist. Those who knew Zvi Goffer for more than a few months understood his tendency to boast. We took what he said with a grain of salt. That is markedly different than being a knowing conspirator in a serial insider trading scheme. Zvi actively and deliberately misled me and numerous others (including dozens of people at his own firm) about the "source" of his information. He would say things like: "My friend's friend is a portfolio manager at Hedge Fund X and he is hearing so and so" or "My SAC guy is telling me Y." These were common refrains. The origins of most of Zvi's calls weren't even capable of being identified.

I suspect that the jury's analysis centered on whether or not I was "tipped" by Zvi Goffer. But as we know, "tips" are not illegal. Tips where the tippee knows that the information is material, nonpublic, and acquired in breach of a fiduciary duty for some pecuniary benefit—that is what is illegal.

Nothing in Zvi's history put me on notice that he was actually involved in an active knowing breach. Instead, he appeared to be just relaying or repeating rumors or research from others. There are whole industries and websites, blogs, other media and analyst research dedicated to these areas of trading. The law has gone from "knowledge" to a more subjective "should have known" to now, in this case, a "could have known" standard. As my attorney Mr. Sommer has spoken about, we traded over 347 stocks together during the time frame in question. Of the 100 or so "calls" Zvi relayed prior to and after 3Com, I probably lost money on ninety-seven of them.

Once we became partners at Incremental, actually working together, almost a year after 3Com took place, I was able to observe Zvi on an everyday basis. I read the riot act to Zvi. I told him that I would have a zero-tolerance policy for any moral or ethical breaches. There is a reason why informant after informant could not point to a single transgression of mine. You can be certain that neither coincidence nor luck had anything to do with that. Based on the number of informants and wiretaps and tremendous resources exerted, it didn't happen for want of looking.

And as for the jury, I sincerely believe these types of cases are too complex. This is not murder, grand theft auto, or a bar brawl. The issues here are too sophisticated, the laws too vague and ill-defined—intentionally so, I might add—and the elements too specialized to be interpreted and analyzed by laymen. They are more like patent cases, which the law is beginning to recognize are incapable of being adjudicated by a jury and therefore better suited to be heard by a judge.

Over the last two years, my life has been summarily destroyed. Everything I've ever worked or studied for has been wiped out. Everything. The firm I built for two years, working eighteen hours a day and investing most of my net worth, is wiped out. Professionally and personally, my reputation has been ruined. I am bankrupt and about to lose my freedom. Starting over my life as a felon, in my forties, with over a million dollars in debt, scares me—but not being there as a father or husband when my family needs me is what truly terrifies me.

I think your honor presided in a fair manner over the trial and I want to thank you for treating my family and me with respect throughout this process.

I understand the rules of the system. And I was fully aware that turning down the government's probation offer and submitting myself to the verdict of a jury engendered certain risks. The fact the jury rendered the decision they did means I have to be punished. I stand here ready to accept your honor's sentencing decision.

I believe in redemption, and will one day make it right, as a husband and father, as a friend and a son, for those who have sacrificed for me.

Thank you, your honor.

And here, instead, is what I actually read:

> I'll be very brief, Your Honor.
>
> Over the past two years, I have had the opportunity—privately—to express my feelings to my family and friends who have supported me throughout this difficult period in my life. So I won't do that now.
>
> Today, I would like to thank the Court for presiding over my trial in a fair manner and treating me and my family with respect throughout the process. When I chose to go to trial, I was fully aware of the risk that a jury would find me guilty, and now I am ready to accept the consequences of that decision.
>
> I believe in redemption and one day hope to make it right, as a husband, father, son, and friend for those who have stood by my side and sacrificed for me. Thank you.

In retrospect, I should have released the text of the statement to the media, but Sommer and Moe were against that. I believe this was ultimately bad advice, as some journalists reported that I had stood and "accepted the consequences of [my guilt]," which is false and incomplete. It felt like the final dagger thrust. The reporting on my trial had involved numerous mistakes. There had even been stories saying that I had worked with Raj at Galleon. So many things were wrong, but they were out there now, and could hurt my reputation for years to come.

After my statement, I sat down and looked at Moe. He mustered a smile, but I could tell his heart wasn't in it. He had been here before.

For Moe, sentencing was never enjoyable, even when he was standing with the government on the winning side. There is something about sitting in judgment of one's fellow human beings that weighs heavily. Perhaps it should. Moe had been a lead prosecutor in the Ronell Wilson murder trial, in which Wilson was convicted of killing two undercover New York police officers on Staten Island back in 2003. Moe wrote to then US Attorney General Alberto Gonzales, arguing that life in prison was sufficient punishment for Wilson. Gonzales told Moe to seek the death penalty or resign immediately from his job.

Now my fate was in the hands of the Honorable Richard Sullivan.

After my statement, he asked the prosecution if I was of "a different caliber" than the other defendants. They said I was, and the "least culpable." Over a hundred letters of support had been offered for me—"the most I'd ever seen for a defendant," Sullivan observed. He also conceded that my verdict had probably been a "close call," and one that "could have gone either way." But he also said I should have known better than to get mixed up with my codefendants.

Then, for a moment, he said nothing more. This was it. I knew the sentence would come next.

I was given thirty months, followed by three years' probation. It was basically the same sentence received by Nu, who had made more than $1 million, used a prepaid phone, written cover-up emails, and doled out illegal cash.

The wind went out of me. I could feel hearts sinking behind me.

Sullivan stood and exited the courtroom. The government prosecutors grabbed their Redweld folders and headed for the doors. I knew that Moe and Sommer's promises to file an immediate appeal were sincere—it was par for the course, after all, and more work for them. In a daze, I turned around and saw my poor parents, my father red in the face, struggling with tears, as well as my mom, who remained impressively strong-looking, considering her broken heart. Lisa was surprisingly stoic—jaw clenched, glassy-eyed. She was the one I hugged first. I needed that strength to face what I knew awaited me outside—the cameras, the klieg lights, the microphones.

"Mr. Kimelman, Mr. Kimelman! Over here, over here! Do you have anything to say about the decision?"

Looking straight ahead, believing that my head was held high, with Lisa by my side, I'd officially crossed over. I had become a convict. There was nothing more to say. That was it, my two-year wait was officially over. I was going away.

There were forms to fill out, and interviews with psychiatrists, doctors, the media, and representatives from the Bureau of Prisons. I was also occupied with legal matters for my appeal and lots of goodbyes, capped off by a positively funereal "going away party" at a dive Irish bar near Times Square. As I shared my last drink with friends, their stories about careers and families echoed in my mind. As my life would disintegrate, as I would be trapped in a new hellish limbo, the larger world would keep spinning.

A couple of days after my sentencing, and two months before I had to surrender myself to federal authorities at a prison in central Pennsylvania, Peter Lattman from the *New York Times* called me up. He said he was writing a story on me and requested an interview. I was hesitant, but also did my due diligence. Lattman, a seasoned, savvy, and serious journalist, struck me as someone I could really talk to. I mean, what was the worst that could happen: He writes a scathing piece and makes me look bad—me, whose face had just been on every major news network in the United States and beyond, beneath the all-capped word: GUILTY! I'd tossed the dice over much bigger things in my day, including my very own freedom; this one seemed about as harmless as could be.

As I learned writing this book, it's as much about what you leave out of a story as what you decide to put in—and this was clearly the case with the Lattman article. Sommer was firmly against it, believing all media was bad media, but Moe, to a degree, felt that humanizing the so-called "beast" might not be a bad thing, especially in light of what the federal prosecutors and the FBI had done to make me look like a monster.

Lattman's article made the rounds. Some of the reactions were expected, others were definitely not. Lisa, at least, got great exposure—mostly because of her flattering picture. Long red hair, curvy body in a clingy dark dress, and porcelain skin have a way of piquing a interest. Suddenly "when does Kimelman report" became the question du jour, as the underlying tenor was "Perhaps poor Mrs. Kimelman will need some company," as at least one FBI agent reportedly noted.

Preet himself said he was making the article mandatory reading for all Assistant US Attorneys, so they would understand and appreciate the power they have and the lives they can impact.

That last line of mine in Lattman's article is one of the truest, most painful things I have ever said, let alone thought. *"It's the kids that'll kill you."* Concern for my children was all that went through my head as I sat in the back yard, waiting to report. It stayed with me through the long quiet hours, the days and nights, the weeks rolling into months, lying on my cramped prison bunk, hands behind my head, staring at the peeling ceiling. And it stays with me now, three years on, a convicted felon but a free man.

In the article, Lattman mentioned that we still had yet to tell the kids. Looking back, I'm not even sure when exactly we told them. It was such an emotional time. Maybe it was that October, right after the sentencing, or closer to "departure time," in December, when Lisa and I sat down on Cam's toy-cluttered floor and finally talked to him and to Syl about it. (Phin was simply too young to understand, and too disruptive.) Among the Tyco trucks, G. I. Joes, and stuffed animals, I tried to explain to my children that, in life, we are held responsible for the things we do, and sometimes for things our friends do. I said it's important to surround yourself with good people. I explained that Daddy had chosen some of his friends poorly, and they had done some bad things. Maybe not *very* bad. They didn't hurt anyone, or kill anyone. But they did cheat at the game we were playing, ignoring the agreed-to rules. And because I was their partner, I had also been held responsible for the things they'd done. So now—I told them—I have to go away . . . to a prison camp. I will probably be gone about a year. But I *will* be back, and life *will* be normal again. Mom will be here, Grandma and Grandpa, and Chris (Lisa's sous chef, who became a true friend to our kids), Brett (another Iona grad and occasional prep chef), and Annette (or "Netta," our Czech babysitter). All of them will be here. And you can call Daddy and talk to him on the phone every night, and we can write letters . . . and . . . And there was a lump of pain in my throat the size of a baseball, which no amount of swallowing would get rid of.

I don't know how I got through that without breaking down and bawling. It was the hardest thing I've ever had to say or explain to anyone, ever. It was also hard to process their looks of childish confusion. The gently furrowed brows. The utterly innocent frowns. They did not cry at the time—they were, I think, still processing—but they were clearly saddened.

I encouraged them to ask questions, as Sylvie's therapist had suggested. (And let's be clear: the *only* reason Syl ever needed to start seeing a therapist was because of my arrest, trial, and subsequent incarceration. That's on me.)

As it turned out, the kids' questions would come later, in the following weeks. They were heartbreakingly simple, Cam's especially. "Can you explain why you have to go?" or "Why can't you just stay with us and be my dad?" or even just "Why?"

Oh Cammie, I will always be your dad. But the "Why?"

That was the question. That was what I was still trying to figure out myself.

The more challenging questions came from Syl: "If you didn't do anything wrong, then why do *you* have to go to this . . . camp?"

Talk about a rock and a hard place. Her queries forced me to explain the difference between "I didn't do anything wrong" and "I did something that was later ruled illegal." That can be a lot for a kid to try to understand.

Again and again, as I spoke with my children, I found myself going back to an old refrain.

"I did something wrong because I chose bad partners. I knew they weren't nice people, but I went into business with them anyway because I thought they could make me money. That's called 'greed,' and it's something I hope you won't fully understand for a little while."

I might have told them what Lou Mannheim told Bud Fox in the movie *Wall Street:* "The main thing about money, Bud, is that it makes you do things you don't want to do."

Looking into their confused eyes, it finally crystallized for me in a way that pride and stubbornness hadn't allowed it to in the previous two years while I agonized over the decision to fight or fold. In this waking nightmare, the dark alleys were mostly of my own making.

It would now fall entirely to me to walk out of them on my own, and make sure my children had a father when this was all over.

CHAPTER TWENTY

SURRENDER

"Sometimes the wrong choices bring us to the right places."

—Unknown

WHILE I WAS FINISHING THIS BOOK, one of the biggest hits on TV was the Netflix original series *Orange is the New Black.* Anyone even remotely familiar with the plot—which is based on a true story (at least it started that way)—might wonder if there are parallels to my own trip upriver. In the show, an educated woman is sentenced to a minimum security prison. Out of her element, she is forced to adapt to a strange, surreal, unnatural, sometimes dangerous and often inhuman world. She's even ratted out by her former partner, who also ends up in the same prison, making for an awkward situation, to say the least.

All of these things were true with me.

And yet, I was also miles away from *Orange is the New Black.* First, Piper Kerman, who penned the memoir of the same name, was actually guilty of a crime. True, she was lured into breaking the law by her lover, Cleary Wolters, who was a much bigger fish among international money-laundering drug smugglers. But being blinded by love, or lust, will not change the basic legal facts of Kerman's case. And as I have tried to make clear—and as the evidence amply demonstrates—Zvi Goffer did not lure me into a life of crime. He simply decided that he would break the law and then, once arrested, would not do a goddamned thing to help me once I had been taken down, despite his knowing full well I wasn't part of his scheming. For almost two years—two fucking *YEARS*, from arrest to trial to sentencing—Zvi could have come forward and tried to make things right, to say I was not involved, that he never told me he was trying to bribe lawyers, etc. And this is why Zvi's words to Pete Bogart, outside the courtroom on the eve of the verdict—*"Why is Mike even here?"*— will haunt me for years to come.

When I was going through them, experiencing them, I believed that my prison experiences were novel and unique. They weren't.

What I now understand is that prison is about leveling everything, regulating everything, and wearing you down. What takes over, behind the barbed wire, is the mind-numbing monotony and depression—and *all that time on your hands*. It gives you an uncanny, unique ability to reflect on your poor choices, with no real distractions except getting through the day in one piece. Some cold evenings, your internal monologue becomes the greatest punishment of all.

That, and separation from the ones you love.

It took me three interminable days at Lewisburg FPC (official name: United States Penitentiary, Lewisburg) until I finally found the courage to take a shower. Every kid that grew up with a television set knows about how you should never drop your bar of soap in prison. I learned the hard way that walking into to the shower in only a towel and flip flops was also a very poor idea.

"Hey, Jew with the tattoo, you got a nice ass," was the immediate response from the peanut gallery.

A guard pulled me aside, warned me that I was "inviting trouble," and said to cover up until I was actually underneath the showerhead.

Clearly, I had a lot to learn. I was prisoner #62876054. They didn't tattoo it onto my forearm, but in a metaphorical sense it sure felt that way—and still does. Even today, I can't say or hear my number without breaking into "Look Down" from the musical *Les Miserables*.

That I had even attended a Broadway show differentiated me from 99 percent of the other inmates in the facility.

Located in the Susquehanna Valley of central Pennsylvania, Lewisburg was minimum security and gave us views of a lush landscape that always struck me as something out of a Van Gogh. Not quite Saint-Remy de Provence, but we did have our share of starry nights. I wondered why the government built prisons in such beautiful (and relatively valuable) locations. Sing Sing, nestled on the bucolic banks of the Hudson River, is another example. "The Camp," as Lewisburg was known within, was also not too far from my alma mater, Lafayette College. With a rival school that was our college football nemesis literally visible in the distance on clear days, it was a stark reminder of how far I had fallen.

Lewisburg had seen some heavy hitters over the years. Gotti, Capone, and Hoffa were just a few who had called it home. Illustrious ghosts who roamed the halls unseen.

On my first day on the inside, my deer-in-the headlights expression spoke volumes. One observant inmate smiled and asked, "Hey, did your lawyer lie to you too, and tell you that this was a white-collar camp?"

Yes, I confirmed. He had.

But to be fair to Sommer, most lawyers know next to nothing about the post-conviction process. This explains why "prison consulting" is a budding, burgeoning industry.

Adjacent to the "camp" was a maximum security federal penitentiary, which housed roughly one thousand of the Bureau of Prisons' most violent inmates. On my first day there, a surly guard warned me that if I misbehaved I would be sent there, pointing up the hill to the imposing structure.

"That's a gladiator camp," the guard explained, when I didn't react. "We pull people out of there with holes in them every night."

The guard wasn't joking. I could hear the screams from behind the walls there at all hours, and it sounded terrifying. By comparison, my five hundred camp compadres were relatively tame.

Even though Lewisburg was technically a "camp"—or a "country club prison," as law-and-order hardliners disdainfully dubbed it—there were some extremely tough convicts there, men who were being "reintroduced" to society after stints at maximum security prisons. I had to learn to interact with them.

One of these men was known as Irish. He was into his twenty-fourth year behind bars and was rumored to be associated with the Aryan Nation. Most recently, Irish had been serving time for credit card fraud and drug possession. His reputation preceded him. Those who (quietly) spoke his name told me he was a genuine "career criminal" who had spent literally half his life in jail. I learned this included an unimaginable eight-year stretch in solitary, at a prison out in Arizona. I also overheard that he was scheduled to be released around the same time as me.

One day soon after my arrival at Lewisburg, I found myself standing next to Irish in the yard. Because I was new and did not know any better, I tried to strike up a conversation. Some part of me said that maybe this man had had a rough life and could use a friend.

"Hey man," I said. "I know we don't know each other but I'm Mike. I know you've been locked up forever and are getting out soon . . . I just came off the streets so if you ever want to have a conversation or pick my brain about what it's like out there, or the job situation, I'm happy to do that all day."

These were words and sentiments and customs wholly foreign to him. That much was obvious to me immediately. He just stared at me as though he were considering killing me, and then stalked off without saying a word.

Then, about three weeks later, I ran into him again. I didn't know what else to say, but made the split-second decision to double down. I made the same offer, and mentioned that I would be happy to talk to him about things like using computers and smart phones and other things he might need in order to find a job.

He stared at me again, but this time he said: "I might do that."

Then he stalked off again. And I relaxed again.

Two weeks after *that,* Irish sought me out and said he wanted to take me up on the offer. It never became a scheduled thing, but whenever we ran into each other, I told him everything I could about life in the outside world in the 2010s. I talked about how to get jobs, and what kind of jobs there were for ex-cons. I talked about what jobs you could do if you didn't "know computers" and how to get those jobs. I talked about finding housing and managing money and everything else I thought might be useful. I never asked anything from Irish in return.

Day-to-day life at the camp felt like Groundhog Day—with each activity strictly regimented and stripped of all spontaneity. You faced the steady, mind-numbing cadence of automatic moves and static schedules. From meal to meal, prisoner count to prisoner count, time seemed to lose meaning as days and weeks blended into a wretched, indistinguishable blur. Surprises were few and far between.

I initially shared a three-bunk cubicle with two sizeable black inmates. On the outside, I never paid much attention to race. In prison it was a big deal, playing a role in everything from where you sat for meals to what you watched on television and who you watched it with. I didn't give a crap about the color of anybody's skin, but my cubicle-mates treated me with total contempt. They may have truly hated white people, or just hated me personally, but I expect they were simply acting out the way the culture of the prison expected them to act toward me. Their glares told me I was not welcome. One of them, Bo, was older, enormous, and borderline obese, with the worst sleep apnea you could imagine—an ear-splitting rumble that drove me nuts. The other was basically—and, in retrospect, amusingly—almost an exact clone of Bo, but on a much smaller scale. I never knew if he also snored, but if he did, nothing could be heard above Bo.

Trying to sleep on my bed (or maybe it should be "bed") was pure torture. It was a steel plank half the size of a twin, the mattress no better than a worn yoga mat. It had been used for years before I inherited it, and I would wager the ranch that some poor soul is sleeping on it tonight. The SUV I'd driven my three kids to school in was bigger than what was now my home. Framed pictures weren't allowed, so I taped a few shots of my family on the inside of my locker—wanting to keep my private life private, and images of my kids away from any leering pedophiles.

That was it, my home for the next thirty months. A long, long way from the leafy suburb of Larchmont, New York. The only thing I had to look forward to while serving time—the one thin ray of hope that kept me going—were the family visits. They were my best link to the outside world, to any tangible sense of life as it used to be. Yet, during my entire time at Lewisburg—remember, we're talking almost two years, for good behavior—Lisa came to visit me just twice, both times with the kids. Never a letter, and not nearly enough phone calls—and those seemed designed exclusively to remind me how difficult everything had become because of my incarceration.

Lisa's tone in these calls always made me recall very specific exchanges we'd had in late 2009.

One happened a week or so after my arrest. We were in the car, and we were pulling into our driveway following a visit to her Grandma Gladys out on Long Island. The three kids were dead asleep in the back of the SUV, with nothing but a deafening silence between Lisa and me all the way from the Whitestone Bridge.

Then Lisa had suddenly sighed and said: "I just don't know if I can 'be' with somebody who's guilty."

I looked over at her. Her eyes were red from crying, glassy with resignation.

I gripped the steering wheel tightly, twisting and choking the leather. For the first time since I'd been cuffed and perp-walked, I couldn't prostrate myself anymore. It had been a week of apologies, of trying reassure her that we would get through this intact.

I was done.

"Jesus, Lisa. I've apologized again and again, over and over. I don't think this is fair, or right, and I'm confused too. But I didn't rape or kill anyone. I played a tip—what thousands of people on Wall Street do every day, and what you've never had a problem with before. Look, this situation isn't what I expected either—not in my wildest dreams—but I gotta tell you, honey. 'I'm not sure I can be with you if you're guilty,' doesn't work for me. This marriage was for better *or worse*. In sickness and in health. Our vows—remember those? Or is all that 'bullshit,' as you're telling me now. If you can't be on my side, or with me, then it's on you. But I'm done apologizing. I'm done second-guessing myself. I'm done asking why, or what I could have done. I've got nothing left."

Lisa turned her head away from me, and said nothing. The kids slept on. But I was suddenly worked up, and continued:

"Remember when you mistakenly didn't pay sales tax on your business for a couple years and I had to talk to our accountant to fix it? Did you *intend* to break the law? No. But do you know that's still a felony? Do you know Wesley Snipes is doing three years for not filing a tax return? If you were arrested for that, do you think it would be fair if I said to you, 'Sorry but I'm just not sure I can be with someone who is guilty?' I didn't even break the law, Lisa. I may have chosen a really fucking bad person to go into business with, but I didn't break the law."

Realizing I had just sworn like a sailor, I looked back at our kids again. Still comatose. Thank God for that.

"I told you, Mike. I never liked Zvi."

"Yeah, you did tell me that. And good for you for spotting it. Bravo. But that was *after the fact*, Lisa. That was when it was already too late."

"Something was so slick and oily about Zvi."

More Monday-morning quarterbacking.

We were home. I yanked the keys out of the ignition and stepped outside, into the cold November night air, and took a deep breath.

From that point on, communication between my wife and me changed forever. Something was gone. Something was different. It was small, but it was there. Her life as she knew it had been upended, destroyed. She was scared and confused. Our future had gone from consistency and complacency to total uncertainty. She felt alone, with three little kids that might soon depend entirely on her for their needs. I got it, and my heart ached for her, and for the fear she was feeling. But I needed her, too. And she was emotionally gone. Checked out.

The other memorable exchange occurred a little later, when I asked her opinion on the government's offer to me—plead guilty and serve no time.

I wanted my wife to weigh in on the most important—and difficult—decision of my life, of *our* lives.

She was totally unable to do so.

"How can you not have an opinion?" I asked in frustration. "The Decision" consumed me at that moment, simultaneously devouring my stomach lining and what was left of my sanity. Everything rode on it. Each day it consumed my waking thoughts.

"I have an opinion," she allowed, in an even-keeled, remarkably relaxed voice. "I'm just not going to tell you."

"What the . . . You won't share that with me?"

"Nope."

"Can I ask why?"

"You already know *why*, Mike."

But it seemed to me that I did not.

"I do? Humor me. I might have an idea, but I'm tired and depressed and don't feel like playing the guessing game on something this serious. This is our lives. I'm the one that can end up in prison, but it's still *our lives*."

After a long pause, while she obsessed over a platter of spring rolls that I wanted to sweep onto the floor, she looked over at me with those beautiful green eyes and said: "I'm not going to be responsible for the outcome. I'm not going to allow you to blame me for the next forty years, as you sit there, miserable, because you took the plea, or because you fought it out in court and lost. This is your decision, and yours alone."

I waited for that all-important "but don't worry sweetheart, you know I'll support you" . . . but it never came.

"That's it, Lisa? Are you serious? You want me to make the most important decision of *OUR* lives completely on my own?"

"Mike, you are the biggest grass-is-greener person I've ever met. When we were in the city, you wanted to move to Westport or Larchmont. Remember that?"

"We were trying to have kids. I didn't want to raise them in the city! I love the city, but I like trees . . . and driving . . . and clean air . . . not having to worry about a bum spitting on my child in a stroller. And the Towers had just crumbled within walking distance of us. On friends of mine."

"No, I understand that," she said. "But then even when we settled in Larchmont, you would regretfully throw out Los Angeles every once in a while, just to torture me. Then it was Sarasota. You're always unsatisfied with the choices you made, Mike. You always think a different decision would have been better."

She went back to work at the butcher block, carefully rolling the transparently thin spring rolls. For the moment, I gave her only stunned silence. What was there to say?

"Nothing is ever good enough," Lisa continued. "Nothing was ever the right choice. And that's when *you* make the choice. I'm not going to allow you to turn *me* into the scapegoat for your unhappiness, whether you're in jail, or you're a confessed felon who regrets not fighting for your good name . . . because *your damn wife didn't want you to.* I don't want that burden. I can't, Mike."

I stepped back. Decided not to reply. There was no point in continuing.

While Lisa would only visit me twice in prison, my parents came every eight weeks or so. They'd fly in from their home in southern California, head out to Larchmont to pick up their grandchildren, and then drive the four hours west to spend the weekend at a Hampton Inn in Lewisburg. I thanked God for my parents, who were broken up about my situation, inside and out, yet never failed to remind me of their unwavering love and support. Without them, I never would have been able to get through it as well as I did. Eight weeks was one hell of a long stretch to be alone, but I could manage that. Once a year, frankly, would have driven me to some sort of edge I'm grateful I never had to face.

For the kids, going to visit dad in prison seemed like a vacation . . . of sorts. They would swim in the hotel pool, eat the foul processed food out of the vending machines, play Hangman and Go Fish, or just chill out with me. All at once it was amazing and uplifting, but equally awful and heart-breaking. How can you entertain three young kids, or have them truly enjoy themselves, when they can't really *do* anything with you. You're just sitting on folding metal chairs for three straight hours. Boys of three and six aren't much for sitting still and talking anyway. To have been able to go outside and toss a baseball or football, or to wrestle, would have been pure bliss. Yet for me this was life. This was my taste of the real world, as we inmates called it. And each time the visit was over and my children left, escorted by Grandma and Grandpa, I was emotionally drained and despondent, counting down the days until I might see them again. Then it was back to the dreary, debilitating monotony of my shared cell.

You get a strange sense of how your kids are aging when you're incarcerated. I received drawings or letters once in a while. I guess that these creations came at the urging of my parents, because the return address was always in my mom's scratchy handwriting. I wrote to them regularly, and assume they still have the letters, but it's a subject I don't want to raise with them. Still, what do you say to kids at that age, to the children you love more than life itself? At a loss for words most times, I generally kept it simple.

"Daddy misses you a lot and loves you to the moon and back, forever and always."

And so forth.

I wrote to Syl in a little more detail, trying to joke about how the prison food was gross and telling her that she had to be good—helping her little brothers and listening to her mom—and always emphasizing how much I missed her and that I would see her soon.

Soon . . . what a dangerous word to use with a child. A child's sense of time is so different than an adult's. I'm sure the term soon lost all meaning for her.

My two boys seemed to age normally, though it was as inevitable as it was painful that I would miss so many of their milestones while in prison.

Cam, who invariably smiled, seemed more subdued during his visits. That initial burst of enthusiasm when they entered and saw me was never anything short of miraculously uplifting . . . but things had a way of fading after a few minutes. It was painfully apparent that seeing me in this situation had caused him to lose some of his typical spark.

Syl, already a bright, complicated kid, became even more so. She was smart and picked up clues. "Why does it say *prison* camp?" I didn't know what to tell her.

It was painful having them see me in "uniform"—head to toe brown khaki—or having the guards bark at them, which inevitably happened. There was an older guard, a spiteful drunk, who seemed to burn up when he saw what I had—three beautiful children and parents that loved me. Said guard would snap at them, yank away their coloring books, yell about a chair being too close to an aisle, or caution a kid whose only crime was being excited about getting an ice cream from the godawful vending machines.

In prison there were arbitrary rules for everything. You got used to it as an inmate, and then it was hard to see outsiders—like people you loved—confronted with it. They would also change rules constantly. I think it was just to keep us on our toes. On some days rules were enforced, and on others they weren't. It depended on who you got as a guard, and what kind of a mood he was in. There was a large sign posted in the cafeteria—No Removing Food—yet inmates would openly walk out with a pint of milk and an apple, or an extra slice or two of Wonder Bread to feed the ducks, and no one seemed to care. But if one of those COs got in a fight with his girlfriend, or was chewed out by his boss, suddenly walking outside to finish a mushy apple meant you'd be written up and cited and have privileges revoked (no shopping, no visits, no phone).

Heaven help you if you complained about anything; you'd disappear to solitary for a week or never to be heard from again.*

During one visit, that bitter old alcoholic guard decided he didn't like my three-year-old son slowly rolling his McDonald's Happy Meal plastic car down

---

* While I was never sent to solitary, I heard from those that had been that it was, even in a minimum security prison, nothing short of torture. Yes, actual torture, like the UN/CIA definition of torture: huge fluorescent lights shining on you 24/7, the heat turned up beyond bearable, or else ice cold. There was food and sleep deprivation, and only sporadic showers. You had no contact with others, and could only leave your cell for an hour a day, tops.

the table, so he snatched it roughly right from Phin's hand. You should have seen the look of shock on Phin's face, and the tears that followed. Phin looked violated and quickly became inconsolable—it was something I will never forget. To be forced to watch, powerless, as this piece of human garbage went out of the way to hurt my child, was beyond painful. My only option was to fantasize about what I might do if I ever ran into him on the streets.

Once, my brother flew out to Chicago to visit, and the guard at the front gate said he wasn't on the visitor list—except for the fact that one's immediate family is *automatically* on the list. Someone had removed him. All they had to do was look on the computer; my probation report listed two parents and a brother—all automatics.

"We printed the list for Kimelman, and if he was on it, he would have been on it."

This garbled nonsense was, verbatim, what they said to him.

Then they sent him away without even allowing me to see him. The fucking gall. The financial and emotional cost of a flight from Chicago, two nights at a hotel, cars to and from the airport, just so a guard could have some adolescent fun at my expense. And there was never any recourse, no right to complain, nothing you could ever do. Sometimes the guards would punish every visitor and his family, simply because one inmate had been busted smoking a cigarette. It's a level of pitiful sadism that's still hard for me to fully fathom. My parents were also turned away once, with my kids in tow, after a 3000 mile flight and four-hour drive, just because another inmate had been caught smoking. They made us all suffer, inmates, families and children, for one man's carelessness. From my vantage point in the yard, I could see my three-year-old and six-year-old sons sobbing hysterically as they were escorted back to the car.

Try doing time with that image seared into your conscience on a loop.

But now I must admit something. I've been holding out on you. There was one other factor about life at Lewisburg that made it close to unbearable. One other detail that—had I disclosed it earlier—might have obscured your ability to appreciate the other, nasty aspects of the place.

This missing detail is the presence of Zvi and Nu.

That's right. Both Goffer brothers were also inmates at Lewisburg.

I'll start with Nu.

Always the weaker of the two brothers—a man whose poor liver must have howled through the long prison nights, begging for its fix—Nu remained the faithful, unflinching sidekick throughout his time inside. Zvi's power over him would never wane. It had existed as long as long as I'd known the two. It would exist in prison as well.

At Lewisburg, Nu and I had the distinct pleasure of spending nine months together in the RDAP, or the Residential Drug and Alcohol Problem. When I got sent into the RDAP (Nu would arrive about one month after me, a total wreck), I was moved from my cellblock known as "Vegas"—a totally lawless place where literally any vice was available: alcohol, drugs, gambling, even women*—to what was purported to be a medically strict environment. Yet despite its being quieter and stricter than Vegas, there was still illicit gambling, cellphone use, and most amusingly, obvious drug and alcohol use. I had done my best to get in the program as soon as I'd learned of it. Not only would it mean time away from snoring roommates; I would also receive six months off my sentence.**

The building that housed RDAP looked like a rundown greenhouse or barn. It had been built as temporary housing in the 1950s with a five-year designated lifespan, but was still standing. There was limited heat, and they shut that off in March, so we had to spend a solid two months coping with nighttime temps that were often down to twenty degrees. It was like sleeping outdoors. I wore two sets of clothes, a hat and gloves, and still had to wrap myself in newspapers at night to keep warm. The windows could not have been any thinner, and most of the walls were uninsulated aluminum sheets, barely half an inch thick. And when it warmed up—you guessed it—there was no AC. The greenhouse-like window orientation meant we could expect

---

* A few of the more entrepreneurial inmates had once used a contraband cellphone and Facebook account to meet a local prostitute whom they smuggled into the prison (don't ask how). The pro ended up getting angry and going to the authorities after several inmates demanded unpaid freebies. That was the only way we found out it had even happened.

** And it paid off: along with an additional three months taken off for good behavior, I was able to "walk" in twenty-one months, as opposed to serving the thirty months Sullivan had sentenced me to.

experience temps above 110 degrees during summer. The air was stale and miserable, with around two hundred souls surviving in a space the size of a basketball court, stacked with bunk beds. It was very tight quarters. At night, if you leaned over even slightly you'd smack the person sleeping next to you. Nu slept no more than twenty feet away from me. Despite this, we hardly communicated at all. We might give one another looks, or bump shoulders occasionally in passing, but that was that. No real contact. Nothing to say. Just frustration and a good deal of mutual antipathy. I blamed Nu in part for my place here. I'm sure he blamed me for his.

In sharp contrast to me, Zvi seemed to have been born for success in a prison environment. Somehow he managed to have an iPad and quickly became known as a reliable source for cigarettes and alcohol. Zvi drank regularly, yet always avoided getting caught. He acted as a bookie and took bets on things. But perhaps more than anything else, he succeeded inside because of his ability to spin tales.

Zvi boasted about having $300 million stashed overseas, in Israel and elsewhere. He played on the inmates' gullibility, promising them jobs and payoffs if they helped him out with this or that. When a few of the less-gullible inmates asked me if Zvi's stories were true, I asked them whether a guy worth $300 million would have hired an ex-public defender from Florida, as opposed to any of the top white-collar attorneys in New York City, who all would have chomped at the bit to represent him—for the right price.

'Nuff said, fellas.

Yet Zvi seemed to acutely understand that he was free to make up anything he wanted. He was an artist, and prison was a blank canvas. For a while, this did not concern me. I might have felt pity for the other inmates he duped, but they would eventually learn the truth about Zvi the hard way. Just as I had. But then word reached me that—among his many tales—Zvi had said that I was a rat who had informed against him.

Zvi spread a rumor that I was the one who ratted our group out, and that the only reason he and Nu and the whole guilty bunch were behind bars was because I had squealed. Such rumors could cost you your life, even in minimum security. (The only thing worse than being a rat was being a child molester.) And the threat did not end once you were released. Plenty of prison justice got carried out years later, on the outside.

I couldn't let this bullshit go unchallenged. To save my own life, I had to resort to prison tactics myself.

I sent my new friend Irish to have a word with Zvi's people. He was only too happy to oblige.

To say Irish looked intimidating would be an understatement. He towered at six foot three, 260 pounds, and was covered in tattoos. His hair was shaved into a buzz cut, and he moved like a tightly wound bundle of in-your-face swagger. But the most threatening part of him might have been his eyes. He had the icy stare of someone who had done things and seen things beyond the imaginings of most people. His eyes made him look a decade older than his forty-three years.

At first, Irish's "inquiries" got us nowhere. All we learned was that it was rumored Zvi had paid someone to hurt me. This might have just been talk, but I wouldn't have put it past him. Life is cheap on the inside, and many people with nothing to lose are willing to provide a beatdown for very little money.

Then another rumor found its way to me. It concerned something I wouldn't have thought *anyone* capable of—not even Zvi, if I hadn't heard it myself and also had it relayed to me. Zvi said he was going to pay someone on the outside to rape my eight-year-old daughter. And he had added in person that, once he got out, he might even rape her himself if the opportunity arose. Even if this was pure psychotic bravura—nothing but a power-play smoke-screen created by a sicko to boost his standing in prison—it was still an unbe-lievable new low. It spoke volumes about the kind of man Zvi Goffer was. He would do anything, hurt anyone, to make himself even slightly more powerful and comfortable.

The threats played on my worst fears. This was, of course, by design. Inmates hate the fact they cannot be personally present to protect the ones they love. For months, Zvi's threat made my headspace into a constant nightmare. Would I soon receive a call telling me that some monster had hurt my Syl?

Post-sentencing, I'd had a recurring, vivid nightmare. I'm with my family. We are up in Vermont, with my college buddy Stan and his family. The prop-erty is vast and breathlessly beautiful—trees, mountains, and cold clear streams running through it. We're camped in a log cabin, getting ready to barbecue, while our kids toss and kick balls, or climb small trees. Lisa and Stan's wife Rachel walk up the hill towards us, smiling, carrying flowers. Stan is playing with his son, Harris. Phin and Syl are nearby. But where's Cam? I slowly spin around to find him, making a 360-degree circle, my hand over my brow, a visor to block the late fading sun. I do not see him, and soon become panicked.

"Stan," I yell. "Is Cam over there?"

Stan looks all around and says he doesn't see him.

I yell to Lisa: "Is Cam with you?"

"No, I thought he was with you!" Her voice cracks.

Cam was just here, watching a darting chipmunk. As loud as I can I yell, *"CAM!"*

Nothing but the echo of my own desperation. My heart begins to race. I tell Syl to watch Phinnie and start jogging back towards the cabin.

"CAM!"

Maybe he went in to get a drink, or use the bathroom. If he's in the house, he'll be okay, I realize, so I reverse away and begin running toward where I last saw him. Maybe he's just lost. I get around a hill and the land flattens out. I can hear a creek, and then I see the creek, and then I see Cam, standing in the creek, body upright, arms above his head in his black bubble North Face down jacket, his feet touching the bottom of the creek, clear and calm enough so I can make out his red hair and his yellow SpongeBob T-shirt. My boy's not moving. I run as fast as I can, praying I'm not too late. Cam can swim. What happened? Did he panic? Did the freezing water disorient him? How long has he been like this? Is he dead? The odds spin through my head. If it's been ten minutes, he's dead; if it's two I can still save him; but if it's more than that, he might have brain damage. Will I be able to resuscitate him? Crying, scream-ing, I dive into the water . . .

And the icy coldness of the creek always jolted me awake. I sat up in bed, barely able to breathe, my chest constricted. I would bolt into the bathroom, nauseated, feeling like I might throw up. I'd certainly never thrown up over a dream before. It felt so real that I had to see Cam right away. When the dream happened, I would have to go glance at him in his room.

So when I was faced with an *actual* threat to my children from an incarcer-ated monster, I felt determined to exact the worst sort of revenge. Somehow. I would skin the fucker alive, and relish his screams. I'd pour salt on his wounds and keep him alive until his body could take no more, and then I'd castrate him. Things like that. These were my fantasies.

In the months that followed, Zvi's threats came and went. Nothing ever happened. Over the rumor wire, I heard that Zvi was ready to take back what he'd said. He wanted to let bygones be bygones. I didn't know whether or not to believe it.

As it turned out, these overtures of retreat were just a calculated move designed to protect Zvi's hide. Word had reached him that my guy Irish could really do some damage. This was confirmed when Irish got sent to the hole, and Zvi felt emboldened again. The threats started back up.

Then another strange twist. Zvi learned through third parties that I was spending time writing. That I was working on the manuscript that would eventually become this book. The wheels in Zvi's mind began to turn, and he worried about what the larger world might think of him after his release if I told the truth about him. He soon sent out new olive branches via third parties.

Having to deal with Zvi was the worst part of prison—but probably also the most fitting. It was my partnership with him that had been my undoing. I'd ignored the aspects of his personality that had always pointed toward evil and psychopathy. The confirmation that I had been a very poor judge of character was something that confronted me daily.

And then, when I thought I might have seen the worst, seven months before my release, Lisa served me with divorce papers. This was connected to the threats from Zvi because of the way it came to my attention.

A Pennsylvania state trooper arrived at the prison and I was summoned over the loudspeaker to the "Bubble," the guard office where you never wanted to be called. Of course, I expected the worst—that Zvi had indeed been able to orchestrate something horrible happening to one of my kids.

The trooper asked me to confirm that I was Michael Kimelman, then handed me a blue-backed envelope. It was about the size and shape of the menu for a Chinese food restaurant. I opened it and immediately realized what it was.

Thinking like a lawyer, I asked the trooper what would happen if I refused to accept it. The nearest CO said, "That's easy; I'll put you in the hole until you beg to accept it" and flashed a sadistic smile. I should have expected no less.

It turned out that Lisa had prepped the kids several months earlier, telling them that I wasn't going to be coming back home to stay with them. To her credit, she told them I would have my own house nearby, that we both still loved them, and that I would always be their dad. I'm sure it was horrible for them to hear, and for her to say. (The next time my parents brought my children to visit, Cam asked point-blank why I couldn't come home to them when I was done serving my time. I had had weeks to think about it, and still had no answer for him.)

Talk about feeling trapped and powerless. I couldn't understand why Lisa needed to do this *now*. I couldn't help wondering why the hell her friends, brother, even her father hadn't tried to convince her otherwise. I was heading home soon enough, and a sober man to boot. A different world and life lay before us. My head would be clear for the first time in almost twenty-five years. Was it a second chance with her I wanted and thought I deserved? Maybe. Maybe it was a third chance, or even a fourth. Maybe we'd both lost count of what we felt we owed each other. But with the future of three little ones—*our* three little ones—on the line, was one more chance too much to ask?

I asked her to wait until I got home. If it didn't work once I was back then fine, I wouldn't contest a thing and move on—while also telling her that if she did this now, by abandoning me in this hellhole with nothing to think about but this pain for the next seven months, then I doubted that I could forgive her. Our marriage would be over.

In the days after being served with my divorce papers, I felt genuinely abandoned, lost and alone, drifting inside my cage. The feeling did not ease. I simply learned to maintain. I focused on my release, which was growing nearer and nearer, and was soon right around the corner.

Then, at the last moment, another twist.

Just a few days before my release, Lisa got in touch to say she had had a change of heart. She wanted to pick me up with the kids, and to try and reconcile. I was skeptical. Heartbroken. I did not really respond.

When she did come to pick me up with the children (no running into one another's arms like in a movie, just me slowly walking out the prison door to the car and never looking back), I still couldn't commit. Communication was hard. I told her I wouldn't rule anything out, but it had to be different. I wasn't going back to what we had before. She had to understand that. Our previous style of togetherness was over forever. This would be something entirely new.

Despite losing almost everything in life, I fought to remain positive after my release. I wanted to be an optimist, who understood he had a second lease on life. I couldn't spend my new life on the outside with someone who saw the glass as half empty—or with a defeated, depressed person. I did not hesitate to remind Lisa that she had abandoned me at my lowest point, when I needed help the most. I made her understand that such an act could never be immediately forgiven.

We tried for a while.

Every time it seemed like there might be a chance of making it work, some small tiff would set off our massive geysers of resentment. It didn't take much for the old, angry Lisa to come out (or the old, angry Michael). I couldn't handle the Jekyll and Hyde of it.

In the end, if I'm being honest, I was never able to fully forgive her for abandoning me in prison, for not visiting me, and for not keeping the faith that things would one day get better.

I ended up moving into a small two-bedroom apartment in Mamaroneck, New York. And that, as they say, was that.

CHAPTER TWENTY-ONE

REHABILITATION

CAN YOU REHABILITATE A MAN WHO considers himself unjustly convicted? What does "success" look like in that situation? What is the system supposed to do?

When it comes to my case, I still believe any respectable journalist, judge, or legal scholar examining the facts will conclude that I got a bum rap. My mistake was trusting people. I trusted the people I went into business with. I trusted that presiding judges would be impartial and fair. Even after the FBI stormed my home during a pre-dawn raid, I still trusted that this was all just a big, strange mistake and that justice would prevail.

Truth, justice, and the American way. Cut to the Stars and Stripes billowing in the breeze. Boy, did I misread that one. To me the preamble of our Constitution now reads, to use an appropriate British expression, like a bunch of cock and bull.

Spend any time in prison—even in a minimum security prison—and you will regret not doing whatever might have been in your power to prevent those circumstances from happening. You will regret that decision every single morning when you wake up on that cramped bunk with a half-inch slab of foam between you and the steel planks—sore and knowing you'll be just as sore each night you lie back down and try to sleep. You will regret it in the shower, or hovering over a rust-stained toilet, or watching your back.

I didn't have to be here. Fuck me and my stupid pride.

But it will be too late.

You will regret it long after you're released. You will regret it when you see how your children have grown without you, and how your actions have damaged what should have been an era of innocence in their lives.

And yet . . .

Even now, as a divorced man struggling day by day to rebuild my life, some part of me still believes that the time will come when my friends and family will tell me that, despite it all, I did the right thing. I even dare to dream that, someday, my beloved children might tell me that as well.

Or if they disagree, that they at least forgive me.

One day they will read this book and understand their father, warts and all. They will see me for who I was: someone who worked too hard to give his kids and his wife a "better life," who drank too much, who thrived on risk and competition, but most of all, someone who cherished the time he spent with them and tried to live a life by example. They will see their father as flawed—as all children come to see their parents when they grow up. I dare to dream that, when this happens, my children will conclude that I was, in fact, caught in a maelstrom, unfairly tried and unjustly convicted.

That if I had, in the end, taken the government's offer and pled guilty, everything I would have said to my kids, or myself, about my fundamental innocence would have been compromised, forever tainted. My word would have meant nothing—to them, who mean everything to me.

In June of 2014, I sat down and wrote an angry but lucid letter about my plight. I considered submitting it to the *Wall Street Journal* or the *New York Times* as an editorial. But then I thought twice. The ugly truth is when you're on probation, you're still a prisoner. The "system" can still snap its fingers and send you back to hell.

So instead, I sent it to Walter Pavlo, a journalist at *Forbes* who focuses on white collar crime. He asked if he could publish it, and I said sure, as long as it was anonymous. He prefaced my piece as follows:*

Recently, I received a submission from a defendant who had faced U.S. prosecutors in court, lost the case and completed his/her prison term. The person, who wishes to remain anonymous (supervised release and exercising free speech can be at odds), gave me permission

* http://www.forbes.com/sites/walterpavlo/2014/06/11/a-former-defendants-view-on-judge-selection-the-wheel-of-misfortune/

to share their views here on my blog. Like all of you, this person is now just an observer, except that they have the experience of having been on the front lines of a federal courtroom.

I called the piece "The Wheel of Misfortune." I present it here, in a slightly edited form.

There has been a growing and long overdue realization that the US mass incarceration policy is an economic and human tragedy. The *New York Times* recently ran a long front page story for two straight days, along with an editorial* ("End Mass Incarceration Now," May 25, 2014) calling into question a system that subjects first time non-violent offenders to disproportionately harsh sentences, and compels innocent defendants to plead guilty to avoid those same life-destroying sentences. We as a society spend four times more to imprison than to educate our citizens, an unsustainable trajectory with a total tab well north of $60B. The statistics are haunting and familiar. The US imprisons 25% of the world's incarcerated, despite having less than 5% of its population. The government puts up a head-scratching conviction rate of 98%, year in, year out. Heavily encumbered by widespread institutional racism and deep structural biases in favor of the government, arguably the system itself is a gross distortion of our Constitutional rights and traditions.

Closer to home, US Attorney for the Southern District of NY Preet Bharara has put together an 80-0 record in insider trading cases. As if widespread structural bias and a 98% guilty conviction rate wasn't enough, a new and rarely discussed trend has emerged. One of the most vital determinants in the outcome of a criminal case tends to be which judge the defendant "draws," or rather what judge is "wheeled out," as they like to say in New York. That's right, if you weren't aware of this, the Southern District of New York, the pre-eminent Federal Court in the country, still alleges to use an actual

---

*   http://www.nytimes.com/2014/05/25/opinion/sunday/end-mass-incarceration-now.html&
assetType=nyt_now?_r=0

wooden wheel covered in index cards in order to determine which cases will be assigned to which judges. A wheel like you might find in an Atlantic City casino or on the popular game show *Wheel of Fortune*. The major difference, of course, is the currency being wagered here: it is the very life and liberty of the defendants themselves, as opposed to mere dollars and cents. Now it appears that the "wheel" may be rigged, or rather, never really spun at all.

One might ask, what's the big deal? Well, as the 2nd Circuit Court of Appeals recently voiced, it might be a very big deal indeed. In the cases of Anthony Chiasson and Todd Newman, two hedge fund analysts convicted of insider trading, the stratagem by the United States Attorney's Office (USAO) to place key cases before a specific judge may blow up in their face and tarnish their perfect record. During recent oral arguments, 2nd Circuit Judge Ralph K. Winter was critical of the government's apparent manipulation of the system to steer cases before a judge named Richard Sullivan, which he viewed as potentially paramount to "judge shopping." Why would the government want to do this? The answer is simple, obvious, and inexcusable—to make their jobs easier. Most judges have spent the majority of their careers as former prosecutors, and the government perspective has been heavily imprinted upon their psyche. It's like asking Bill Belichick to referee a New England Patriots game. While most judges are deemed pro-government, some are considered so friendly to the government, that I've personally heard stories about normally stoic AUSAs actually high-fiving each other on learning their cases have been assigned to a certain judge. Judge Sullivan just happens to be one of those judges.

In the recent 2nd Circuit hearing, AUSA Antonia Apps stuttered when challenged by Judge Winter as to how a disproportionate number of these cases ended up with Sullivan, a judge who requires a lower burden of proof by the government with regard to tippee knowledge. Statistically, there are fifty eligible judges, yet in seven major recent insider trading trials, Sullivan heard four of them, a resounding 57% ratio. That's like spinning a Vegas roulette wheel and hitting Green-00 on four out of seven spins. A simple statistical analysis yields a probability outcome of 6,000,000 to 1 if the wheel was truly random. The next time Preet goes to Vegas, I'd like to bankroll him. Either he's the luckiest man alive, or more likely, he's got his thumb on the wheel. Not surprisingly, AUSA Apps could only muster a weak argument, claiming judicial efficiency in having two totally different trials with different defendants heard by the same judge, an argument quickly dismissed by the appellate court. If, in fact, judicial efficiency was the USAO's goal, then why didn't they look to have the case of Zvi Goffer heard before Judge Holwell, the judge in the Raj Rajaratnam case that was tried just a month earlier, and which had many of the same legal issues and parties? It seems, therefore, that the USAO only cares about judicial efficiency when it makes their job easier by being in front of one of their preferred judges.

Judge assignment not only has serious repercussions for defendants who exert their constitutional right to a trial—it similarly affects those who plead guilty or cooperate with the government during the sentencing phase. The discrepancy in sentencing in the Southern District of NY is huge. As history has proven, defendants receive very different sentences based on which judge they draw (for instance, Rajat Gupta got two years from Judge Rakoff, while Zvi Goffer received ten years from Judge Sullivan).* Now it seems that a defendant cannot blame their fate on a bad spin of the wheel but, rather, on a rigged system allowing the government to steer cases to their preferred judges. Isn't this the type of gaming of the system that the USAO is supposed to despise and look to prosecute? Haven't they paid repeated lip service to a "fair playing field" as the justification for the recent round of insider trading prosecutions? Is there no shame, no sense of decency?

With SAC Management's Michael Steinberg sentenced last month, this topic once again climbs to the forefront. Steinberg's attorney,

---

* Gupta was a man of immense power and wealth, a chairman at McKinsey, on the board of Goldman and a confidante of the Clintons, getting only two years, even though the tapes were damning, while Zvi was a comparative nobody, hustling and cheating for a comparative pittance.

Barry Berke, focused on this travesty at the indictment stage, asking Judge Sullivan to allow the case to be randomly assigned to a new judge. Berke claimed Sullivan had given prosecutors an easier burden to meet in past insider trading cases compared to rulings by two other judges. He rightly identified this as a "significant legal issue," and claimed the government's indictment gamesmanship "violates the letter and spirit of the district's rules, due process and basic fairness, and creates the appearance of impropriety." Sullivan said he would "consider" letting Steinberg's case be reassigned, telling Mr. Steinberg "Don't believe Mr. Berke, I'm not as bad as he says." However, Judge Sullivan refused to allow random assignment of the case. Will there be any punishment for the prosecutors who potentially broke the law? At least an outside investigation? Will Sullivan only get a slap on the wrist? Preet's focus is now on corruption in Albany, so maybe some angry state politicians will take the lead.

Sullivan's refusal to recuse himself may have a silver lining for Steinberg. If the 2nd Circuit's oral arguments in the Chaisson-Newman cases are any indication of things to come, Judge Sullivan's stubbornness to allow a random assignment of his case may have gift-wrapped a new trial for Steinberg, and Messrs. Chiasson and Newman as well. Only time will tell.*

So the next time Mr. Preet Bharara touts his perfect record, and an overall conviction rate of about 98%, perhaps take a step back and ask yourself how, in an allegedly fair and impartial adversarial system, could something be so close to perfect? Perhaps because the government was stacking the deck all along?

Pavlo published this almost verbatim. Not only did my article allege something unholy in Preet's unseemly judge shopping—a pure desecration of the enshrined, "Justice is Blind" tenet that allegedly upholds our system—but it

---

* The sad truth is had Sullivan recused himself, even with the correct legal jury instructions, these guys probably still would have all been convicted. Juries want blood. Your "average Joe" is still struggling, and there remains no easier target or scapegoat than a seemingly smug rich guy who allegedly "cheated."

showed that evidence of bad behavior was everywhere, and it could be unearthed with even perfunctory research.*

One month later, in July, Preet suffered his first real defeat, after eighty-one straight convictions, when a jury acquitted Rengan Rajaratnam, Raj's younger brother and protégé. Rengan had worked for Raj at Galleon. He had originally been charged on five counts, with two dismissed before the trial and two quite serious fraud charges dismissed mid-trial. And no, Sullivan was not presiding. No surprise there. After four hours of deliberation, the jury found Rengan not guilty of the lone conspiracy charge, citing that the entire trial seemed to be all about Raj, and that nothing seemed to stick to Rengan specifically. All poor Preet could do was take it on the chin, and as of the fall of 2014, he has moved on from insider trading cases.

I dared to hope the tide was turning.

When it came to my case, this was only the beginning. On December 10, 2014, the Second Circuit Appellate Court overturned the convictions of Anthony Chiasson and Todd Newman, traders who had been convicted by Bharara in 2013. In their decision, the same Court went out of its way to publicly slap and chastise Judge Sullivan as being *the only judge in the entire circuit* that refused to properly instruct juries on tippee** (*e.g.:* me) knowledge as required by the law. (During trial, we got the sense that Sullivan was a prosecutor in drag, donning the black robes of a judge. Now, everyone

---

* Judge Richard Sullivan was actually Preet Bharara's boss for a time and the two were friends. During Sullivan's confirmation hearings, Preet is the aide to Senator Schumer who welcomes Sullivan and they have a verbal lovefest on the record prior to his testimony. *"I should note that while Mr. Sullivan was with the Southern District of New York, he supervised my chief counsel, Preet Bharara, right here. You probably read his glowing article in Time Magazine. His mother enjoyed it very much, he informed me. But Preet has only had wonderful things to say about Rich Sullivan. I guess that is why it says "Rich."*

** "Accordingly, we conclude that a tippee's knowledge of the insider's breach necessarily requires knowledge that the insider disclosed confidential information in exchange for personal benefit. In reaching this conclusion, we join every other district court to our knowledge—apart from Judge Sullivan—that has confronted this question." —2nd Circuit Court of Appeals in *U.S. v. Newman.*

else was finally starting to also see a smidgen of what we had witnessed firsthand.)

The same day those convictions were overturned, my buddy Peter Bogart published the following on his Facebook page:

> My close friend and former colleague Michael Kimelman lost his insider trading case in 2011. He had turned down probation because there was no credible evidence against him. Evidence did not matter. The Government was on an insider trading crusade and Mike was road kill: he lost and went to federal prison. The jury was clueless. Mike lost his reputation, his law license, his CFA license, his money, his marriage, years of seeing his 3 young children, and 3 years of his life. Today they finally figure out that he did absolutely nothing wrong under the law, and that his jury was wrongly instructed on the law. I professed his innocence then, and I do so again today. Where is the justice for Mike?

Choked up, I thanked Pete for his unwavering support—from the moment of my arrest until that day—and added: "Same facts, same judge, same incorrect jury instruction. I guess I didn't need to go to prison after all . . ."

But it all felt bittersweet.

When Judge Sullivan's peers are questioning his tactics, and when Bharara is being soundly defeated, it signals that the times they are a changin'. Yet for me it was too little too late. Knowing full well that the charges against me were measures weaker than those leveled against Rengan, Chiasson, and Newman, and even Steinberg, did not fix my family or reverse my time in prison. That makes for a hollow victory from where I'm sitting.

I had still been vilified in the press and made a poster child of the "corrupt culture of Wall Street."

I had still lost everything.

Occupy Wall Street wanted blood, and they had gotten mine—the blood of a proprietary trader. But what about the big guns? The Goldman Sachs and JP Morgans, the Wells Fargos and the Banks of America? What happened to them? Were Jaime Dimon's Park Avenue digs raided? Was he handcuffed and perp-walked, fingerprinted and tried before a jury of his peers? We know the answer to that one. In fact, his stature and power, and that of Morgan—and all the big banks, really—seem only to have to have increased since the initial crash that triggered the Great Recession. America has always been about amusing the sheep, rather than shooting the elephants in the room, as Lewis Lapham once famously observed.

The culture of corruption and collusion between the Federal Reserve and the biggest banks—once the domain of eccentric conspiracy theorists—further came to light in a big way with the revelations of Carmen Segarra, a brilliant lawyer who dug too deep into the matter, under the original request of her bosses at the Federal Reserve of New York, whose offices are also on Wall Street. When Segarra raised a red flag about how Goldman Sachs seemed to run roughshod over the Fed, she was summarily fired.* She fought back, filing a lawsuit, which a judge dismissed. But then Segarra revealed tapes that she had made during her investigation—tapes that now demonstrate her claims with dazzling clarity.*

And consider too the "settlements" with Bank of America, Morgan, and others, $16 billion and counting in the case of Bank of America and Countrywide, due directly to the sleazy subprime mortgage scam that caused millions of Americans to lose their life savings, their homes, and often their futures. There is no doubt, no doubt at all, that laws were broken by these banks, by entities but also by individuals at the highest levels. Yet no arrests were made, no careers or lives destroyed among those at the top.** In the Morgan settlement, because the firm was not required to admit guilt, they were able to write off part of the settlement as legitimate losses. What this means is that the US taxpayers had the honor of picking up part of the tab. It boggles the fucking mind. To add insult to injury, there was the Washington bailout of Wall Street that we've all had to pay for as well in one way or another.** (Or

---

* One exchange has Segarra's boss literally begging her, "Why do you have to say there's no policy?" and then demanding she change a report that embarrassingly noted that Goldman had no "conflicts of interest" firm-wide policy. The "oversight" and evident regulatory capture came to light in the NY Fed's investigation of the Kinder-El Paso deal which featured Goldman wearing far too many hats (advisor, principal, shareholder) without disclosure in a supposedly arms-length transaction.

** See Michael Lewis's *The Big Short* and the resultant Adam McKay movie for an excellent narrative of this travesty.

will have to pay for, given the federal government's ever growing $19 trillion debt and market distortions from zero interest rate policy.) The phrase "too big to fail" has become part of the average American's financial lexicon. I would humbly submit that "too big to be held accountable" belongs there too. No entity should be too large or important to answer for what it has done. Simply put, that is a luxury that we as a country simply cannot afford.

So how did it end for us? For those of us were *not* too big to prosecute?

Raj is still in prison, and his appeals have failed. However, prison may have literally saved his life. Formerly, he was massively overweight and had health issues. His outrageous appetites cannot be indulged where he is today. But will his reformed behavior extend his life long enough that he will ever see the outside of a prison cell again? That remains the question.

Nu, like me, has now been released. I haven't heard a peep from him and I don't ever expect to. I believe he's living off of his wife, who is still a lawyer. In prison, Nu kept himself going by talking about all his big plans for the future. When he got out, he was going to go back into business and do it right this time. He was going to raise millions, and do X, Y, and Z with it. These were pipe dreams. If you're a felon convicted of a financial crime, the only way you *might* get a job on Wall Street again is by being so brilliant and charismatic that a firm would decide you were worth the added risk. And that's just not him. Nu is lucky if he's working construction.

And then Zvi. Fucking Zvi. The human shredder himself.

When this book is published, Zvi will have another year or so left on his sentence. He's the only guy in all of this that I still have any residual anger toward. Looking back, there were so many good things he could have done. So many opportunities to be a decent human being. He could have walked forward and said this was on him. He could have given me a deferred prosecution. He could have put his family first. He could have decided not to gamble with other people lives, *in addition* to his own.

But he did none of these things.

Prison's a horrendous place as it is. It might have been just tolerable for me to be there without him. Instead, he took a bad situation and made it *unbearable.*

These days I'm a pretty Zen-like guy and I try to forgive everyone. But I haven't been able to forgive Zvi.

I don't know what will happen when he gets out, but I hope he chooses to just disappear. Gets smart and chooses to form a new life somewhere far away. And while that's a pleasant fantasy, that may be *all* it is. A fantasy.

This is a man whose memory runs deep, and who has threatened me and threatened my children. Will Zvi try something one day? I'd like to say "no," but I know his stupidity all too well.

My dream is I never think of or hear from him again.

But instead, I keep tabs.

Just before dropping dead of a massive coronary (at around the same age as I am now), F. Scott Fitzgerald famously wrote that there are no second acts in American lives. It's a poetic, powerful turn of phrase. Sometimes I think about how it applied to Fitzgerald himself. He became a celebrated, best-selling writer in his twenties, and then spent the next two decades unable to recapture that initial success. Does it come as any surprise that he basically smoked and drank himself into an early grave?

As a nation, we tend to forget quickly, and we turn our eyes to the present and the promise of the future. Yet aphorisms are not always correct, even famous ones about second acts. Some things, some people, do change. I plan on being one of them.

I can honestly say that, following all of this—my arrest, trial, incarceration, and release and divorce—I am beginning a "second life." As an innocent man, this second life is not exactly an act of humble contrition. Though I'm still plenty humbled. For the foreseeable future, it's an uphill battle. I'm a forty-two-year-old man who once helped create a $40 million company from scratch in eighteen months. Now a friend is on the lease to my apartment and my brother is on my electric bill. I can't get a credit card, or open a bank account, so I use a prepaid debit card like the "unbanked" or "unbankable." I am technically both. I continue to send out my résumé and get called in for interviews, only to return home and agonize over the results of the background check. But I'm hardly waiting on others to make something happen for me, and my status hasn't stopped me from grinding, pushing forward, and trying to do better for myself and my family. I am motivated to keep trying in part by the knowledge that I am now sober. Even in the midst of the incalculable stress, depression, fear, and emptiness of prison, I knew in my heart that I had been operating for the last twenty years at a 60 percent capacity, at best. The saddest regret of all is what might have been. How would my life have been different if I hadn't leapt into a black hole of vodka at so many different turns?

I didn't know the answer to that question. But what I *did* know is that the past is the past and the present is the present, so I doubled down on the present and got busy.

Coming out of prison, I hit the ground running. I was eventually able to get some work from a guy sympathetic to those within the clutches of the System. I started writing more and developed a TV show called *Coming Home*. It has landed a development agreement from a heavily respected NY production company. There were LA firms that wanted it too, but because my travel was limited to midtown Manhattan, NYC it was. We shot a sizzle reel and the initial success led to two follow-up offers for other shows, including a scripted episodic series based on the life of a client. (I started a management firm to complement the production company and handle some of the talent I met while "away." There is a whole well of pent-up literary, entertainment, and entrepreneurial talent that's been bottled up in the System for years just waiting to prosper if given the shot.)

I still need permission to go anywhere. I can't go to Brooklyn, New Jersey, or even Connecticut, which is ten minutes from my apartment, without advance permission. Luckily probation isn't permanent, although it's a definite pain in the ass.

Worse though, may be the distance that has grown between me and those who knew me before this chapter in my life. They try. They mean well. But they can never truly understand. To them, my claims seem exaggerated, unlikely, or mistaken.

Upon her return from Oz, Dorothy had this to say to those who thought she was delusional: But it wasn't a dream! This was a real, truly live place. And I remember some of it wasn't very nice.

I hear you, Dorothy. I hear you loud and clear.

EPILOGUE

On Dec. 10, 2014, the 2nd Circuit Court of Appeals ruled in *U.S. v. Newman* that insider trading requires that insiders who passed confidential tips did so in exchange for personal benefits of some consequence. Essentially, the ruling forces the government to prove that the *tippee* had knowledge that the tipper breached his fiduciary duty in providing the material nonpublic information.

The ruling overturned the convictions of hedge fund managers Todd Newman and Anthony Chiasson, whose trial was also overseen by Sullivan. The appeals court said Sullivan instructed jurors incorrectly on the law.

The Newman case also resulted in the overturn of the conviction of Michael Steinberg, who was tried and convicted in front of Judge Sullivan. An additional seven defendants also had their convictions overturned.

In March of 2015, Michael Kimelman filed a motion to have his conviction overturned as well. Citing the similar facts of his case and the incorrect jury instructions provided by the same Judge Sullivan, Kimelman asked that his conviction also be set aside. Under the law, the motion must be made to the same judge that originally ruled on his case—Judge Sullivan. The motion has sat on Judge Sullivan's desk for almost two years and has not been ruled on as of the time of this writing.

PUBLISHER'S NOTE

During this book's final production process, the motion that had sat idly in Judge Sullivan's chambers for almost two years was finally addressed. On January 17, 2017, Judge Sullivan denied Kimelman's motion.

What is surprising is not the denial (what judge wants to overrule himself?), but that Judge Sullivan chose to rule on procedural grounds and inexplicably wait two years to give a ruling he could have given in thirty days. In refusing to address the motion on its merits, Sullivan claimed that Kimelman's attorneys could have appealed his admittedly improper jury instructions and elected not to.

Kimelman's attorney, confident of ultimate victory after appeal, insisted that Judge Sullivan's reading of *US v. Newman* was too narrow, and noted that, "Mr. Kimelman is actually innocent under the proper legal standard and has every intention of pursuing an appeal."

The ruling hardly came as a surprise, as this is the same notoriously pro-government judge who, against all mathematical odds, had been "randomly selected" by Preet Bahara to hear Kimelman's case, along with a handful of others, during the height of the "Occupy Wall Street" frenzy. We believe Judge Sullivan's opinion is biased, inaccurate, and shall be exposed as such and vacated on appeal.

ABOUT THE AUTHOR

Michael Kimelman is a graduate of Lafayette College and the University of Southern California Law School. Formerly an associate at Sullivan & Cromwell, he was the founder and managing partner of Incremental Capital, a New York-based hedge fund with over $250 million in assets, which closed shortly after his arrest. A serial entrepreneur, he is currently consulting and launching new ventures in the technology, retail, and entertainment spaces. He actively volunteers his time to several causes, including prison and education reform. He lives in Mamaroneck, New York.